LEAVING YOUR
LIFE
IMPRINT

LEAVING YOUR
LIFE
IMPRINT

*An Amazing Story that **Will Inspire Your Own!***

KENNY MAUCK

Copyright © 2019 by Kenny Mauck

Leaving Your Life Imprint:
An Amazing Story that Will Inspire Your Own!

All rights reserved. No part of this publication may be reproduced, distributed, or transmitted in any form or by any means, including photocopying, recording, or other electronic or mechanical methods, without the prior written permission of the publisher, except in the case of brief quotations embodied in critical reviews and certain other noncommercial uses permitted by copyright law.
Quantity sales special discounts are available on quantity purchases by corporations, associations, and others. For details, contact the publisher at the address above.
Manufactured and printed in the United States of America. Distributed globally by Boss Media. New York | Los Angeles | London | Sydney

ISBN:
Hard Cover 978-1-63337-318-1
E-book 978-1-63337-319-8

Library of Congress Control Number: 2019942050

BOSS Media rev. 2nd ed. Date 10/01/2019

To my mother Melonee and my Pa Paw Nichols

DISCLAIMER

The people, events, and places depicted in this book are based on a true story of my family's journey and were retrieved from my research of the facts—names, dates, and events. Additionally, I have tried to recreate conversations with others who have shared their memories with me and from my own memories. To tell the rest of the story, at times I used my own creativity of how I imagined the story went or could be.

Although the author and publisher have made every effort to ensure that the information in this book was correct at press time, the author and publisher do not assume and hereby disclaim any liability to any party for any loss, damage, or disruption caused by errors or omissions, whether such errors or omissions result from negligence, accident, or any other cause, or alleged to have been caused, directly or indirectly, by the information contained in this book.

Contents

FOREWORD		1
ACKNOWLEDGEMENTS		5
INTRODUCTION		11
CHAPTER 1	Passages	27
CHAPTER 2	Uncharted Waters	43
CHAPTER 3	Facing the Headwinds	63
CHAPTER 4	Batten Down the Hatches	91
CHAPTER 5	Wade in the Water	109
CHAPTER 6	Course Corrections	127
CHAPTER 7	Finding Your Sea Legs	149
CHAPTER 8	Discovery	199
CHAPTER 9	Assembling Your Crew	225
CHAPTER 10	The Admirals Club	251
CHAPTER 11	Captain's Log	275
CHAPTER 12	The Wind in Your Sails	299
ABOUT THE AUTHOR: KENNY MAUCK		319
CONTACT INFORMATION		321

Foreword

FIVE MINUTES WITH KENNY, AND YOU would definitely get it. Kind. Engaging. A dreamer. Passionate. Look-you-in-the-eye type. The kind that makes you feel like you are the only person in the room.

I've watched him from a distance for a long time. One thing is certain, you can't deny the love he has for his family and the love they have for him. That says something, and so do his focus and work ethic, commitment to making a difference, and the hand of favor that has been on his life. It's compelling. And he is on a new mission. He wants to teach you a critical life skill. As you jump into these pages, I am confident you'll find the journey worth your time.

What will your legacy be? How will others remember you? Family members? Coworkers?

Pictures matter. An inheritance matters. But there is something really special about memories to share, stories to tell, and the imprints we leave. As I have heard Dr. James Dobson say numerous times, "An inheritance is something you give to someone, and a legacy is what you build in someone."

In *Leaving Your Life Imprint*, Kenny challenges you to take a hard look at your life, that deep search that forces you to look at what has and what really does matter, a Psalm 90:12-17 heart-wrenching cry to the Lord that awakens within you to "number your days" and live them well.

That's because we do live in stories. There is a reason, a purpose to this life. Unfortunately, we can get lost or confused along the way... maybe distracted, disconnected... and we can't make sense of the story in which we find ourselves. The result? We miss out on moments and don't pass on the gift that God wants us to share with those we do life with or for those who come behind us.

As you read *Leaving Your Life Imprint*, find your story. Then go to work. It's never too late to dial it in. Leave a life imprint.

To anchor my life, I often read James 4:14: "Whereas ye know not what shall be on the morrow. For what is your life? It is even a vapour, that appeareth for a little time, and then vanisheth away" (KJV). Here today... and then gone... just like that.

Live your life on purpose. Don't miss a moment. Kenny lives like that.

Warmly,

DR. TIM CLINTON
President, American Association of Christian Counselors

Executive Director, James Dobson Family Institute

Acknowledgements

FIRST OF ALL, I WANT TO THANK MY WIFE Raye Ann for your support, love, and endurance over the last three years while I wrote *Leaving Your Life Imprint*, for helping me start our legacy company and being its first employee, for being married to a dreamer the last thirty-five years, and letting me fulfill God's call on my life. I also want to thank God for gifting us with six awesome imprints, our adult children Landon, Megan, and Kelsey, and our three grandchildren "Awesome Easton," "Super Cooper," and "Princess Gracelyn Hope," as well as those yet to be born.

Also, special thanks to my parents Louie and Melonee Mauck, married sixty-four years now, as well as my big sister Candy, a rock in my life and someone with whom I share cherished memories to this day. Also, my brother-in-law Brad, someone I consider closer than any brother, and their sons, my two buffed police-officer nephews Nic and Ryan and their families. Lastly, my sister Tammy and her two girls Vickie and Vivian, as well as my father and mother-in-law Ernie and Ann Robertson, and brother-in-law Brent and his wife Dina Robertson.

Pastor L.H. Hardwick, my deepest appreciation for you allowing me the opportunity to direct our counseling services at Christ Church and for reminding me in a famous sermon to keep my promises. Also, thank you for you leading your two sons Mike and Steve, who taught me by their example and support what skills are needed to lead.

Then there are five amazing people who are part of BOSS Media. First Michelle Borquez, who was a great encouragement to me throughout the writing experience and brought together a great team of people like Allison Stevens, Michael Saltar, and Diana Acosta. Special thanks for Sherrie Clark's amazing contributions and editing.

One of the most wonderful blessings was having Ken Abraham, an eighteen times *New York Times* best-selling author, help guide us throughout critical stages of writing this book. Then there's my friend Dave Ramsey, my fellow Eagle (a band of brothers and group influencers he initiated) who has helped promote the launching of our book by allowing use of his nationally syndicated radio station, interviewing via podcast with national speakers like former Attorney General Alberto Gonzales, Dr. Tim Clinton, and then meeting with Dr. James Dobson about our shared passion on leaving a legacy.

I would be remiss if I didn't thank my biggest influencers and mentors in my life, such as Don Evans, my business and life coach Bill Campbell, my high school track coach Don Marsh, Tennessee

House of Representatives Mark White, and so many other influential people from church, government, and community.

Thank you to my lifelong friends from childhood through college, Greg and Tom Gardner, Pat and Kim Campbell, Kerri Powell, Ken and Stacie Tucker, and Melanie and Butch Leix.

I would like to thank those who helped me start and/or have remained faithful as leaders with Life Care all these years in leadership: Sean McPherson, Jim Carter, David Thomas, Rebecca Rahman, Christal Wise, Christy Scruggs, Myrna Kemp, James Davis, and Tory Woodard. Also, Maryann Killion, Dominque Miller, and Ken Graham served as part of our psychiatric, nursing, case management, and counseling staff.

I want to give special mention to Mignonne Sawyer, one of the best therapists I have ever had the opportunity to work with, a wonderful Christian who specialized in caring for women's issues, depression, and multiple-personality disorders.

I want to thank LifeCare's past and present board of directors, Eagles, and LifeCare Heritage and Foundations, Bill Campbell, Don Evans, Dan Finley, Bruce Boder, Jeff Parish, Eddy Richey, Ron Doyle, Dan Scott, and advisor to the board, Dave Ramsey.

*In memory and gratitude, board members Ernest Robertson, Landy Gardner, and Dave Cavender.

With deep appreciation, I want to thank my other Eagle influencers Dan Miller, Gene Riley, Don Scurlock, Jeff Mosely, David George, Aaron Walker, and Tom Summers.

Thank you to my cousins Mike and Brenda Berner, Rebecca Foster, Ronnie and Lanora Foster, Lauren Cantu, Mark and Tammie Foster, Joy Gardner, Lauren Hodge, Dionne Dismuke, as well as Ken Johnson, Jeff Johnson, and other Mauck-Nichol family members.

I am also so thankful for the great opportunity to meet and share the imprints of generational prayers with Dr. James Dobson, a true Christian hero of mine.

Finally, and most important of all, I want to thank my Lord and Savior Jesus Christ, for without a doubt, He is the ultimate and eternal imprint on my life, the "Keeper of my redemptive story," one that will live beyond my lifetime.

* * * * *   (Represents five-star friends and family not mentioned)

Introduction

HAVING JUST PENNED my last sentence of this book, I sit slowly sipping my hot tea. This coupled with the sun rising quickly has created some appreciated warmth on this brisk morning. My faithful sidekick, Manny our Miniature Pinscher, lies snuggled and curled next to me, snoring lightly.

This ritual of ours began some eighteen months ago as I began writing my family's story. God has provided an amazing inspiration and backdrop for me with a serene pond behind our home and a variety of wild game to accentuate it. As I look up, a doe has walked down to the pond from behind the trees to the water's edge. She seems mesmerized by viewing herself in the clear glassy water. Like this doe, I find myself in a season of reflection, the prime of my life, a time of seeking what really matters, and just as importantly, what really doesn't.

When I started researching my family, I did not intend to write a book. I was simply inquiring to find some basic information—dates of birth, locations, ports of entry, and death certificates. Yet as I have worked my way through my ancestry, I slowly began to pull away from the research. I started experiencing some anxious and troubling thoughts and questions about my own mortality.

One night, my anxiety, accompanied by racing thoughts, heavy breathing, and sweating, got so bad that I was suddenly awakened from a deep sleep. I quickly sat up, planting my feet down on the floor to make sure I was still alive. This overwhelming thought caused me to frightfully ponder these words, "One day, this heart of mine will no longer beat, and this body will breath its last breath. My whole life is passing right before my eyes so quickly."

While sitting up, I asked myself, "Is this just me, or do others experience these mid-life mirror-of-the soul questions?"

Thankfully, a few nights later I found some solace one restless evening as I recalled God speaking through the Psalmist David. He assured and calmed my restlessness by branding these inspired words onto my heart, "Teach us to number our days ...." (Psalm 90:12-17).

I realized at that moment, God wasn't responding just to David or myself. This message was for all of us—friends, family members, and anyone else willing to intentionally embrace, cherish, and fully take in each day of one's life.

This idea of living each moment was even more pronounced in that even during times of celebration over the last fourteen months, I have lost some of my closest family and friends: my first-cousin Landy near Thanksgiving, our dear friend's daughter Kristi on New Year's, my father-in-law Ernie on my birthday, my Aunt Marciel on Christmas, and Dave Cavender in the early part of 2019. Life is truly a gift and needs to be lived with purpose and intention. It's part of numbering our days. A dear friend of mine intentionally numbers his days by beginning his daily prayer with this: "Lord, thank you for the gift of life."

Striving to communicate my story has been part of my attempts to heed God's words and number my days. As this book has progressed, profound questions have risen within me about how we now communicate with each other daily in this modern electronic age. Have our meaningful interactions now given way to texting and social media, changing how we connect to and with our dear friends and loved ones? We seem to be totally enraptured by social electronic media, even breaking up or discussing life's most intimate matters. Our world is now fully accessed by a simple touch of our finger that involves less human interaction. We can even do our banking, grocery shopping, watch movies, etc. by a few simple clicks.

Could these wonderful items of convenience also create the unintended consequence of us moving further away from each other, preferring instead to text rather than to speak? Are we losing those special places of time to express our love, to make amends, or to simply laugh and cry with one another? Why do we wait until death to even consider sharing life's most applicable stories with our children?

Three Epiphany Moments that Inspired Me to Write *Leaving Your Life Imprint*

The first epiphany that steered me to ultimately write this book started in January 2014, as a doctoral student at Trevecca University. I was assigned to read the *New York Times* best seller *The Last Lecture* by Professor Randy Pausch of Carnegie Mellon. Randy's doctor had given him an end-of-life notice due to an aggressive cancer. So with little time left, he decided to do a video and write his memoir.

However, Randy's wife wanted him to concentrate primarily on their children during his final year. Instead, he decided to write the book, thinking his children would be too young to remember him. In the latter chapters, he surmised, "Why didn't I take the time when I had it to write my story?"

The seconds, minutes, hours, and days spent on the book was meant to give to his family something by which to remember him. Unfortunately, it competed against his wife's wishes, to spend time with her and the kids with what little time he had left with them.

As a result of his decision, though, Randy was able to give to people like me some simple yet amazing insight: If you have a life story, don't wait until the end of life to begin sharing it.

The next epiphany moment came on November 14, 2014, when my wife and I were invited to participate in Christ Church's sixtieth anniversary service in Nashville, Tennessee. I was asked to share about Lifecare, our legacy faith-based nonprofit company my wife and I founded while attending and serving on staff at the church. (At that time, Christ Church was only one of the few Nashville mega churches.)

The church was founded by one of the kindest, most loving, humblest, and most caring men I have ever known, Pastor L. H. Hardwick. After our Lifecare board presented a plaque to both Pastor Hardwick and the church's current pastor, Reverend Dan Scott, in honor of this church anniversary, I spoke.

Before sharing about Lifecare, part of my own legacy, I briefly spoke about Pastor Hardwick's own legacy story. I have come to realize that one should never give one's legacy story without first giving preference and acknowledgement to the one who inspired and imprinted their own.

So, I began by describing Pastor Hardwick's humble beginnings, like marrying his first wife Montelle on Christmas Eve, December 24, 1950, when she was nineteen, and he was eighteen. (He later married his second wife Carol in February 2007. Ironically, Carol had been Montelle's dear friend and thus the only one Montelle had given approval of should he ever remarry). Pastor Hardwick began preaching at the age of eighteen, and his joyful and humorous wife Montelle helped him start his first little church on the corner of Rose and Sadler streets.

In a podcast last year, I interviewed Pastor Hardwick's sons Mike and Steve. Both had been significant to the church's success as well.

Mike stated with a chuckle, "Two of the four families who started the church were from our own family. My mom's parents and our family were half of the church's total members."

For years, Pastor Hardwick never had enough money to pay himself a salary, so he worked as a chaplain at the state prison and taught his boys how to get up early and help him sell Krispy Kreme Donuts, box lunches, and dinners as ways of helping support the church. Funds were needed to run the buses for children and those families in need of a ride or for various other necessities of the church.

Mike and Steve remember their dad cutting grass in his suit on hot days. Why? Some days, there wasn't much time to change clothes between a funeral or a hospital call.

These small yet important steps of commitment and sacrificial events created building blocks that were being carefully laid. They had become part of the Christ Church imprint in that integrity and servanthood was at the core of the church's early days. After years of working and volunteering for the church, eventually Pastor Hardwick was given a small salary.

I stood on the platform and looked out over the large crowd attending that morning. I jokingly shared that as a counselor, the odds of him marrying at the age of eighteen and remaining a pastor at one location for fifty years was slim to none. We all had a good laugh. I asked everyone to please stand and give honor and thanks to this great and faithful servant of God after all these years.

As the congregation gave him the great standing ovation he so rightly deserved, I felt inadequate to even be part of this service.

Why? Well, for one reason, I remember the gracious acts of service he displayed, regardless if it were toward a homeless person or peering over the shoulders of others while listening to the great Billy Graham speak in his office. Pastor humbly put Reverend Graham in his own chair and made sure all his needs were personally met. The life of this wonderful man from Finley, Tennessee, had not only left an imprint on my life but the lives of hundreds of great pastors and thousands of church attendees he had met along the way.

However, the highlighted call on my life in the mid to late 90s was a specific sermon Pastor Hardwick had given titled BHAG ("Big Hairy Audacious Goal"). It was this very message that caused me to make good on the promise I had previously made five years earlier to God and a little nine-year-old African-American boy named "Carlos." God had used that to prompt me to realize He was actually calling me to reach out beyond our local church and community for Christ. So, if God could use a young man from the small town of Finley, maybe he could use me as well despite the painful inedible bad memories left by one of my family members.

This time, I knew I had to fulfill the promise I had made as a therapist to that child in 1992. I had tucked this promise down deep inside my heart due to the enormity of what I knew it would take to fulfill it. In fact, it would take a miracle to fulfill such a huge call and goal to which God had called me.

At that time of fulfilling that promise, little did I realize that God would not only be faithful to me but to thousands upon thousands of children and families we would help over the years. This 2014 celebratory service would prove pivotal and another motivation to write this imprinted story.

Looking at Obstacles as Opportunities

Winston Churchill once stated, "One should look at obstacles as opportunities, not problems."

Had it not been for Pastor Hardwick, his two sons Mike and Steve, the teachings of Dave Ramsey on finances, Dan Miller explaining the importance of creating a well thought-out mission statement, my cousin Mike Berner helping me with policies and procedures, and my first cousin Landy giving me a thirty-day loan to meet payroll, our legacy company LifeCare would most likely never have happened. Fortunately, I also had a dad, a father-in-law, and dear friends serving on my board to help fill in the gaps during those early foundational years.

Still, how does one build a new company, realizing you have limited management skills necessary to run it? For example, I had no business degree, limited resources, and no staff. Well, as you journey with me through this story, you will see how God's favor and mercy were prevalent every step of the way.

Looking back, I realize now after employing many hundreds of employees and managing millions of dollars, it had to be God's favor that allowed us to serve thousands upon thousands of our state's most poor, vulnerable, neglected, and abused children, as well as those with rehabilitative, physical, and special exceptional supports. This book will help show you how after twenty-two years and building two nonprofits, God made the impossible possible, despite the great weaknesses I posed.

Completing Our Will—The Final Epiphany Inspiration in Writing this Book

At the beginning of 2015, after some prodding from one of my fellow friends and facing my mortality, my wife Raye Ann and I decided to have an attorney draw up a will for us. I felt the attorney would give me some peace by ensuring that we carefully divided up our investments, buildings, land, and other assets to our three children equally.

When it was completed, I left our attorney's office with some initial peace, knowing it was finally done and our children would be fine. This sense of peace ironically would be short-lived in that on the drive home, I felt something was still missing. Surely, there had to be something more meaningful to give to my kids and grandkids.

I kept mulling these things over in my mind, yet I still did not want Raye Ann to think I wasn't happy with our completed wills. As the months continued, it kept bothering me that I wasn't giving something of real substance to my children about my life or that of their ancestors.

So, around the early part of 2015, ancestry.com popped up on my screen at work, and I began to ask myself, *How can I share a story with my kids about their heritage and that of their descendants if I haven't even taken the time to find out about my own ancestors?*

A few days later, I made the decision that it was time I commit to doing some real significant research about my family's heritage. I had been told my family was of German descent, but I had no idea if this was folklore or fact. No matter what, I was now committed to find out.

I became inundated with a multitude of questions. Did my family come from Germany, and if so, where? Who was the first person in our family to come to America? Why did they come here?

My search and journey for meaning had begun. Over the next two years, I began my new routine early in the morning to write or do research while giving Manny his uninvited snuggle space. I began by diligently searching online and in libraries to find various family historical sites and books. I sought permission from ancestry.com to enter the family trees of some possible downline relatives who may have some stories or facts that could support my research. Other family trees I found with maternal or paternal downlines were also important. However, the ancestry.com site and outreach to my immediate and extended family, including that of my parents, evolved into hundreds of more questions and thus became an everyday goal to try and find out as much as possible.

My Admitted Addiction

As time went on, I got up early, went to bed late, drove my wife and kids crazy, asking them to turn down the tube and keep my dinner on the stove. I soon realized my original intention of just charting births, deaths, and who begat who was not enough. So began the next level.

Within nine months, I was now in the deep guts of research and was beginning to form some of my ancestors' stories. I was like a little kid discovering hidden treasures in a candy store. For years, I had done family trees as a therapist that were helpful in the counseling process, but this one tree was of specific significant interest in that it involved my own flesh-and-blood relatives. It felt as if I was bringing history back to life again. I was making a connection between family members and the generations to which they were linked. Finally, I was finding out about parts of my family story I never knew existed.

As I began threading the stories as far back as the early 1700s, it was as if I was watching an old black-and-white reel-to-reel projector, watching real pictures and matching faces and stories. A storyline was forming together, no longer a bunch of disjointed accounts, but with people and stories that were intimate, funny, sad, full of loss and joy, ones that were becoming part of my own extended story I never knew existed.

I started bringing tissues, and Manny tried to stop the tears. I found myself smiling, laughing, hurt, and frustrated. Most importantly, it was all coming to life now. My family story was starting to make sense. My questions were finally being answered, and feelings of hope were replacing uncertainty as I watched what seemed like treasures unearthed from the sea and brought to the surface. I strongly empathized with some of these real-to-life stories that would stretch from me, my father, and every grandfather up the chain, all the way up and back to my sixth-generational great-grandfather.

I found out our family truly did come from Germany and in what town they lived. Eventually, the names of Hans, Frederick, Samuel, Joseph, William, and Tom were no longer just distant relatives; they had become part of my own heart. The good, the bad, the ugly, and the beautiful parts of my family's story were no longer hidden away in layers of words and pictures with no connections. Each one of my grandfathers was suddenly alive and now in a full panoramic view.

All these characters were not only flesh and blood, but I could see some of them in my own friends, colleagues, coleaders, and coaches and in therapists, administrators, business CEOs, blue-collars workers, artists, educators, and friends in ministry, many with whom I have had the privilege to work.

Some of my relatives, who you will read about in this book, would need to develop a new language and new culture and encounter others who also shared experiences of risk, exploration, lack of money, and loss. Some experienced similar things to that of other families as well. Most remained faithful as couples, yet some did not.

Our Trip to Germany...

Prior to beginning chapter one, I wanted to conclude this introduction by briefly sharing an amazing trip my wife and I recently took to Germany that touched my very soul. I hope as you read about it, you will see how these last few pages set up the entire book. I hope it will create that sense of inspiration with you as it did with me.

Germany—Going Back to My Homeland

On September 13, 2018, Raye Ann and I travelled to London, England, on an overnight eight-and-half-hour fight from Nashville. After a several-hour layover, we flew onto Frankfurt, Germany. We would be celebrating our thirty-fifth wedding anniversary primarily in Italy, but we had scheduled three days in Giessen, Germany, some fifty-five miles northeast of Frankfurt. It was here where our Mauck (Mock) family and imprinted story began. This was the place where Hans Peter Mock, my sixth-generational great-grandfather, was born in 1707. His Lutheran parents were Wilhelm and Sophia Mock. (The spelling of Mock, Mauk, and Mauck evolved over time. The German and English phonetics caused translation problems in regards to spelling, intonation, and blends.)

During our one-hour flight from London to Germany, we flew over the English Channel. I had just figured out how many miles we would have traveled internationally, over 4,571 miles to get here.

It would have taken me approximately nine hours in total to travel from Nashville to Frankfurt and close to another hour to get to Giessen, ten hours in total. In comparison, the trip from Giessen, Germany to Philadelphia, Pennsylvania, in 1733, took my sixth-generational great-grandfather Hans Peter Mauk a total of approximately 150 days, or nearly 4,000 hours. To think it took me less than half a day to get there in comparison to a twenty-five-year-old coming on an English passenger boat was overwhelming.

Soon, I would be attempting to trace the actual steps of Hans Peter. The thought of bringing that to fruition was suddenly very surreal.

As we drove to Giessen, I realized I was on the autobahn with cars passing me at some 140 miles per hour. Experiences like this, Hans would have never imagined in the 1700s. The temptation to speed was too appealing. I soon discovered that driving at 120 miles per hour in the slow lane for a few minutes was very exhilarating.

We checked into our small bed and breakfast, a large older home. The keeper of the home spoke limited to almost-no English. Not knowing any German, I quickly saw the immediate barrier Hans would have encountered when he first came to America. It must have taken him six months, maybe even years to learn a language about which he and our ancestral family knew nothing.

Our German meals at the inn were very different. A common lunch or dinner in Giessen would include sausage, rice, homemade cheeses, tomatoes, and cucumbers. Breakfast could consist of cereal, eggs, yogurt, meat, potatoes, or oats.

I also learned that in Germany, there was little to no ice. They believed in serving you drinks from glass bottles. They didn't use plastic cups, forks, spoons, or knives. It was nothing but real silverware, plates, and glasses. Any less was considered offensive.

Preparing a meal was the time to converse and meant to be special. Life seemed simple despite the modern changes in this little city that had once been a village. We did recognize how Americanized we were that one-night we celebrated with pizza.

First and Second Full Day in Giessen...

The first day, we relaxed from our long flight. The next day, we met the local Lutheran lady pastor of Giessen who spoke English. Though knowledgeable about her local large Lutheran church, she could not determine which church my generational great-grandfather Hans and his family attended.

She pointed on the map that was laid out on a nearby table to where the local river intersected north and south from the roads at that time. Hans would have likely departed from that area. The west side of the river would lead him eventually down river to the Rhine.

Last Day in Germany, September 15, 2018

Our last day in Germany was the most rewarding. The downtown city map indicated where our Mauck family would have shopped for goods as farmers. The beautiful Bavarian town, at one time part of a war-torn country, was now adorned with beautiful brick churches. Modern enclosed walkways were diagonally structured with intersectional areas that led to shops. Clean cobblestone streets were surrounded by old and new buildings accessorized by Germanic-style shudders and gables. This once little village town was now a quaint city, but at a one point, it was an eyesore due to the ravages of war and death. However, one would never know due to the town's total reconstruction and modernization after World War II.

The most rewarding and emotionally fulfilling experience was locating the Lahn River whereby my sixth-generational great-grandfather Hans Peter Mock would place his little family canoe and start down the tributary to the large English passenger ship named *Samuel*. This ship would have been waiting for its passengers to board on the Rhine River sometime in the late spring of 1733, to ultimately head to America.

As Raye and I followed the map, sure enough, we came across the railroad and roads that intersected near the waterway downtown as the pastor had told us. As we entered a small tunnel underneath the railroad tracks, my eyes suddenly gushed with unexpected tears. There in front of me was the quaint tributary from where Hans Peter Mock would have left. I then knew exactly why I had to come some 4,500 miles away from home.

A beautiful walkway lined the river where kayakers rowed in unison, cutting through its serene surface. A restaurant next to the pier and trees complimented the ambiance of the congenial Lahn River and its view. I was captivated by it all.

As a couple passed by us, I whispered to my wife, "Raye, it's overwhelming, isn't it?"

"Yes," she whispered back, "it is."

"This is where Hans left at twenty-five years of age. Hard to believe we are here seeing this place in person?" I slowly backed away while eyeing the view. "I want you to know the tears you see from my eyes are not about me or for me; they are for him. His parents had saved most of their entire life for the one and only ticket to America for their son, and he was a young man eight years younger than our own son when he left."

I thought about how everything Hans had ever known in his life, he would now be paddling away from—his home, friends, and pastor. On that spring day when he said goodbye to his parents, they and he knew it would be the last time they would ever set eyes on each other again. The parting must have been the toughest thing he had ever been asked to do.

Still, Hans Peter Mock made the brave decision to travel to America in the spring of 1733, to ultimately honor his parents' wishes for him to have a better life and to find a place where he could freely worship without the fear of religious persecution. In Germany, the Lutheran people worked hard as farmers, yet they were treated like dogs beneath the table. Not only would wealthy kings and landlords look the other way when others took their land, but they would torture the Lutherans because of their faith as well.

I imagined him wanting to avoid being seen by those oppressors, so he probably had to travel by the moon shining on the water at night and hide in the cove as needed during the day. As he travelled down this long tributary, he had to eventually connect with the much larger Rhine River.

Little did he know what would soon be facing him!

The very spot where I stood seemed like a place of providence. It was here where Hans determined if our name, our faith, and our way of life would continue or die, if he would turn around and go back to a place where our family had suffered greatly for their faith.

I would capture this place with my camera to keep it as an imprint to share with my family, signifying this as the very place where my sixth-generational great-grandfather would last see his home and family. I realized while standing on this very spot that few, if any of my past relatives would have this opportunity to come to this iconic spot since most of our family had passed away. My dad was the only Mauck left to share it with.

Hans hoped to make it to America. He would never know that some 285 years later, his sixth-generational great-grandson Kenny Mauck would come and visit our original home of ancestry where he began our story. On behalf of all the Maucks now living and worshiping freely, I was humbled to be here celebrating his life decision in risking it all by journeying to America.

(As you travel onward through this book based on my family's true-life story, an application section at the end of each chapter has been created with interactive questions to assist and support you in developing your own story.)

CHAPTER 1

Passages

> "What can we gain by sailing to the moon if we are not able to cross the abyss that separates us from ourselves? This is the most important of all voyages of discovery, and without it, all the rest are not only useless, but disastrous."
>
> — THOMAS MERTON

A S I AM STANDING ON MY BACK DECK, a large crane dives perfectly over the pond, spearing a fish within seconds. I watch with fascination as he skims beautifully over the water before landing effortlessly with his prize breakfast near the far bank.

Our backyard is the best place I have found for inspiration to study and write. Early in the morning or late in the afternoon, the flora and fauna that surround my home provide a spectacular creative backdrop.

Here in this beautiful setting primed for reflection and introspection is where I have realized the importance of story. What started as the simple desire to document our family history, including the migration of our German ancestors to America in the 1700s, has become a life-changing, eye-opening journey for me. The most impactful was the information I uncovered about the life of my multi-generational grandfather Hans Peter Mock and his voyage to America in 1733.

Hans Peter Mock: 1707–1771
(My Sixth-Generational Great-Grandfather)

I can only imagine that at only twenty-five years old, Hans was probably both scared and excited as he embarked on the ship *Samuel* in the spring of 1733, with 291 passengers, including the captain, Hugh Percy. He was in good company with most of his traveling companions consisting mostly of Lutheran families and couples with dreams and aspirations that come with traveling to a new land, but he was only one of a few individuals traveling without a friend or family member.

This British passenger ship had been carrying passengers back and forth for nearly a decade. It wasn't large by today's standards, especially with so many travelers aboard, measuring a mere 140 feet by 30 feet by 15 feet. Still, even the cramped six-foot by two-foot individual sleeping quarters housed three floors below deck wouldn't deter those coming to America.

As a result of these conditions, each of the travelers would acquire their own story, including my ancestor Hans. As I dug deeper into his, I felt like I was unwrapping a gift that led me to a missing key piece of the treasure map of my life. Here is his story through his journal:

July 3: Our ship left Germany in early May and is now fully sailing out into the Atlantic Ocean and bound for Philadelphia. These days are beginning to run together. It is difficult to tell one from another. Can this be over a month and a half that has passed? It does not seem that long. But I count 45 days, all ordinary other than a few slight overcast days, wind, and slight rain that quickly passes. Otherwise, sailing has been unhindered for the most part.

My new friend, an older grandfatherly type by the name of Thomas, and I had a game of cards on deck and talked of his dreams of owning a tavern in the new world. Thomas looks like he could be one of the rough sailors onboard. I sense secrets lurking beneath the surface, more like something he is running from rather than the new life so many onboard sprint toward.

This morning, dark, even ominous clouds are coming toward us on the horizon, but our Captain Percy seemed unconcerned.

Throughout the afternoon and into the evening, the winds have picked up considerably since we are now out deeper into the ocean, more so than any other day thus far. So I have returned from above the deck to my quarters a little early for the night.

July 4: The wind is stronger, and the waves have gained strength. Captain Percy and our first mate met at the bow of the ship this morning, away from the eyes and ears of passengers. I now can see some concern as they observe the dark clouds that appear to have gained on our ship's position overnight.

We caught a westerly wind for a good part of the day, but even that has not pushed us out of reach. I fear we are losing ground to the approaching storm as the waves and wind continue to intensify. They have become too strong for our Lutheran leaders to pray on deck, which till now has been the normal pattern. They chose to instead pray within the safety of our quarters this morning. Overnight, I heard the wind and waves pick up considerably.

July 5: Captain Percy and the crew have been working through the night to fasten down more items on deck. The dark clouds that were once at a distance a few days ago have all but surrounded us now. Thomas and I snuck atop deck to a sheltered spot out of the way. We watched Captain Percy shout many orders as the crew quickly obeyed, tying down loose sails, repairing damaged lines, and scrambling to secure all doors and windows as the captain kept an eye on the horizon through his telescope. The captain then met with the entire crew briefly, the contents of the meeting I could not ascertain, but my fears were confirmed when he went below deck to meet with the Lutheran leaders.

Thomas and I followed down a different set of stairs to hear the captain's loud warnings and instructions for the leaders and other passengers. Every man will be needed to help in order for us to survive this storm, so be prepared if and when they called. As he turned to leave, he whispered to one of the Lutheran ministers, "We could use some prayer as well, Reverend."

The pounding rain grows louder as if it will bore right through the hull. The winds drive us over waves quickly now as if to thrust us over the edge and plunge us to the ocean floor. I cannot sleep for the roughness and the fearful cries of the elderly and children and listening to the crew yell, "Hold the wheel steady."

July 6: Few if any slept last night, and prayers for sunlight to break through the storm that next morning were unanswered. For what we could now see by day was proof of those things we heard by night. We assisted the crew the previous day by securing the upper deck of the Samuel. The strong winds and hard rains proved too strong. The deck was scattered with ropes, broken oars, buckets, and bindings with several large cloth sails that would need to be resewn and then reattached by several men.

Even our living quarters were impacted with wet shoes, clothes, and hats. The captain asked that we nail down items above our beds. His eyes were bloodshot from the late hours. Though his words were meant to console us, everyone was now fully awake to the sobering reality that our fate was no longer in his hands. All the men, including myself, were needed to help prepare for the next round of storms.

A prayer meeting was called by the Lutheran women near the stern of the Samuel. Now, all its passengers, crew, and the ship itself were being fully battered and needed something that none of them could control. A sovereign act from God is what each hoped for now.

July 8: Thomas and I have spent the last two days bailing out water with buckets. The storm still rages. Evenings seem worst in that the wind and rain have fully blown out most all the lanterns and candles. The children continually cry, and mothers are distraught by not being able to console or quiet them. Sleep now gives way to daily survival.

July 9: Day 4 of the storm and day 3 of the women, children, and elderly trapped below deck to avoid the danger outside. Sickness and anxiety are settling in. All are desperate for fresh air or something other than the putrid stench from what feels like imprisonment.

July 11: A tragedy came upon us last night. They believe a little five-year-old boy was lost at sea. Most all the crew looked for him for hours to be sure. The unfortunate combination of nightfall, the great gust of wind, hard rain impacting eyesight, and wet decking near the guard rails contributed to the child's death. It seems the little one briefly escaped the hold of his mother and father in order to gasp one more breath of fresh air. Unfortunately, the wind had caused the father to quickly shut the door behind him just after the child lurched away from his hand. Once the father realized what had happened, he re-opened the door to save his son but lost any and all sight of him. My heart grieves over this child's death. God, I do not understand.

Cases of pneumonia and food poisoning plagued the ship as we lost several of our elderly over the last week as well. Sleep continues to evade me as I hear the wails of mourning parents and loved ones.

July 13: Early this morning while it was still dark, the storm violently tossed me from my bed, causing me to hit my head. Yesterday, the winds seemed to settle ever so slightly, only to regain more strength later in the day. In fact, it snapped three separate masts and slammed them to the deck, killing one of our crew. No one, not even myself or Thomas, is permitted above deck today. Waves send water down the stairwells into our quarters below, and we cannot keep up with the bailing. Our ship creaks as if it is breaking in two. Thunder shakes the hull.

July 15: Morning. The waves are overrunning our ship. The storm is winning this fight. Captain Percy has instructed us to keep items that float within reach should he order the call to abandon ship. With the loss of Samuel's four masts and the severe damage it has undergone, we are at the mercy of the storm. Some elderly have prayed what I consider their last prayers. But like myself, most of the men and women labor tirelessly, passing buckets up to the deck to return as much of the water back to the sea.

I cannot eat, as I have been throwing up for two days in between bouts of bailing out water. Although my faith is still strong, I am prepared to leave this earth. All of us are at our end physically and mentally. So tired.

Evening. I am thirsty but still cannot eat due to not being able to keep solid food or drink down. We continue to take shifts, bailing water without pause. I rest whenever I can. Exhaustion is my constant companion.

I have finished the letter to Mama and Papa and sealed it inside an empty whiskey bottle I found while cleaning the deck. For 12 days, torrential rains and winds have given us no reprieve. Even now, the ship rises and falls, creaking and moaning on an unfortunate constant motion fed by the strong gale winds and seas. It's as if a monster has arisen from the depths of the ocean, relentlessly battering us over and over again. Even though my faith and hope have not yet failed me, my body and mind have nothing left. So, I pen these last remaining notes in my diary to record the dire circumstances we now face and will toss the bottled letter into the ocean toward Germany in hopes it gets to my parents. I fear the storm and waves are overtaking us and that we will not make it through the night.

(To whoever may find this letter, most likely found after my death at sea on the Samuel, please see this letter is delivered to my parents, Mr. Johan Wilhelm and Sofia Elizabeth, of the Village of Giessen, Germany, not far from the Lahn River.)

Dear Papa and Mama,

I write this letter to you as I believe my time is short. Our ship has become disabled due to damage caused by violent storms, and I fear these moments may be my last.

Mama, Papa, do not let sorrow overtake you. Instead, focus on the good memories we have had. My life as your only son leaves me with nothing but the greatest appreciation and affection for you. I have no regrets, nor should you. Your selfless, sacrificial gift of sending me to a better life in the New World is a testament of your love for me, and I am forever grateful.

Mama, you prayed the night before I left for an angel to accompany me on my journey at sea. That prayer has been such a warm blanket to my soul! I was hesitant to come to America because I didn't want to leave you behind, but you and Papa insisted I take the money you have worked so hard to save, enough for one passage, and go. You saved me from a life of war and oppression that my friends will surely endure. You wanted more for me than a life of shame and ridicule that our Lutheran people have greatly suffered from. I too want more, to build a life for my own family as you and Papa did for me and to carry on the Mock name.

I hope you will be proud at the risk we have all taken, seeking a new homeland where I can freely confess Jesus Christ as Lord and not be persecuted for our faith.

That last night, I prayed as well, asking God for peace and favor if I was to go the next morning to America. He answered, giving me complete peace as I came downstairs and shared our last meal with you and Papa.

Papa, I wish I could have been stronger for you when it was time to say goodbye. But hearing you and Mama pray, it was too overwhelming, and I could not hold back my tears. If I don't make it to America, please know I did my best.

If it is God's will that I awaken in heaven, I will await both of you at the gates. To live, it will take a miracle sent from God above. If He chooses to send one, I will continue to make you proud. It is in His hands now!

I love you.

Your dearest son,
Hans

July 19: *I woke yesterday from what seemed like a horrible dream to people gathered all around me, smiling but with concern in their eyes. George and his wife Mary sat next to me and gave me a small glass of water. They told me I have been semi-unconscious four days, sick from food poisoning and thrashing around from delirium. They have been caring for me, helping me to consume small amounts of water.*

I have no memory of it. I wondered for a moment if I was still dreaming and if I was truly alive. I am weak, but since waking, I have been able to keep down a spoonful of beans and barley.

I was surprised to see the sun shining through the open door at the top of the stairs.

July 20: *Today, I am well enough to walk on the deck with assistance. I am still not strong, but I am glad for the breeze that breathes new life into my being. Most of the masts that had been snapped by the storm are repaired.* Samuel *is on its way again* as the sails flap beautifully in concert with the wind. Sea air has replaced the stale and horrible smells associated with 12 days of being isolated below the main deck of the boat.

As I rounded the stern on my slow assisted walk, I realized I am not dead. I AM NOT DEAD. I shouted, "I AM ALIVE!" I startled a baby who began to cry. What a beautiful sound.

July 21: All is well with the exception of my friend Thomas. I inquired today of his whereabouts, but no one knows. No one knows who he is. George and Mary have said they only took care of me but did hear me mention his name as I talked in my sleep. But there is no Thomas on this ship. I am at a loss for an explanation.

August 1: I feel I have healed completely. I have been visiting the sick and weak below deck, helping where I can. The captain was glad to see me up and about again.

Four adults and three children died from an accident, pneumonia, and food poisoning. Even so, today was a special day. A baby was born, something we can all rejoice in. I see thankfulness in the faces of my fellow passengers for the miracle of surviving. Like this baby, a new life now awaits us!

August 17: The captain has told us we are just hours from entering the harbor of Philadelphia. Upon hearing this, I stood at the bow of the boat, arms lifted toward heaven, thanking God as I thought of Mama and Papa. Even now, I cannot hold my emotions back. My parents' dream of their only son living in America will come true. My hope of carrying on the family name lives! No longer will I live under persecution for my faith.

May these written words ever remind me of the sacrifices made for this new life for myself and for generations that follow. I live to serve my God, to make my parents proud. May God help me make my life count for something greater than just myself.

Here I sit impacted by Hans Peter. Although I may be generations disconnected from him, I will forever be closely connected to him after finding his redemptive story. Our choices, our journeys, and yes, our stories represent legacies unfolding before me like a beautiful tapestry. Hans' story is woven with excitement, adventure, and harrowing experiences, all leading to a new life of freedom.

Mine reads a little different, yet it's been an exciting one as well. It includes a promise made to a little inner-city boy and a catalyst by a beloved and respected minister named Pastor L.H. Hardwick from Christ Church in Nashville, Tennessee.

I met nine-year-old Carlos in 1992, during my early years as a counselor. He had been removed from his home at four years old after being found alone caring for himself and his two-year-old brother. His childhood had been anything but childlike, raised by a crack-addicted mother who paid for her habit by working the streets.

Being left for hours, even days at a time, was not new for Carlos. Also, during those infrequent times Mom was home, she was not engaged with her children or emotionally present; she was high. When neighbors finally called the police because of the constant crying day in and day out, the officers found two emaciated young boys who hadn't seen their mother in two days.

In the newness of my career, Carlos' situation was hard for me to reconcile. I couldn't even begin to understand how any child could be living in such conditions, even though I knew at the same time he was one among many kids who did. Although his story was unique, it was not uncommon for kids living in inner-city housing.

I felt overwhelmed with the desire to take care of not only him, but every child like him.

I remember watching Carlos on the playground that summer and hoping his foster-care parents could adopt him someday. He and I bonded together that summer, playing basketball, hopscotch, kickball, and tag. Although Carlos couldn't talk well or had limited motor skills, he wanted attention. Unfortunately, he often went after attention in the wrong way.

He didn't play many games with the other children very often. He was abused and wasn't sure who he could trust. He had a long way to go in the area of trust and understandably so. We couldn't take back the physical and emotional trauma from his past, but we were working to give him a better future through the time he and I had spent together, the programs available to him, and the care of loving foster parents. I did my best to help him heal and give him hope and a sense of security.

I watched him bounce a ball against the wall for a while before finally asking him to join me. We laughed together as I shared how much I appreciated getting to know him.

My voice broke as I hugged him, trying to hold back my emotions. I whispered, "It's going to be okay." I told him I was sorry today would be our last meeting at the school, but I would inquire about how he was doing, even if we couldn't be together any longer. I didn't realize it would mean never seeing him again. So after hugging him on that hot summer day, I made a promise to him in my heart that I would dedicate my life to helping young boys and girls like him, but do it from a place of Christ's love.

I walked behind Carlos and the other children as they walked to the waiting vans. After returning to the playground, I sat down on a large rock. "God." I whispered, "whatever it takes, even if it means building an army of caregivers who loved like Christ did, I will help children like Carlos in some way the rest of my life."

After that experience, I did continue to work with children, both as a teacher and a counselor. But it wasn't until five years later that Pastor Hardwick's empowering message titled the BHAG ("Big Hairy Audacious Goal") would stir a passion and an unquenchable fire in my heart, bringing my promise to God and a little boy named Carlos to life. At the time of the sermon, I was Director of Counseling at Christ Church. But that day, the Lord called me with the help of that sermon to begin what is now called LifeCare, a nonprofit that would help many children and begin a new chapter in the Mauck family story.

Navigating Your Story

Let's talk about story.

"Your story matters." Although this is a current buzzword/phrase we constantly hear in churches and the counseling community, your story *does* matter. I believe that statement. I wouldn't have had a job as a counselor if I didn't!

Every day, every week, every month, every year, sentences, paragraphs, and chapters are added to your story. The choices you make, the things you do, the places you go, the people who come into your life all add lines to your story. But that's just the surface. It's in the past events of a person's life where their story takes on a whole new level of meaning.

We can't talk about a life story without bringing up legacy. Legacy is the story passed down. It's the story you leave behind. It's the story that is left to you.

You don't have to share your story with the world, but share it with someone because again, all of us have a story. It has been passed down *to* us, created *through* us, and passed down *by* us. You inherited a story. You are creating a story, and you are leaving a story. Legacy is all of these things. It's your extrinsic life story of the past, present, and future coming together and moving forward from you.

Legacy and life imprint are intertwined, but not the same. Understanding imprint is vital to your story and the legacy you are creating. *Imprint* is both a noun and a verb. It's something that happens *to you* and something left *in you*. It's a mark on your soul and becomes part of your spiritual DNA.

An imprint can be both an impression in the mind and the effect of an action. When you *make an imprint* on someone through your choices, words, or actions (or lack thereof), you are participating in shaping someone's way of responding to life.

An imprint is something done *to another* and left *on another*. The result is a mark, an indelible impression, a *lasting effect*. It's a mark left intentionally or unintentionally whether or not either party realizes it. It's a life-branding of affirmation from those who love us, then passed on to those we love and to those yet to be born, ones we call a "loving imprint in-waiting."

Imprinting also happens through the events we live through or live in, such as wars, natural disasters, and economic, cultural, or religious influences. This process has been happening for generations, shaping and leaving a mark on your family and ancestors. And it will continue down for generations to come, long after you and I are gone.

Imprinting impacts an individual on a psychological and emotional level and is often accompanied by pictures or words that directly affect how you live your life. It impacts your story and the legacy you leave. The story imprinted in you, combined with your life story, is your life imprint.

Your Children's Inheritance

My original intent in researching my family history had been to simply make sure my family actually knew their history, that something existed on paper telling them from where and whom we came.

However, as I started researching, reading, and documenting my family history, the therapist in me spoke up and said, "This story is a mess!" Thankfully, its only part of my story.

My internal counselor saw that in the lines of my ancestral history were identical issues through which I've helped people in my office for years. Patterns that emerged on the pages of their stories were the same patterns I saw written in my own life story.

That counselor voice in my mind read the risks, the losses, and the addictions surrounding the names and events that had shaped my ancestors, their decisions, and ultimately my family. The Scripture passage in Proverbs 13:22 (ESV) that says, "A good man leaves an inheritance to his children's children" suddenly came into a new light. The relationship between story, legacy, and imprint jumped off the pages, and I heard a voice say, "This is your children's inheritance."

During Christmas 2017, I had the opportunity to share some of my findings—ancestry and stories—and my thoughts with my children and grandchildren. I told them of the bravery of their seventh-generational great-grandfather Hans Peter Mauk, of his parents' courageous choice, and of his fascinating journey to and life in America.

I shared heartbreaking stories of loss with a sense of gratitude for the sacrifices made by our flesh-and-blood ancestors who had a direct impact on our life today. To my surprise and joy, my family was wholly engaged, laughing, listening, and asking questions.

My hope is that I have rekindled a timeless tradition of storytelling in my own family that will continue for years to come. My prayer is that this inheritance of understanding our legacy blesses my family generation after generation.

Charted Steps

Your story is like mine, full of an inheritance of rich treasures and truths waiting to be discovered. Generational and eternal gifts are just waiting to be opened by you and then your children and your children's children. But for there to even be a gift, you have to start the journey.

I began this book with the history of Hans and his journey. His story and my story create beautiful bookends, if you will, to a chapter in my family's life imprinted story. As we fill in the middle, we'll discover the keys to unlocking your true story.

Many things imprint a person's life. We'll dive into those and leave you with a few steps you can do to explore your story further.

IMPRINT—Your Family History

1. If you don't already have a journal, pick one up or fire up the laptop and begin noting what you discover about your own family, generation by generation. Start with your parents and then your grandparents. Find a family tree template online and start filling it in.
2. If possible, be intentional about finding time to talk to family members about what you are doing. You'll be amazed at the information they have tucked away just waiting to be shared! Ask your family about important things they heard about your family. Then check if it's true. Sometimes our loved ones can be right on but other times not.
3. Cover this process in prayer. Lay your inheritance at the feet of Jesus and ask Him to guide you, speak to you, and do His work in you through your family story.

CHAPTER 2

Uncharted Waters

> "Two roads diverged in a wood, and I—
> I took the one less traveled by, And that
> has made all the difference."
>
> — ROBERT FROST

MY HANDS ARE TIGHTLY cupped around my mug, absorbing the warmth on this chilly morning. The sun continues its ascent, further unveiling the beauty of the landscaping against the forest clearing behind my house.

The scenery is one of the many things I love about our new home and neighborhood, which is nestled among tall forest trees, with many areas left in their natural state. I wonder how much it resembles the forested areas of the home Hans left in Germany.

I recently had the opportunity to visit the hometown of Hans in Toms Brook, Virginia. I imagined Hans stepping out and surveying his new home after arriving and settling in, feeling humbled and thankful, much like I am feeling today. In my mind, I can see him giving a deep sigh of satisfaction, of thankfulness as he admires the view of the Shenandoah Valley and the One who created it. As I mused, I wondered if he was in awe of the provision along the way as he reflected on all that had transpired and brought him to that place, possibly like me right now, a peaceful moment while anticipating what the future held.

Hans Peter Mauk (Mock): 1707–1771
(Continued from Chapter 1)

Upon any immigrant ship's arrival in Philadelphia, Pennsylvania, male passengers would be taken ashore by the captain or his designee, presented to the authorities, and required to sign an Oath of Allegiance stating their agreement to abide by the laws of the land before they and their families could officially enter the New World. So, when *Samuel* arrived that August 1733, Hans Peter signed and received his papers of allegiance.

Within a year, Hans moved to Toms Brook, Virginia, where he turned to the family business of farming and raising livestock. Eventually, he opened one of the first German-owned lumber mills.

On April 30, 1739, at the age of thirty-one, Hans married a young woman of German descent named Juliana Rheinhart. Together, Hans and Juliana took pride in working the land, starting the town's first sawmill, and caring for the house they built. Five children blessed that home between 1739 and 1760: John Peter, Catherine, Frederick, Henry, and Andrew.

The story surrounding Hans acquiring this first piece of property is one of both providence and sometimes humor. A primary example was when a local magistrate with thousands of acres of land hired Hans to assist him on his farm.

Back then, colonial court systems were modeled after the British judiciary systems. A magistrate was a local official, usually a British landlord and often referred to as the "justice of the peace."

One evening during the winter of 1742, and after a few too many brews at the local party, the magistrate was so drunk, he couldn't mount his horse after many attempts. The horse became agitated. A small crowd began gathering at the spectacle.

After several more failed attempts, Hans intervened, settling the animal down and assisting his employer in mounting his horse. In front of those witnesses, the man gushed his appreciation to Hans and promised a prized parcel of land for his trouble and kindness.

Interestingly enough, Hans did acquire property later that same year on June 23, 1742. It was a beautiful 168-acre parcel on Opequon Creek, deeded from Joist Hite on behalf of the magistrates. Hite managed thousands of acres for the British landlord. Hans Peter would later bequeath 100 acres of this land to his second child, my fifth-generational great-grandfather Frederick Mauk.

A Declaration of Faith

On August 1, 1745, nearly twelve years after first setting foot on the soil of the American colonies, Hans became the *first naturalized American German Lutheran citizen* in the Shenandoah Valley of Fredericks County, Virginia, an act that would make history and set a precedent.

After signing the Oath of Allegiance, Hans had a choice between two pathways to citizenship. The first and shorter path involved swearing allegiance to the Crown of England *and* to the Church of England. This pathway too closely resembled what he had left Germany to escape. Under the tyranny in Germany, he had had firsthand experience seeing his family and friends refuse to accept state religion and suffer the consequences. Those who would not convert lost their homes, land, and sometimes their lives.

So instead of taking his local Oath of Allegiance to the King of England, supremacy, and abjuration required by the British monarchy, Hans had learned from his family's past experience and chose the second pathway to citizenship. He understood that after seven to ten years of residing in Virginia, he would be grandfathered in as an American citizen *without taking the oath*. This choice allowed him freedom to choose his Lutheran faith.

One of Hans Peter's first acts as a naturalized citizen was to be baptized by a Lutheran minister. Why was this so important? The oath from here on would be to God first, and secondly, to king and country. These two symbolic acts, his grandfathered affirmation as a naturalized American citizen and baptism by a Lutheran minister, empowered Hans Peter Mauk.

Finally free from a life of bondage and tyranny, I can see the letters to his parents back in Germany. Not only would he let them know he had made the trip safely, but also that the voyage to the promised land of America had been worth every risk and every sacrifice made by them.

Frederick Mauk: 1749-1830
(My Fifth-Generational Great-Grandfather)

Frederick Mauk was born to Hans Peter and Julianna Mauk in Tom Brooks, Virginia, in 1749. As a young boy, Frederick was enthralled by his father's stories.

As was the custom in those days, after dinner the family gathered around the fireplace for a time of storytelling, singing, or Bible reading. The most beloved stories usually came from the oldest family members—grandparents, great-grandparents, aunts, and uncles—of their growing-up days, the hardships faced, risks taken, and of family generations removed. Folklore, humorous tales, and songs were the entertainment in the evenings. Legacy and heritage were intentionally passed from generation to generation in this fashion, something often lost in today's culture.

Picture a spellbound little boy, enraptured by stories of his father's long and harrowing voyage to America on the passenger ship called *Samuel*, of his grandparents' great sacrifice and earnest prayers over his father. I can see him sitting at his daddy's feet, eyes wide in wonder, silently hanging on to every word as his father acted out his exploits and adventures after landing in America, imagining that he too was a passenger on *Samuel*, a sidekick in his father's travels. Those times probably caused Frederick to determine that he would also be an adventurer, a risk-taker, and follow in his father's footsteps.

An 18th-century house flipper of sorts, Frederick enjoyed improving the homestead wherever he was, and he found it profitable. He had an impeccable work ethic, no doubt learned from his father as he worked by his side growing the family lumberyard. Frederick appreciated and was grateful for everything he had. He knew from years of hearing his father's stories that life would have been different in Germany.

Frederick met and married the beautiful Margaret Schwartz of the German settlement Tom Brooks in 1775. Her focus was on their three children Peter, Samuel, and Catherine, while Frederick focused on working with his father Hans by building out the town's first sawmill.

One thing Frederick did not excel at, however, was the English language. In fact, his thick German accent provided many funny misunderstandings and left his family in stitches from laughing so hard, such as the time Margaret had asked him to pick up some necessities in town, including newspaper. (A little context for you...

newspaper performed a dual function in those days. Not only did it keep you informed, but it eventually made its way to the outhouse for other purposes.)

Frederick headed to the general store where the conversation might have gone something like this:

"Gerd morning, sir. I need pepper."

"Good morning, Mr. Mauk. We have that right here," answered the shopkeeper, pointing to the spice rack which held several different kinds of pepper. "Black pepper?"

Frederick glanced over to where the shopkeeper pointed. "No, I need *pepper*," he corrected him gently.

"Um, well, then, white pepper?" The shopkeeper removed a small glass container and held it up for Frederick to see.

"No, no," Frederick said, waving his hands and slowly repeating, "Pepper."

"Oh," the shopkeeper said, nodding his head in understanding. "Red pepper?"

"Nein!" By this time, Frederick was more than a little annoyed. "I'm looking for pepper for my outhouse! *Newspepper!*"

The storekeeper chuckled and pointed to the papers hidden on the far end of the counter, amused by his humorous customer, the funny German, Mr. Frederick Mauk.

Frederick the Traveler

Four years after his father Hans, the family patriarch, sadly passed away from a heart attack in 1771, the Revolutionary War broke out in April 1775. Frederick saw the writing on the wall. British soldiers commandeered homes, property, and even people. He remembered the stories his father had told of citizens forced into servitude and allegiance to kings and warlords in Germany and to the Church. Freedom of religion and freedom from this kind of tyranny had been Hans' parents' motivation for sending their son to America.

To Frederick, it somehow seemed merciful that his father and mother had both passed away, not having to witness the very thing that caused him to flee Germany. After North Carolina patriotic forces defeated the loyalists in 1776, Frederick took his family out of war-torn Virginia, to the safety of North Carolina. Once the Revolutionary War was over in 1783, they went back to Virginia.

Comparatively speaking, Frederick moved his family more than the average American, from Virginia, to North Carolina, and back to Virginia, to eventually landing in Ohio, in his later years of life. Moving an entire household long distances isn't easy today, but it most definitely was not a practical decision in Frederick's day, especially repeatedly. Interstates didn't exist. Cars hadn't been invented yet. The family wagon was just that—a real wagon—not a minivan. Travel took significant time and effort and was risky.

Sometime after the birth of their third child Samuel in 1785, Frederick and Margaret packed up the children and trekked to Philadelphia, to the port in which his father first landed. He wanted to see and smell where his father came to America, to hear the sounds, see the sites, and touch the soil that young Hans had first set foot on. Now that his dad was gone, he was trying to feel in some tangible way what his father must have experienced upon first arriving in America.

Frederick had the heart of an adventurer and ultimately understood not only the risks in the stories that his father Hans shared but also the value of those risks. His father's stories truly inspired him, as evidenced by the way he lived his life and what he named his children: Catherine, Peter, and Samuel.

His first two children, Catherine and Peter, followed tradition and were named after his immediate and extended family. But he broke tradition with his third child, my fourth-generational great-grandfather, by naming him "Samuel" after the ship that brought his father to America. He was fascinated by this ship.

In Hebrew, "Samuel" means, "God has heard us." This name encapsulated everything for Frederick, from the earnest prayers and enormous sacrifice of his grandparents, Wilhelm and Sophia, to his father's long journey to America and deliberate "silent" naturalization and baptism. It meant freedom of religion, freedom of choice, and the payoff of faith and risk.

More of My Story: A Leap of Faith!

Once the Lord spoke to me through that "Big Hairy Audacious Goal" sermon, I was all in. I created a mission statement. For weeks and months through numerous sleepless nights, I prayed and labored over this new vision.

By that time, I was working as a counselor at Christ Church. After long days at the church, sometimes ten-hour days, I must have been running on adrenaline. After dinner, during the late evenings, I threw myself into writing out the programs on paper along with the guidelines and services we would offer. I even included job titles with blanks underlined next to them and mused, "Well, Lord, I wonder who You'll put there? Do I know them yet?"

Finally, the time had come to take the dream from paper to reality, to put feet to the pavement and move to what would become LifeCare. I needed to start acting like a company even though we had no money, no employees, and no office. It was my "Samuel moment," knowing God was with me.

I began our charters and bylaws with the Tennessee Secretary of State. I performed some research and found out we needed approximately $750 to submit to a CPA to apply for our 501 (c) 3 nonprofit application. At that time, my wife and I had $100 in checking and about $650 left in savings. It was a sign!

Naturally, this would require me to drain both of our accounts on the same day. I appeased that little voice inside my head that suggested I could ask my wife's forgiveness later. I had waited a long time to keep my promise. It was now or never. So, I took a leap of faith and turned in the application.

After a few days, I mustered up the courage to tell Raye Ann at breakfast precisely what I had done. I wanted to leave nothing but the truth on the table.

As I picked at the food on my plate, I braced myself and waited, expecting her to respond, "*You did what?!*"

But my gracious wife calmed my concerns, because while understandably surprised, Raye simply instead said, "Well, okay, but you do know that's all the money we have."

To which I looked down for moment at my plate and then back at her with my sheepish smile and responded warmly, "Yes. I do."

For me, the early years seemed more like a comedy of errors and mistakes than the startup of a God-given dream, and yet at every step, my faith was steadfast. As I walked out that promise to God and Carlos, He met me every step of the way, even when I didn't exactly get it right.

For Raye Ann and myself, those first years were similar to some of my generational grandfathers, both faith-stretching and yet humorous. I'm sure that more than once Raye, who would eventually become our first employee, looked around thinking, "Are we on *Candid Camera?*" Or maybe it felt more like her and I in a never-ending episode of *I Love Lucy*.

For example, we got our first call for a referral to have one of our staff work in a home with a family. Unfortunately, our Poodle Rascal was barking the entire time as Raye kept apologizing.

Everything but the Kitchen Sink

At our first board of directors meeting in 1997, LifeCare's charter and bylaws were approved. I tightly held to my chest those dreamed-filled pieces of paper. Even without names or faces, the dream now felt alive and real. For the first time, I could see our faith-based company was no longer a baby waiting to be born. It had become a full-fledged toddler overnight, needing more space to move and grow. I slept well that night.

I won't lie and say it was easy convincing my down-to-Earth, realist, financially savvy, and organized wife that we needed to now convert our dining room into an office, our breakfast nook into a copy room, and get this venture going. Even more challenging were the weeks after receiving our first grant contract of about $20,000 from the Metro Government of Nashville, a contract that opened the door to receive more referrals, which meant helping more people. It also meant needing even more office space.

Once I realized this, I began looking around the house, trying to figure out where to go. I landed in the garage while in my daydream state. I surmised, *Yes, the garage would make the perfect office space.*

I explained what was happening and what I thought was needed to Raye Ann, hoping she would react the same way she did when I told her about depleting our checking and savings accounts. When I shared about how we needed the garage, I realized by the look on her face that I needed more time to sell her on the idea.

Because incredulously, she exclaimed, *"You need what?"*

Now, you have to understand that my wife believes garages are for cars, and she liked to park hers in ours. It was a tougher sale for sure.

I immediately realized I forgot to tell her about the benefits from having the office in the garage, that it was not a problem but a solution. So, I put together my facts regarding all the positives and took her out there to see the vision, where I carefully laid out the plan and had her dream with me.

I said "This is going to be your office. We'll have air conditioning here, carpet, drywall. Of course, we'll have to come up with the money for materials, but our fathers can help with the labor, which is free. And best of all, we don't have to have the office in our dining room and breakfast area." Albeit a little reluctantly at first, she began to share in the dream by nodding her approval.

However, once the garage renovation was finished, I still realized working for the church was still my main priority. I would volunteer my time as LifeCare's President over the next five years without pay to ensure successful growth. I needed to maintain the integrity of my main position at Christ Church as the Director of Counseling.

Finally, in the fall of 1998, we were able to take Raye Ann on as our first full-time paid employee at a modest hourly wage, and we had hired four contracting staff who I trained to work in the homes to provide the services.

I'm quite sure it was not an impressive financial offer to Raye when compared to her career history and background as an executive assistant at General Motors, but it was a start and more than she would receive as a substitute teacher. Baby steps!

Time to Jump!

Between 2000 and 2001, it became apparent our small company was ready to leave the port of Christ Church and set sail alone. In January 2000, I met with the leadership at church to discuss my leaving and the next season for the counseling ministry Barnabas that I helped create in 1994.

Next was the LifeCare board of directors. Steve, Pastor Hardwick's son, and I came up with a mutually agreed-upon timeline, one that included a gradual downsize in both space and financial support. The time to take the LifeCare leap of faith was now.

Seasons such as these are bittersweet, and growth always has pains. Late in the fall of 2000, I had a meeting with all the volunteers and staff of Barnabas to get them up to speed. I shared my heart of wanting to leave on a good note and this being a calling, not another position or job. First, I wanted them to hear it from me. Secondly, I wanted to give them time to consider their own options. Many tearful and difficult conversations took place. Most understood, but that didn't necessarily make it any easier. In fact, in hindsight, it would have been much easier on my family and those I worked with if I had stayed.

I was taking the greatest risk of my life by leaving my job there to take on a whole new ministry venture. I had no idea Hans Peter Mauk even existed then. What an encouragement his story would have been at that time in my life had I known.

In some ways, I felt as if I was abandoning my teenage child, Barnabas Counseling Ministry, for another baby. Yet seeing God's hand in all that we accomplished and realizing it was God's plan got me through the early challenges.

I knew it was time to focus solely on LifeCare. Even though leaving had been a process, the risk weighed heavily on my choices and decisions during that time. Emotionally and financially, I would soon be free falling into the arms of God and letting Him catch me... the ultimate trust fall. That's a terrifying and exhilarating place to be.

Now was the time to jump.

Navigating Your Story

I've been in some risky situations in my life. My cousin let me fly his plane once. Without telling me, he flipped the start switch, killing the engines and sending us into a death dive toward Earth. I screamed. It was a joke and one I wasn't sure at the time I'd live through!

I've jumped off the high cliffs of Blue Hole in Jamaica, a considerable risk for someone with a fear of heights. I tried slalom skiing, emphasis on *tried*. It wasn't pretty. Admittedly, none of these hold a candle to the enormous risks surrounding Hans Peter Mauk coming to America. However, when I took a chance and made the decision to come to Nashville, I was the same age as Hans when he embarked on his journey. Then when I took a leap of faith and started LifeCare, I was the same age as Hans Peter when he became one of the first naturalized citizens in the Shenandoah Valley.

Faith and risk are two core values, and I most definitely want to pass on those experiences and understanding of both to my family. Faith is the substance of things we know and believe are going to happen because God is in it. Sheer risk is like rolling the dice, jumping off, and relying on a trust built on one's past experiences. Imprints from my journey that started with Hans and Frederick stood out as a thread woven down through my family's story. In my experiences, the best one can hope for is realizing that faith and risk, if used as God intended, go hand in hand.

Risk implies the possibility of loss or injury. Risk is often calculated as high or low. When we decide to take a risk, we are relying on our estimation of the situation, our knowledge. We determine whether or not we have the strength emotionally, physically, or financially to make it happen.

Faith takes risk to another level. Faith stretches us from the depths of our soul, a place where we are in communion with the One eternal source, God, who is greater than all of our abilities and knowledge. Faith calls us to a deeper trust that involves letting go of what we know and what we can do and *relying on God to reveal Himself and take us beyond ourselves in His time.*

By Faith

If you haven't read Hebrews 11, take a few minutes and read it now. (I'll wait...)

What an amazing chapter on faith. Verse 1 reads, "Now faith is confidence in what we hope for and assurance about what we do not see" (NIV). Faith is the belief that something we hope will happen happens, even when we don't have all the answers, all the evidence, or all the information. The chapter continues by laying out a spiritual lineage of faith, a lineage that is a part of my story, a lineage that is part of your story, an inheritance in which we all can take part.

By faith, Abel. By faith, Enoch. By faith, Noah. By faith, Abraham. By faith, Moses. By faith, by faith, by faith.

Every listed forefather of our faith was given a promise. Faith is the hope that the Lord's promises are true, that the vision He gives you is real and will come to pass, *even if you never get to see it.* Keep in mind, not one of them saw the promise come to pass in their lifetime.

My ancestors have forged a legacy of faith as well. By faith, Wilhelm and Sophia. By faith, Hans Peter Mauk. By faith, Kenny Mauck.

In those last days before launching into our new adventure with LifeCare, many asked me, "Why?" Why would I leave a position that had been such a benefit to the church and so secure for me?

Fast forward about seventeen years to when I was on a trip with Raye Ann, and we were driving back from Virginia. Once we entered Tennessee, we drove through about seven different counties.

Tennessee is a beautiful state, and as I admired the rolling, tree-covered hills, something occurred to me. "Raye Ann," I said, "do you realize that in all the counties we have passed through since the state line, one of our staff has touched or changed the life of a child or family for the better?"

It was surreal. Maybe it was on that day, the day before, during the previous week or month, but someone from LifeCare was providing medical assistance, counseling, case management, or trauma-related crisis support. Perhaps someone got a better place to live, help with meals, prescription assistance, a child was hugged to remind them that they are remembered and special, or someone dealing with depression was helped to choose one more day; they considered living instead of committing suicide.

That little baby of a company we started at our dining room table in 1997, has grown into one of the larger faith-based licensed mental health care companies in the country. For over twenty years, LifeCare has provided counseling, in-home case management, site-based psychiatric care, primary care, adult and rehabilitative daycare, and 24-7 community living support services to over 100,000 Tennesseans, and we continue to grow each day.

With our recent merger with Omni, LifeCare is now part of a broader management organization that has over 1,500 employees operating in three states with plans to expand into five to ten additional states over the next five years. By faith, Kenny Mauck...

By faith, you.

In All Things

They say hindsight is 20/20. Looking back over my life, I find that to be true. At every hill, every valley, every fork in the road, I can see God in His sovereignty moving me in the right directions, His mercy correcting my course when need be. So many things that seemed mundane or outside of what I would have considered my "wheelhouse" were opportunities for training and growth. He was equipping me to be able to walk in my own imprinted story, forging ahead with his footsteps to guide me.

The leadership and management skills I gained during my time as Director of Counseling at Christ Church and the Barnabas groups of encouragement were valuable to what I do at LifeCare, such as preparing and overseeing staff meetings, coordinating family conferences, booking speakers, managing a larger ministry at a megachurch, and overseeing dozens of volunteers and paid staff.

And budgeting. I always knew how to spell the word; I had just never done one before. Fortunately for me, Pastor Hardwick's sons Mike and Steve were in the world of business finance. Mike took the time to come in and train our entire staff on the ins and outs of budgeting. We were challenged as leaders to look at the needs and set aside our wants when the bottom line demanded it. Steve showed us how billing church members' insurances for their sessions could drastically help our bottom line.

Recently, I had Mike and Steve over, and we reminisced and laughed about old times. Both men have become good friends and successful businessmen. I shared with them that lessons learned about keeping a company financially solvent, having positive cash flow, and all the other financial tools they added to my arsenal had been invaluable to both the Barnabas ministry and me as I grew LifeCare, and they are continuing to pay dividends today.

One of the most valuable skills the Lord gave me the opportunity to hone was listening to those who came into my office needing help, listening to the stories of children similar to Carlos, or listening to the paid staff and volunteers. By learning to listen, I also learned to ask the right questions and discern the needs of clients, parents of children, and staff who helped shape the services and support that LifeCare provided.

What started with a promise and a mostly blank organizational chart spread all over my dining room table has grown exponentially beyond my imagination. When I remember who and where I was in 1994, and then look at where the Lord has brought me to today, I am so thankful for His provision of training in preparation for what was to come.

I love Romans 8:28, which tells us, "And we know that in all things God works for the good of those who love him, who have been called according to his purpose" (NIV). All those in-between years, the promise of God working all things for good kept me going when I would begin to doubt. I would pull that verse out when I got weary or couldn't see where I was headed.

God works all things for good—the good and the bad, life experiences, job training, mistakes made, and lessons learned. I believe it is so important to "do all things as unto the Lord and not men" for this very reason. Your entire life is a training ground, preparing you to walk out your legacy for the ultimate purpose of bringing glory to the Father.

You have no idea what He has in store for you, what legacy He is working out for you. Don't you want to be ready when it's time?

Do Not Fear

As I look back on the stories of my ancestors, I have to wonder about the fears Hans Peter had to work through: fear of leaving the familiar—his home, his family, his country; fear of being lost at sea. Sailing was no easy feat and had no guarantee of arrival in those days. Would the ship make it? Would they have enough food, enough water? Did he have a fear of the unknowns of a new country? Where would he live? How would he live? Would he find work? Would he be able to make it on his own? What about his parents?

Can you imagine sending your only child on a voyage on which he quite possibly could die, knowing you may never see him again?

When I stepped out from under the umbrella of Christ Church, I had a few fears of my own. Would I make it? Was I really hearing from God? What if I failed?

Scripture has so much to say about fear, or more specifically, about not being afraid. Joshua 1:9 commands us to be strong and courageous and not to be afraid or discouraged. God will be with us wherever we go.

Isaiah 41:10 also says, "Do not fear, for I am with you" and adds, "I will strengthen you and help you" (NIV). One of my favorites is Philippians 4:6-7, "Do not be anxious about anything, but in every situation, by prayer and petition, with thanksgiving, present your requests to God. And the peace of God, which transcends all understanding, will guard your hearts and your minds in Christ Jesus" (NIV). What could be more reassuring than the transcendent peace of God that passes all understanding?

One of the most tangible examples of risk, faith, and fear in Scripture comes from Matthew 14:25-31, the story of Peter walking on the water.

> 25 Shortly before dawn, Jesus went out to them, walking on the lake.
> 26 When the disciples saw him walking on the lake, they were terrified. "It's a ghost," they said and cried out in fear.
> 27 But Jesus immediately said to them: "Take courage! It is I. Don't be afraid."
> 28 "Lord, if it's You," Peter replied, "tell me to come to You on the water."
> 29 "Come," he said.

Then Peter got down out of the boat, walked on the water and came toward Jesus.

30 But when he saw the wind, he was afraid and, beginning to sink, cried out, "Lord, save me!"

31 Immediately Jesus reached out his hand and caught him. "You of little faith," he said, "why did you doubt?" (NIV).

In the middle of a frightening, intense storm, Peter *believed* that it was Jesus walking on the water. When he was told to come, he took a step of faith and a huge risk. There was wind, waves, the small vessel being tossed about, water smacking the hull, probably spilling over the top. (Sound familiar?)

But Peter took a deep breath and stepped out into the whipping wind and choppy waters, and in faith, *walked on water*. Peter could not have experienced this life-changing moment without first having faith, and second, taking a risk by leaving the safety of the boat.

Charted Steps

Writing my own story has helped me realize the importance and even responsibility of passing my ancestors' stories down to the next generation. Unbeknownst to Hans and his parents, their choice set an example when it comes to risk and faith that still impacts our family today. I want my grandchildren, great-grandchildren, and future generations to understand that a choice made hundreds of years ago is relevant to their lives today.

As you are reading this book and discovering your family heritage, I hope you are beginning to understand that chapters, paragraphs, and sentences are providentially written to learn from and grow. Even the seemingly insignificant has relevance.

These stories are the imprints and legacy of your flesh and blood relatives, those with whom you share DNA. They are vital keys to a sacred treasure chest of meaning, purpose, and understanding for you and your family.

Friend, we've covered two very important imprints in this chapter:

IMPRINT–Risk
IMPRINT–Faith

It's now time to break out that journal and family tree and put pen to paper. Ask the Lord to guide your thoughts and show you His hand and His purposes in your legacy story, your life imprint today.

1. Who was the family ancestor who started your family's new beginning? For me, finding this person and following the path through the generations of my family has been like opening up a treasure map to follow. Who are the brave folks you need to thank for bringing your family legacy to life?
2. What challenges or roadblocks did they face? What risks did they encounter? What was going on historically and culturally during that time?
3. Think of a time in your life when you took a big risk. How did it pay off? If you can't think of one, then how has the story of Hans and his parents encouraged you in the area of faith and risk?
4. Is there something now—a vision, a dream, a word—the Lord has given you that you need to act on but have been holding back?
5. You don't have to have all the answers, but if you wrote down an answer to the last question, what is a first step, your "leap of faith," you can take to move you toward that vision?

CHAPTER 3

Facing the Headwinds

"I am not afraid of storms, for I am learning how to sail my ship."

—LOUISA MAY ALCOTT

THE SUBDUED GRAY AND PINK HUES of dawn are softly fading, welcoming the golden tones and brilliant blue sky of the day. Manny is curled up next to me, curiously watching me as I write.

Admiring the ever-changing color palette, I'm contemplating the impact of how one event can transform an entire family for generations. This is exactly what happened to the Mauck family through my fourth-generational great-grandfather Samuel Mauk. To tell the story well, we need to revisit Frederick and his wife Margaret briefly from a slightly different angle. There is so much more to uncover.

Frederick Mauk: 1749–1830
(Revisited)

As we saw in the previous chapter, Frederick was like his father in that he liked to take risks and was driven to succeed. That adventurous spirit in Frederick looked much different in comparison to Hans.

Hans came to America and settled down in one place, the Shenandoah Valley. Frederick, on the other hand, preferred not to stay in one place. He loved to travel, to explore new frontiers, and to set things in motion.

The counselor side of me recognized Frederick as the classic middle child, a person seeking affirmation by outward action and accomplishments. Internally, Frederick was a restless heart trying to find his destiny through exploring. It was as if every day of his life, he was a ship seeking a port but not finding it. Unlike his siblings who seemed content to listen to and just be proud of their father's sacrifices and true tales, Frederick desired to seek out and create his own adventurous life story.

This internal need manifested outwardly in the way he lived his life. He always searched for the more perfect place to live. He was driven, no matter the cost, to find an exciting identity like his father had. Quite possibly, and tragically, Frederick's drive contributed to some of his most significant losses in life—the illness of his wife and the death of one of his children.

One of Frederick's way of dealing with Margaret's failing health was to think of another venture or mountain to cross. He had not lost a loved one as close as his father Hans. He couldn't imagine the love of his life getting so ill. Nearly half of his years on this earth had been spent with Margaret by his side. She had been his partner in adventure and was the mother of his children.

As a therapist, I would identify Frederick's life following Margaret's dementia as a significant break in his character. Margaret and his family were his life. Without them, he felt there would be no more trips, no more adventures, no more land purchases, or homes built.

Frederick used to spend a lot of time with the family, enjoying his grandchildren. Samuel and his siblings watched as their father quietly mourned and gradually distanced himself from the rest of the family as their mother lost more and more strength with each passing day. When Margaret became bedridden, the spirited, go-for-the-gusto man who Peter, Catherine, and Samuel had known growing up seemed to have now lost the wind in his sails. I'm sure they wondered if they'd ever see that side again.

Fresh Wind

The great migration to the West began in the early 1800s and expanded greatly thereafter. The West was the new frontier. Every year, adventurers seeking new beginnings, new challenges, and new lands set out with their families and worldly possessions in a steady stream of wagons from late spring to early fall. With every caravan's departure, adventure called to Frederick's spirit, slowing refilling his sails

Frederick served in the military for a brief time during the War of 1812. His knowledge of the forest would prove helpful in training the troops. Although he was never exposed to the fighting, he appreciated his abilities of knowing how to survive. After the war, he returned home to be near his children and wife in Virginia.

Frederick's youngest son Samuel had met the young and beautiful Catherine "Caty" Hoppers. The couple had one son, Peter, before marrying in 1813, and two more afterward: Joseph, the middle child, and Paris, the youngest. Paris died shortly after birth, and little was known about his passing except that it took Catherine several years to overcome the loss.

At family gatherings, Samuel, Catherine, and Peter watched as little by little the father they once knew came back to life. When I think of those times, I envision Frederick sitting by the fire after dinner, telling tales of the Wild West, captivating the hearts and minds of his grandchildren just as his father's stories had captured his heart and imagination.

Catherine and her husband John's two boys, along with Samuel and Caty's sons, would sit at their grandfather's feet, hanging on to his every word. Whereas Hans' stories were adventurous retellings of what had been, Frederick wove wonderful tales of what could be, full of excitement and adventure.

After the children went to bed, Frederick wanted to continue the conversation with his adult children, dreaming of the life they could have, a fresh start, a new life, a second chance in the beautiful new settlement in Ohio, land as far as the eye could see. Each conversation was more fervent and persuasive than the last as Samuel, Catherine and John, and Peter gave the whole idea of moving to Ohio, more and more serious consideration.

It took a few years, but realizing Margaret was in such poor health and now nursed each day due to dementia, he dreamed like always that a new place and life would be good for her. He would make sure and come back for her in Toms Brook, Virginia, once they were settled. All she needed was fresh air and a new place to live. Frederick not only convinced himself, but Samuel, Peter, and his son-in-law John and daughter Catherine that his dream of moving to a new land was their dream too and that they should all turn that dream now into a reality.

With his family now onboard, the hope of a new start brought new life and a new hope to Frederick. The family began planning for the three-month journey, set to begin in the spring of 1819.

Sparks Fly

After only three weeks of traveling, the rugged terrain of the Appalachian Mountains proved much more taxing on both the family and the horses than anyone had anticipated, including Frederick. The men realized that to make the remainder of the trip, the horses needed several days of rest. So, when they arrived in the town of Scott, Virginia, they made camp and settled in for an extended stay.

The first day in town, Samuel's older brother Peter met a girl, and it must have been love at first sight. For on the second day, he told his family he would not be continuing on with them.

I have to wonder how that conversation went... perhaps heated, emotional. How could Peter do this, abandon them and break up the family, leave them a man down right before a treacherous trip over rugged terrain? Begging them to understand, Peter promised he would rejoin them later in Ohio.

The woman he fell in love with and eventually married was Ellender Sparks. Now, I could not have dreamed up a better name myself. You just can't make this stuff up. Not only were sparks flying between her and Peter, her presence undoubtedly caused sparks to fly within the entire Mauk family as well.

Samuel Mauk: 1785–1819
(My Fourth-Generational Great-Grandfather)

I can only imagine how Samuel must have felt about his brother Peter, who was the oldest, the second-in-command in the family hierarchy at thirty-nine. He was abandoning ship. This left thirty-four-year-old Samuel, the youngest, with the responsibility of successfully getting the family to their destination. I'm sure it wasn't quite what the baby of the family had bargained for on this adventure.

The challenges he faced must have been overwhelming as he probably considered his options of how to make this trip work. Frederick was not a young man anymore, well into his seventies. As hard of a worker as he was, he had already been struggling to keep up with his young sons when Peter was with them. Frederick would be of little help driving, watering, and caring for the horses.

His brother-in-law John wouldn't be of any help either. He and Catherine had their own family and wagon to manage.

Samuel's wife Caty was a city girl, not accustomed to the rugged, unrefined conditions of traveling long distances in a wagon. Plus, she was focused on caring for their young sons, so she couldn't be of any help.

Samuel was out of options, and it was too late to turn around. Losing Peter meant two things. Samuel was now Frederick's eldest son on a trip about which Peter knew more. Secondly, instead of sharing the work that his father couldn't do, Samuel would have to handle both this extra work as well as his own family's needs. Pressure began to build.

The trip to Ohio was taking much longer than Frederick and the family planned. To complicate things, sometimes the trails were marked; sometimes they weren't. Many of the passages were nearly impossible to navigate with a wagon, and the caravan would be forced to turn around, backtrack, and try another route.

The further out of Virginia, and into Kentucky, they traveled, the more complex and difficult the travel became. They had to creep ever so slowly over each mountain and then carefully and cautiously down the other side. The intense focus, energy, and strength required to help the caravan up the mountain and then keep it from tumbling back down left them exhausted and completely spent.

Then Samuel began to fall ill with a deep cough and sore throat that would continue to get worse along the way. With no access to a doctor or medicine on the trail, his illness progressed rapidly in a matter of days. He was no longer well enough to drive the wagon. His elderly father had no choice but to take up the reigns for the final leg of the trip as one of Catherine's young sons kept him awake with coffee.

Each breath Samuel took became shallower and more difficult, every sentence harder to speak. He must have realized the extent of his illness. When they finally entered the small village town of Scioto, Ohio, the last part of the journey, Samuel asked his brother-in-law John to get him medical attention.

The thoughts and emotions he must have had are hard for me to imagine. Samuel loved his family. He must have been sad upon realizing he had uprooted them to move to a new land they knew nothing about, and now he was seriously ill.

Upon arriving, Samuel was more concerned about getting someone from the town to help draw up a will than seeing a doctor. He knew how bad his condition was. The attending doctor realized the severity of what was obviously a bad case of pneumonia and gave little hope. Samuel had to know his time left was days at best, if not hours. Obviously, he wanted to leave something to his wife and boys. Whether or not Samuel and Caty had discussed what should happen if he died, we will never know. The provisions of the will reflected that he knew it would be difficult for Caty to raise the boys alone. She grew up in the city and was not familiar with farm life, so she would struggle to work the land.

If it turned out that she could not care for the property and their boys on her own, Samuel asked that the family step in to help her. Looking through his last wishes, it is evident to me that Samuel fully expected his family to come alongside and assist Caty in raising young Peter and Joseph. He wanted them to become trustees of inherited property until the boys came of age should Caty remarry or something happen to her.

He also asked that Caty arrange for the boys to learn a trade, a skill, something from which they could earn a living and make a life, such as blacksmithing or carpentry. He did not consider farming a profession, so he wanted to make sure they landed a solid apprenticeship with a mentor who would train them well. Hans had been a lumberman and businessman, opening a lumber mill. Frederick knew carpentry and building, and Samuel was a builder as well. He wanted the same promise of success for his sons, especially if he would not be there to mentor them. Having this peace of mind for his sons was important to him. Yet, Catherine's husband John was a farmer.

Samuel completely trusted his family to help Caty prosper and succeed and to keep the family intact. That's what family does, take care of each other, or so he thought.

On August 5, 1819, three days after arriving in Scioto, Ohio, Samuel Mauk passed away. Then everything changed for my family.

I'm sure Caty felt alone emotionally and physically. Her husband had just died. She was hundreds of miles from what had once been her home. She was now left to fend for her sons and herself in a rugged, fairly uncivilized, unfamiliar part of the country. She was probably not entirely keen on being there.

How would she make it here, a young widow with four-year-old Joseph and his older brother Peter and with no experience working a farm or land? In her grief, Caty showed no interest whatsoever in the will. It was completely out of the question for her to take on the working of the land. She was so intensely distraught that she was unable to care for her sons.

In an act of kindness and compassion, Catherine took Peter and Joseph in, hoping after Caty had time to grieve, she would be able to again care for them. Unfortunately for all, this was not the case.

Even with Catherine's help with little Peter and Joseph, Caty's circumstances remained overwhelming for the city girl from Wilkes, North Carolina. She was already uncomfortable living away from her parents. In rugged country with a farm that needed to be cultivated from scratch, no means of income, and no husband, and still the ultimate responsibility of two young boys in tow, she struggled and found it nearly impossible to cope.

In the end, Caty threw up her hands. She completely disregarded Samuel's dying wishes, severed all ties, cut off all communication with and moved on from the Mauk family. Giving up all parental rights, she left the boys with the family.

Within four months, Caty had met and married a local Ohio man, John Halterman, and started a new life. She never looked back, even though the Mauk family always thought she would.

Joseph Mauk: 1815-1891
(My Third-Generational Great-Grandfather)

John and Catherine had not prepared themselves for the possibility of taking Peter and Joseph on a long-term basis. With four children of their own and a new farm to build from the ground up, two more mouths to feed and two more children to provide for was almost more than John could fathom.

They were still trying to recover from those three months of travel, which had been physically and emotionally draining on them all. The few relationships left were already strained and in need of some repair. (Additionally, I have to imagine John felt a little sting and resentment at Samuel's inference that farming would not be a good enough pathway for Peter and Joseph.)

The responsibilities left by Samuel's death, his brother-in-law Peter's absence, and now Caty's abandonment weighed heavily on John. How could Caty be so selfish as to leave her sons with Catherine and him as she ran off to a new life. She knew full well that Frederick would not be able to take the boys in. Since Samuel's death, he had become a hermit, stricken with grief and guilt. Had his need for adventure ultimately caused Samuel's illness? Had he pushed the family too hard, too far, and brought this tragedy on them all?

He moved into the hills of his land. He seldom left his cabin and fell into a deep depression. For Frederick, it was more than the loss of a beloved son. He felt he had lost his story. Samuel was the son with whom he had broken German tradition, naming him not after a forefather but a ship that had brought his father to this new land and started him on an exciting journey. In his mind, Samuel and the ship were one, and with Samuel gone, the journey was now over.

So, with the boys having nowhere else to go, their uncle and aunt, John and Catherine, begrudgingly and out of obligation took them in permanently.

I have found it hard enough for healthy adults to process grief, abandonment, and rejection. How do young children without any life skills or coping mechanisms process such things, especially four-year-old Joseph? He had been ultimately rejected by his mother, felt unwanted, unloved, and even resented by his aunt and uncle, and was dealing with unsurmountable grief he had no understanding of or ability to process from his father's death.

The relationship between Uncle John and Joseph was rocky from the start. Joseph bore the full brunt of John's resentment and anger over the whole unfortunate situation. John gave preference, attention, and affection to his own children and even Peter, who seemed to naturally find his place in the family, while virtually ignoring Joseph's presence, rejecting him even more.

Joseph quickly learned that negative behavior got the attention. As unhealthy as this thinking was, the negative attention to the young child was better than no attention at all. Furthermore, he developed a severe anger issue, manifesting in uncontrollable temper tantrums.

In John's and Catherine's eyes, they already had four children, three girls and a boy named William. According to John, Joseph's tantrums made him a behavior problem that required harsh discipline. A good belt "whooping" was what he needed and quite frequently received. What they couldn't see, or perhaps chose not to see, was the abandoned, hurt little boy seeking love and attention any way he could, even if negative. At the tender age of four, Joseph had lost both his parents that fateful day in 1819. He needed understanding and compassion but received little of it, if any.

The childhood tantrums grew into uncontrollable outbursts during Joseph's teen years. The intensity and frequency of the arguments between him and John escalated, and the chasm between them widened. Finally, John had had enough. The anger spewing from this now thirteen-year-old teenage boy was more than he wanted to handle, more than he cared to handle. He hadn't even wanted him there in the first place.

It was time for Joseph to go. John sent him to a farmer in Elliott, Kentucky, at the young age of thirteen to be a farmhand's assistant. Samuel's request for the boys to learn a trade had not yet been honored, and now, at least for Joseph, it never would.

Joseph was again rejected and sent away to a life of servitude and hard work with little reward, while his older brother Peter remained with the family. They had separated him from the only family he had left, and the anger within Joseph intensified for the new loss he now experienced.

Silver Linings

Every cloud has a silver lining, so the saying goes. While Joseph's life would be better described as a full-force hurricane, there would be a few positive events—silver linings—that impacted his life.

For Joseph, this silver lining would come in the form of his Uncle Peter who had been living in Virginia, with his new wife due to her and her family's wishes. Then in 1829, Peter received a letter from his sister Catherine. She informed him that Frederick was still alive, but his time left was now limited. Peter decided to finally move to Ohio.

Margaret was brought to be buried in Ohio, after her death in 1820, after succumbing to acute complications from dementia. Frederick Mauk died in the fall of 1830, having lived ninety-one years and was buried in Scioto, Ohio, next to his beloved Samuel and Margaret. Most believed he died of a broken heart. It was said Frederick could sometimes be seen overlooking the cemetery from a high ridge.

Enter Uncle Peter.

After Frederick's death, Uncle Peter was named overseer of his father's and Samuel's land and the sole executor of his father's will. He discovered that Samuel had portioned his parcel and inheritance to his two sons Peter and Samuel in his will and that John, Catherine, and Frederick apparently never fulfilled Samuel's wishes regarding his sons. In the process of discovering the story of all that happened in his absence, he also learned what had happened to Joseph as well.

He knew that somehow, he had to make things right, not only to honor his father's wishes but Samuel's as well. He sold what was rightfully his father's land as well as his own and then deeded Peter his land.

At the beginning of 1831, Uncle Peter and possibly Joseph's brother Peter were able to acquire enough information from Uncle John to find out that Joseph, who was now sixteen years old, had been living with a farmer in Eastern Kentucky, near Elliott County for three years and that no one from the family had checked in on him. They went to find him.

Imagine my fourth-generation Uncle Peter and Joseph's older brother, now just about twenty years old, coming down the road and finding Joseph. Meeting him would be strange at first. It had been three years with no contact between the brothers.

His uncle and brother were seeing not just a young man who felt abandoned, but one who was angry, living a life of servitude, alone, poor, broken, feeling unloved by his entire family. He knew by now he had been rejected by his mother, aunt, and uncle and the reason he was separated from his only brother. Where had his uncle and brother been all these years?

His Uncle Peter then told Joseph the story he never knew, one of a father who had loved his two sons, who had cared so much for them that on his deathbed, he planned for Peter's and Joseph's futures. After all these years, his Uncle Peter stood before him, ushering a little hope and sunshine into his unresolved rejected heart. His uncle apologized for not being with his family and for the damage that had already been done.

Joseph now had an inheritance from his father, freedom from the old farmer, and the money to buy a home. He had finally found some tangible financial means that was his. He surmised, "At least my father Samuel loved me."

Joseph would reconnect with his older brother and leave the farmer and find a temporary place to pay room and board from the little money he had saved with the farmer. He would find work by helping other farmers near Edmonson, Kentucky. Within time, he sold his parcel of land in Scioto, a place where he no longer would want to live or visit. He then went on to meet a nice woman named Sarah Holbrook and search for a good piece of land in Eastern Kentucky, in a very small country community town called Moccasin Bend. He wanted a place on a high mountain that would allow him to look back west from where he had come. He would leave Scioto, Ohio, forever, the place of rejection from his family, but his experiences of rejection as a little boy would never be forgotten, no matter where he lived.

Joseph, His New Family and Home

Sarah's family was said to have originally lived in North Carolina, and settled near Elliott, Kentucky. Nicknamed "Sally," she would get pregnant and have a baby three months prior to her marrying Joseph on July 11, 1842. He was twenty-six years old, and Sarah was twenty-one. They then went on to have their second child, my great, great-grandfather William Mauk, in 1846.

Joseph wanted a large family. He wanted to be sure that should something happen to him, none of his children would ever experience the aloneness he felt growing up. In all, he and Sarah would raise ten children together. The naming of the children would speak volumes to me and all who would read them. His oldest, Samuel, was born on April 14, 1842. William was born July 17, 1846, followed by Mary Francis, Sarah, Martha, Amanda, Joseph, Jefferson Davis, Laura, and Sampson.

The naming or not naming a child from a large German family like Joseph's was revealing. For example, Joseph named his first child after his father Samuel, but he purposely excluded naming any of his children after his grandfather Frederick, his uncle and older brother Peter, and his Uncle John. He also intentionally left out his mother Catherine's name as well. He did honor his wife and named one of their daughters after her, and he named a son after himself. He also honored some of his German forefathers by naming some of his children after them, like William.

Intentionally not naming his children after other men in Joseph's life was an emotional line in the sand. It was a familial dividing wall between those who had sowed good into his life and those who had sowed a lifetime of pain from rejection and abandonment.

While Joseph desired to make a change, create a new life, and surround himself with loved ones, raging anger from years of unresolved loss was the one piece of his old life he was not able to leave behind. When partnered with discipline in his home, the outcome was usually punishment carried out with a heavy hand in the form of corporal punishment.

Without warning, switches and belts were whipped out for correction, control, and submission. As a counselor, I would attribute his use of corporal punishment to both his rage and the poor disciplinary example of his Uncle John as well as possibly the farmer with whom he lived. It was the only way people disciplined. From my personal and professional viewpoint, it was tragic for my family.

When Sarah moved passed her childbearing years, Joseph became restless. Children were security and safety for Joseph—the bigger the family, the more secure and safe he felt. I believe he entered a midlife crisis as many men in their forties and even fifties do. He looked back at his life, mistakes made, and opportunities missed, and needed to continue building his empire, which was his family.

During this time, he publicly took up with a younger woman by the name of Mary Ellen Rose and had two more children with her, Sampson and Laura Bell. But it's interesting that Sarah ended up taking care of both of them.

Joseph left each of his children an inheritance with a small piece of his land. However, he did not leave his children a legacy of redemption, purpose, or intention. He had taught them as he had been taught: surviving in this world was harsh. Maintaining a farm and a family business of keeping one's livestock fed and cared for was a difficult daily task, that it was not a trade and would leave his family and predestined generations in poverty.

This mindset was a far cry from the life my sixth-generational great-grandfather Hans envisioned for his family. Hans wanted his faith in God to be the most predominant element of his family's story. He wanted his family to have hope for a better tomorrow, supported by the lumber business he had desired and expected to see his children carry on.

Unfortunately, I can see from this futuristic vantage point that Frederick had missed the mark, focusing so much time and energy on the adventure and chasing tangibles—land and material possessions—that he had failed to pass on the legacy of faith to his children.

Making an almost in-your-face statement to his family who had abandoned him, Joseph would eventually be buried with his body facing Ohio. In his mind, he had fought the odds and survived despite the rejection of his own family. He made sure that through his crowning achievement, a large family, his legacy would continue in name and worldly inheritance. He was saying, "I did okay and made my own family."

More of My Story

In the fall of 2017, I lost one of my closest family members. My cousin Landy Gardner, my Aunt Jo's son and my father's nephew, passed away from stage 4 liver cancer. Landy was always jovial. He brightened every room and life into which he walked. Over the last three years of his life, we grew closer, him serving on our board of directors and us doing more with each other as family.

The morning I received his initial call with news of his illness, I could immediately tell something was up. The seriousness of his diagnoses was in his voice.

Landy told me about the malignant tumors on his liver and his upcoming rigorous treatment regimen. I sat in disbelief, my stomach churning and my world spinning as I tried to process this information. It's true; you never think it will happen to you or someone you love so dearly until it does.

My cousin and I were like brothers. Not being there for him over the next year would be incredibly hard. I encouraged him and cheered him on from a distance. I sent him Scriptures and shared songs that I hoped would lift his spirits and bolster his faith.

At that time, I was in the middle of an intense doctoral program that required hours upon hours of study. I had worked incredibly hard to get where I was in the program. However, as the year progressed, somehow that pursuit of my doctorate seemed less and less pressing knowing my cousin needed both weekly and sometimes daily support. But it was the book by Dr. Randy Paushe that I shared at the introduction of this book that finally made me pull back and leave the program. Time and the lack of it was facing my cousin.

I needed to walk with him as best as I could. The doctoral program was not more important than time with my cousin nor with my own family.

I could no longer concentrate on my studies at the level that was required. Landy needed me, and I needed to be there for him and support him, and those needs won out. I contacted my professors and the Dean of Educational Development and left the doctoral program.

Over his remaining months, Landy and I laughed, cried, and texted daily. We talked about the important things in life. We talked about nothing. We talked about his cancer. We talked about anything *but* cancer.

I listened as he reminisced about what it had been like to be one of the premier interior designers in the country; about the times he did makeovers on our house; about his trips to Ukraine and to Israel; about how he knew better when it came to dressing us for church.

With misty eyes, we recalled his and his wife Joy's choral arranging days, when their arrangements were used by churches around the world, and about the thousands of people to whom he and his choirs were able to minister. He spoke about how proud he was of his two daughters Dionne and Lauren, and how he couldn't wait to be at Lauren's upcoming wedding, which turned out to be a beautiful day!

Landy had a successful round of treatment. The tumors had shrunk, and the doctors were optimistic. He was entering a period of remission, but it was short-lived.

When the news came that the tumors were back with a vengeance, his prognosis was not good. I knew this was probably going to be the end, but I didn't want to accept it. He asked me to be strong and keep the faith. I did all he asked, but down deep I knew it was only a matter of time.

The doctors proposed one more procedure, and Landy prepared for surgery. He was feeling weak and was limiting his time before the surgery to quality time with Joy. He had even asked his daughters to wait until after the procedure to visit. I asked him to please hold off on the operation because he was too weak.

I had an out-of-town business function and told him I would see him afterward. When I returned from my trip, I felt led to call and let Landy know I was heading to the hospital for a visit.

Instead of Landy, a dear friend answered his phone and gently told me that my cousin had just passed away. At first, I was distraught and couldn't respond at all. The hurt of not being able to see him or say goodbye was overwhelming.

I was hoping this moment wasn't happening. He was bigger than life. How could it be? I was in a state of denial. I didn't want to accept the facts. How could I have let this happen? My trip had prevented me from saying goodbye to one of the closest relatives in my life.

Then his daughter Dionne shared his last hours and words with me. Earlier in the week, Landy had told her he had a lot of questions for God. As he entered the final hours of his life here on Earth, she believed her dad had that conversation with God, and God was answering. My cousin, although a believer, was also like doubting Thomas. He had to actually see it sometimes to believe it. God knew this about him, and we believe he was showing Landy the answers to many of his questions. Throughout those hours, Landy would nod and say, "Okay. Okay." Over and over he repeated, "It's so beautiful; it's so beautiful!" God was showing him glimpses of heaven!

Landy passed away on October 28, 2017. I am blessed to have been able to be a part of his life, to watch how he lived his life passionately every day, how he traveled, experienced whatever good things life had to offer, and took risks to live life to its fullest.

I will forever be thankful for the time I was able to spend in celebrating life with him. His zest for life, his passion, his expectation of godly excellence in everything he did, and seeing everyone in his life as a gift permanently stamped a legacy imprint on my heart.

I have actually lost two influential men in my life in the last year. In addition to Landy, my beloved father-in-law Ernie passed away on my birthday and while still in the process of writing this book. My wife and I had some reservations about leaving him for our trip to Germany, which we had planned for over a year. The day before he passed away, he said to us, "It's not like I'm going to die. You two go have fun on your trip."

Ernie was more than a father-in-law; he was a dear, loving example of servanthood. He served me and our entire family his whole life. He was like my right-hand person. When things needed to get done and done well, I called Ernie. He also loved to play all kinds of games. We would play his favorite game euchre until the wee hours of the mornings, sometimes just to see his face light up from watching us. It became a special time for us all.

I have seen my immediate family's experience of processing the grief surrounding Landy's and my father-in-law's deaths run in complete contrast to that of my ancestral family's handling of Samuel's death. We gathered. We remembered the good. We celebrated. We grieved, laughed, and cried together.

Initially needing time alone is natural in the grieving process. I can't fault Frederick for needing to retreat for a time. However, it's equally, if not more important to be with others who can encourage you, cry with you, grieve with you. Lean into the relationships you do have while you process the one you have lost.

For me, grief has intensified the importance of relationships, not just in times of sadness and crisis, but also daily. I love to speak with my parents every day. I consider it a gift to hear their voice and a privilege to be able to still tell them I love them.

I hug my grandchildren a little tighter and fully engage when I am with them. I value each and every conversation with my adult children. Grief has helped me learn to live more in the moment, savor life, and treasure the people in it.

Navigating Your Story

Have you heard the saying, "All families have some level of dysfunction; some just hide it better than others?" My own father was completely unaware of our family history. It's an unfortunate truth that most families hide or don't talk about the ugly parts of their story. Unsavory events become secrets within a family, which in turn become fractures that don't heal, wounds that fester for years, decades, and even generations. A destructive legacy imprint is left with little understanding as to why certain things happen because it's never been discussed or worked through.

It's hard for me to admit that in my own family, my ancestors emotionally and physically abandoned a child. What makes it even harder is seeing that my family didn't know how to deal with their own grief and loss in a healthy, loving way. They are not alone.

As a marriage and family counselor for over twenty years, I have heard and seen countless stories of child abandonment revolving around divorce or the death of a spouse, sibling, or friend. Sadly, it's far too familiar.

The Sins of the Father

Learning about Joseph's unresolved hurt from loss and the anger it birthed has paved the way for a new understanding of my own grandfather and father, and ultimately, my entire line. My ancestral family's abandonment of a four-year-old boy had not only immediate costs to Joseph and his future family, but it incurred so many generational costs as well. Neglect and abuse opened the door for anger and addiction to walk in and take up residence in our family line.

You may have heard a version of the phrase, "The sins of the father are passed down from generation to generation." There are actually many references to this truth in the Bible—the visitation of the father's sins on the children.

I think of Exodus 20:5-6 (NASB), which says, "... for I, the LORD your God, am a jealous God, visiting the iniquity of the fathers on the children, on the third and the fourth generations of those who hate Me, but showing loving kindness to thousands, to those who love Me and keep My commandments."

Also, Psalm 103:17-18 (NASB) reads, "But the lovingkindness of the LORD is from everlasting to everlasting on those who fear Him, and His righteousness to children's children, To those who keep His covenant And remember His precepts to do them."

To me, these verses are widely misunderstood and misquoted. While these verses underscore the "iniquity" piece of generational imprints, they also highlight the righteousness piece. Was the "sin passed down" in my family? Yes and no.

Uncontrolled anger, fits of rage, philandering, and even addictions appeared for many generations in my family. So yes, sins were passed down. This is where I believe these Scriptures are misunderstood or not given their full, true impact and meaning.

My years of training and practice as a counselor coupled with my own personal experiences have taught me that these are also the consequences of choices made by those before me. As I have researched and sought out the Lord for understanding, He has shown me imprints left on my family that became generational curses. When my ancestors acted outside of God's guidelines and purposes through drinking, fighting, and exploits of rage, my entire family suffered this curse many times over.

A legacy imprint was made that had devastating effects. Had Hans Peter's legacy imprint of faith and hope been passed on to his children, the events following Samuel's passing could have written a much different story. The choice of each generation to continue under the faulty imprint or break the curse, and with the Lord's guidance, create a new one, is an inescapable factor.

What If...

So, what if different choices had been made? What if Frederick had embraced his daughter-in-law Caty and helped her see it was possible *to stay, that she didn't have to leave.* What if he had embraced his grandchildren and their mother and been the godly head of the family Hans Peter had been, leading the family through such a difficult time?

When Caty left, what if he had stepped up and taken one or both of the boys when John and Catherine hesitated? At a minimum, what if he had been present from the beginning, active, and a help to John, Catherine, Peter, and little Joseph in finding and adjusting to the new normal and each other?

What if...

What if Joseph's mother Caty had chosen to stay and raise her children instead of run away from adversity? What if Caty had determined to stay with the family instead of marrying another man four months later? What if Caty had had her boys come to live with her and her new husband? What if her choices had been for her boys instead of only herself?

What if...

How different would the story be if Catherine and John had just chosen to open their hearts to Joseph? What if Joseph had sincerely been welcomed and become a part of the family instead of being sent away? What if he had received affirmation and love instead of resentment and rejection?

What if...

Instead, Frederick left his family alone so that he could deal with his own grief. Caty looked out for herself and left. John and Catherine did not open their hearts but instead held on to the hurt of being deserted by Catherine's brother Peter. They resented being put in the position of having to take in her brother's children.

The unintended curse of abandonment and unresolved loss set in motion patterns of running, blaming, pride, anger, and feelings of abandonment within my family.

Look at Psalm 103:18 mentioned above: *"To those who keep His covenant And remember His precepts to do them."* To the chain breakers and those who make the decision to change the legacy imprint from one of running away to one of running into the arms of Jesus, you are the ones who change the spiritual legacy of a family.

Realizing the love and truth behind these Scriptures and how they apply to real life have given me a greater understanding of my family and our issues. Piecing together the story of Samuel, Joseph, William "Wild Bill," and William "Tom" Mauk, of whom you'll read about in the next few chapters, has shed light on some of the reasons why people I loved had such anger, even generations after Joseph.

The importance of teaching our children how to confront fears and work through loss, not run or hide from them or pretend they don't exist, can't be emphasized enough. Even in the middle of the storm, God will guide and change our stories. We aren't meant to face these things alone.

First, we have Him. Our faith in Him, His grace, and His strength can create a love for each other that will become our family's strongest defense when facing a crisis or tragedy. In the end, only He can move us from sufferers of loss to healers of hearts, both our own and the hearts of those we love.

Compassion and Comfort

As our hearts are healed by the Great Physician, we are more and more able to give what I like to call "heaven-sized comfort" to others in their grief. Compassion and love are key in responding to loved ones in the grieving process or who are in the midst of severe trauma. In their grief, they should know they are not alone and have support.

I love the words of 2 Corinthians 1:3-4, "... the Father of compassion and the God of all comfort, who comforts us in all our troubles, so that we can comfort those in any trouble with the comfort we ourselves receive from God" (NIV).

Friends, we don't carry this responsibility alone. This imprint of comforting others comes directly from our Heavenly Father.

Psalms 34:18 tells us, "The LORD is near to the brokenhearted and saves those who are crushed in spirit" (NASB). As we begin reaching out to the God of all comfort, He guides and teaches us how to give heaven-sized love to others. He carries us as we carry others. He draws near as we draw near to the point that if we allow Him to transform us, heaven-sized comfort flows naturally from His heart through our heart to the heart of our loved one.

Comfort and love, even in the smallest measure, let alone a heaven-sized offering, was an enormous, gaping hole in the fabric of Joseph's life. The actions of abandonment and rejection by my extended family members were the very point at which my family, directly and indirectly, contributed to this rift. Too many things got in the way, including their own grief and resentment, and kept them from seeing first the true grief of Joseph, and secondly, the error of their ways.

Charted Steps

Admittedly, this is a heavy chapter. If you've experienced loss or trauma, if you or your family have dealt with abuse, infidelity, or even addiction, especially if there are unresolved pieces, you may have been affected more than you anticipated. Issues within your own family tree that you are still trying to make sense of may have been brought to mind.

If you haven't written a single thing down so far in our journey together, and this chapter has stirred something deep within you, now is a great time to start.

IMPRINT—Trauma and Loss
IMPRINT—Compassion and Comfort

Family connection is so important in times of loss. That said, sometimes so much dysfunction exists in a family that healthy connection is not possible. Many times, dysfunction is only made worse in the midst of loss and trauma. If you find yourself in that situation, leaning into your family of friends may be the healthy direction for you while you navigate reconciliation and relational health with family.

I encourage you to work through the questions below. Take time to talk to a trusted friend, your pastor, or a professional if that's what you need. Don't put off moving toward healing. You may need to change the trajectory of your legacy imprinted story.

I want to assure you that later in the book, we'll address a few other things in dealing with loss and its impact on your family. We'll talk more about the escape of addiction. We'll look at the importance of being a life giver in the healing process and being intentional in making amends with those we may have hurt and who have hurt us, whether the hurt itself was intentional or unintentional. It's a compelling part of our Mauck story and can be a powerful chapter in your story as well.

1. What losses has your family experienced that are still unresolved? Are yours or someone else's actions or inactions a part of the issue? What steps might need to be taken now?

2. What's the most significant loss you have ever encountered? Did you have the support of a friend, colleague, family member, or professional who helped you get through it? If not, consider calling a true caregiver or faith-based professional who can help you walk through it.
3. Have you or someone in your family been abandoned emotionally or physically? After reading my third great-grandfather's story, in some ways similar to that of the biblical character Joseph, what patterns or reactions come to mind from your own life that trace back to you or someone you love being abandoned?

CHAPTER 4

Batten Down the Hatches

"We want Christ to hurry and calm the storm. He wants us to find him in the midst of it first."

— BETH MOORE

YOU MAY HAVE NOTICED THAT for these first few chapters, stories are revisited. Why? Because generations do not stand alone; they build on each other.

This is something I've contemplated in depth during my writing time on the back porch—the intricate connections between generations. The overlapping themes and threads woven between generations are windows into not only my own soul but those of my current relatives and even my children. Learning about Joseph Mauk and his sons has only added to my understanding.

To that end, we must revisit Joseph's story for a moment to have a full picture of William "Wild Bill" Mauk, one of Joseph's sons and my great-great-grandfather.

Joseph Mauk: 1815–1891
(Revisited)

War, Whiskey, and Women

During the Civil War, Joseph was called to join Robert E. Lee's troops. This was a brutal, bloody war where three million Americans fought; six hundred thousand lost their lives.

Joseph witnessed unimaginable bloodshed and uncontrolled rage fighting for his very life on the battlefield. No doubt he heard the screams from the suffering and watched violent deaths, some most likely by the blade of his own bayonet. Perhaps his war experience began to put into perspective what really mattered and brought some level of healing to his wounded heart because Sarah noticed a gradual change in his demeanor with each brief visit home. He seemed to have become more compassionate.

While I believe healing did happen for Joseph along the way, both through his Uncle Peter's actions and his war experience, there is a second factor to consider regarding Joseph's change in behavior. Truth be told, Joseph had traded one "vice" for another. One was developed during the Civil War and would become a side business for him and his older sons Samuel, William, and Peter Commodore. It would more than supplement their income for a time. They would end up making some of the best moonshine whiskey in the eastern Kentucky mountains.

The war experience may have caused Joseph to subside his anger toward the smaller children, but it did nothing to wane it toward the older children. It was teenagers and attitudes he had no patience for now, and he severely beat his older sons.

To some men like my third- and fourth-generational grandfathers, alcohol was the acceptable vice that unfortunately was wrongly attributed to drowning out one's emotional woes. We now know clearly that alcohol is actually a depressant. Drinking it actually makes people get worse, not better.

William "Wild Bill" Mauk: 1846–1916
(My Second-Generational Great-Grandfather)

It's been said that if you walked down Main Street in Olive Hill, Kentucky, someone would somehow be related to the Mauk or Sparks families. Between William moving his family there from Elliot and Peter's in-laws moving from Virginia, they populated the town. Now, I don't know if that was all true, but one thing was true, the sons of Joseph Mauk were a rowdy, ruthless, brawling, women-chasing brood of young men, not a God-fearing, church-going family as their great-grandfather Hans Peter Mauk had been. They worked in the fields every day and made moonshine later when the law wasn't looking or had their heads turned away on purpose.

His older boys not only learned to run the business, but also to drink with the best of those in the county. On any given day, any one of the Mauk boys could drink any customer under the table, and they did and frequently.

However, it was Joseph's son William, nicknamed "Wild Bill," who took the business and lifestyle that went with it to a whole new level. As the oldest son, he was not one of the fortunate younger children who escaped the raging beatings of their father.

Abuse begets abuse, so Wild Bill abused his children when three sheets to the wind drunk. Fear and intimidation ruled his home. The demeaning, shouting, verbal attacks toward his children were known to be worse than the physical beatings.

William was also known to all to enjoy a good chew of tobacco and chase fast horses and fast women. A curse word didn't exist with which he was not well-acquainted. More than once in his drunkenness, he strolled the town square in his birthday suit. Yes, buck naked, not a stitch of clothing. Barroom scuffles, fist fights, foul language, and the occasional run-in with the police were not uncommon occurrences for Wild Bill and his brothers.

Despite his reputation with the women, one did eventually come along who seemed to be able to handle Wild Bill better than most. Mary America Harper, a young Native American Cherokee woman, caught his attention, and the two fell in love and married.

Mary America Mauk was kind and protective over her children. She was artful at redirecting Bill's anger and even occasionally diffusing it. When Wild Bill went on drunken binges, she held the family together, making the children a priority, and continued to farm the land.

She also kept their farm going. Bill had never really taken to farming while growing up. Once the moonshine became part of the family business, he considered the farming business to be for the children and mother to handle.

Still in Control

As successful as the illegal moonshine business was for Wild Bill and his brothers, one would think the family lived well. Pictures I have found on genealogy websites of William's home, however, tell another story. They showed a shack that sat on stilts, dirt floors, very little light, a potbelly stove, an outhouse, and a water pump for a well.

Wild Bill never built a barn for his animals. The small livestock sometimes roamed free inside and outside the house. He, America, all eight of their children, and the farm animals lived together right there in the dirt, demonstrating that he didn't properly take care of neither livestock nor family very well.

My heart breaks for the message it sent to his wife and children. Even at the height of success in the moonshine business, no barn or pen was ever built for the animals, no floor or rooms were added. Nothing was done to show concern or care for his family's living conditions. Any money made was spent on Wild Bill's rowdy lifestyle, betting on the horses, or put back into making more moonshine. The business came first, and the still was always the priority.

Unchanged

When the legal authorities finally began cracking down on illegal stills in that area of the country, Wild Bill and his brothers eventually found themselves backed into a corner. They decided to shut the moonshine business down for fear of incarceration.

Now much older and not having any viable trade to fall back on, Wild Bill and his brothers were forced to return to their farming roots to survive. However, since Bill had never liked it as a child, he gave it minimal effort. His family's living conditions did not improve. The drinking and abuse continued. America and the children continued to carry the majority of the weight around the farm as best they could, eeking out a living from the land without much help from their father. In fact, they were the ones who kept the family from starving.

William "Wild Bill" Mauk died in 1916, leaving the farm to America and the children. According to the coroner's report, cause of death was kidney failure, one of the possible side effects of liver disease caused by his alcoholism. Sadly, Wild Bill drank himself to death, and his children unfortunately had a front row seat to it all. With the children now grown, Mary and her kids took better care of the livestock and obtained farming equipment. America taught her children how to survive, which they would need during the Great Depression that would take place ten years later.

More of My Story

Watching a loved one struggle with an addiction is not easy. Like millions of other families in America, I have battled alongside someone close to me, doing my best to support and cheer on their sobriety.

I've seen the daily battle to remain sober, winning the war one day and losing it the next. I've seen recovery and twelve-step programs embraced and followed, and I've seen them walked away from and rejected. Addictions have no prejudice. They impact rich and poor, regardless of ethnic status, nationality, color, size, or family. Two steps forward, three steps back, on the wagon, off the wagon, I have watched loved ones and patients repeat the cycle more times than I can count.

I have learned through personal and professional experience that family support is helpful, even essential in the recovery process. In addition to someone trained and objective, an addict needs support from those who have walked through recovery before them to be truly successful. Surrounding themselves with those who understand the grip of addiction and those who have been able to overcome and find healing for the underlying causes is just as essential in breaking the chains of addiction.

Wounded People

Much like a wounded animal, an addict lashes out at the very people trying to help. My experience has mirrored this fact, as have the experiences of just about every family member and friend of an addict I have counseled. In guiding those close to the addict who are trying to support the recovery process, I always remind them of this truth: *Wounded people wound people.* I tell them not to expect a logical, or even in many cases, any rational response.

Trying to understand addictive personalities is like *trying to make sense out of nonsense*. One never does. Addicts have to quit lying and admit that they can get better only if they really want and desire to do so. That means changing one's entire life and agreeing to hang with people who will hold them accountable as well.

In the early stages, you are not dealing with someone who is thinking rationally or is in a healthy mental or emotional state. Their outward behavior won't make sense because they're impaired, whether or not they're using. Every good thing in their life is in danger of being damaged, sabotaged, or destroyed because of a wound somewhere that remains untreated.

In the book *Hurting People Hurt People*, Dr. Sandra Wilson discussed this behavior in-depth. Pain experienced in the past leaves a deficit, causing a person to lash out for no apparent reason at someone who has absolutely nothing to do with the source of their anger.

For the families of Joseph and William "Wild Bill" Mauck, this was the unfortunate case. Events that took place, hurts and wounds inflicted by circumstances and family, cut deep into the emotional and psychological fabric and remained unaddressed and unhealed.

Joseph and William probably didn't fully understand why they lashed out so violently. Alcohol was an escape, but I'm not sure they could completely articulate from what exactly they were escaping.

Sadly, I have seen firsthand that it takes years for people from alcoholic homes to heal from the dysfunction of living with an elephant in the room, from hiding the dirty secret from the outside world of what goes on in the home, from the emotional and sometimes physical abuse that goes hand in hand with addiction and families. If professional help is not employed or if healing through the Great Physician is not sought, both the addict and the family can potentially suffer long-term mental and emotional effects and even mental illness.

I believe William did have mental illness brought on by the wounds of an abusive childhood and an addiction to moonshine that only intensified over the years. In those days, help was not as readily available, and mental illness was not understood as it is today. But let me be clear on this point—remaining in a victim state and irresponsible is unacceptable if one is seeking to get help or support. One must be willing to seek and access the help needed. Doing nothing is still living in a place of victimization, and after time, is counterproductive to healing or getting better.

It's a fact; over sixty percent of people with mental illness also suffer from some level of dependence on alcohol or addictive drug. My experiences in the mental health industry offer substantial evidence to support this statistic. When a prescribed psychotropic medication is not readily available, alcohol and drugs are the avenue of escape that many will seek. In addition, many choose to avoid the perceived shame of being diagnosed with emotional problems, rationalizing the overuse of alcohol as a less offensive and more accepted way to cope.

There's only one thing worse than turning to alcohol, and that's losing one's hope to live, choosing a permanent solution to a temporary problem instead of seeking help from those who care.

Imprints of Life, Death, Hope, and Despair
Marco's Mark

After graduating, completing my student teaching, and being a substitute teacher for a year, I ran into the Director of the Career Development Center of Mott College in a grocery store in Flint, Michigan. He asked if I might be interested in applying for a temporary position at Mott College. It was a providential meeting for sure in that I was working temporarily at a private Christian Academy in Brighton, Michigan, but I really wanted to get back into a college position.

Fortunately, the college hired me, and something even better came along within a few months. I got a full-time offer as an advisor with primarily single parents and low-income individuals seeking to go back to college by entering the Academic Development Center program.

Then during my first six months of working as an advisor, one of my most heartbreaking and unforgettable teachable moments happened. Part of my job was helping potential students with academic or language and cultural issues wade through the admissions paperwork and register for classes. Some never signed an agreement to be part of our program but wanted information, such as a particular young Hispanic man, whom I'll call "Marco."

Little did I know that Marco would end up leaving a much different kind of imprint on me. Upon meeting him, I gave him and his brother the necessary admissions and financial-aid information to begin the entry-level requirements for our program. When I saw they had not yet started with the paperwork, I said, "Why don't you either finish filling out the forms here and leave it with our receptionist, or take it home and bring it back?" They both nodded in agreement and left.

Within a day or so, I followed up to see if we had received their paperwork. We hadn't.

The same Friday evening, our oldest daughter Megan **who** was around twelve months old was having an allergic reaction to **the** new formula our pediatrician had prescribed. After hours of uncontrollable crying, several calls to the doctor, and feeling utterly powerless to help her, I finally left Raye Ann with Megan and headed to the local pharmacy. I clutched a paper with the name of another soy-based brand of formula the doctor had recommended over the phone. No, I didn't just head to the pharmacy; I flew. The urgency and stress were radiating out of my body.

I arrived at the pharmacy, and I'm sure my car made a few squeals and screeches pulling into the lot and parking. I flew out of my car and sprinted to the sliding doors and slowed just enough to speed walk through the store until I found the baby aisle. Not even slowing, I grabbed the right kind of formula off the shelf and was making a beeline for the checkout counter when out of nowhere, Marco appeared in front of me.

"Mr. Kenny, I must talk to you right now. Something awful has happened, and I don't know what to do," he pleaded. His eyes looked bloodshot as if he hadn't slept in days or had been on a drinking binge.

Out of the corner of my eye, I saw the cashier listening in while checking out a few customers in front of me. I didn't have much time. I really, really, really needed to get back home with that formula. "Listen, Marco, my wife is home with our baby, who is crying uncontrollably. I really don't have time to discuss this right now. Can you come in Monday first thing in the morning or call me? I'll make sure to clear room on my schedule for you to see me. I will do whatever I need to do to see you first."

Marco and I went back and forth for a bit, him insisting he needed to talk to me right then, me insisting I needed to head home as soon as I purchased the formula. Finally, he leaned in and whispered, "Oh, Mr. Kenny, you don't understand. I have contracted gonorrhea, and my wife doesn't know."

I was so unprepared for this news, but I tried to console him and told him quietly to go to the hospital immediately. He replied, "It's too late. I can't let anyone know about this."

I told him again that I could help him, but please let me just get through the weekend. I assured him I could get him medical attention for this, but it was obvious he wanted this to be resolved now.

For a brief moment, I stopped and looked at Marco as he continued, "I have no one else to talk to. My family would never understand. I can never let my wife know about this, but she's going to find out, Mr. Kenny."

The cashier cleared her throat and snapped me back to my frenzied state of mind. After she told me the amount to pay, I quickly pulled out my wallet. "Marco," I said as I gave the cash to the cashier, "I realize by looking at you how difficult this is, but I have to get this formula home to my screaming baby. Now I'm asking you to understand. I will connect you with the doctors you need, and we can help you with this and keep it confidential. I can even meet you tomorrow. I just have to get back to my baby girl."

I took the change from the cashier and stuck it in my wallet. I gave Marco information on how to call me, but he wouldn't give me a number in which to call him. He told me he was staying with friends and didn't want to give out the number. I repeated for him to call me or to come in first thing Monday morning, and I left.

I felt horrible all weekend. I wanted to help Marco, but what could I have done differently?

When he didn't show up on Monday as I had encouraged him to do, I pulled out his information for his phone number. I was going to call even if his wife answered the phone. I just had an unsettled feeling about everything.

His paperwork was not turned in, and therefore I had no way of contacting him. All week, I kept hoping he would come in, but he never did. On Friday of that next week, my heart dropped as one of our staff members informed me that Marco had taken his life by using a gun.

I was devastated. I was a fledgling advisor having just started my classes for my master's degree in counseling. I had no idea he was so deeply distraught that he would go to such lengths when I left him in the drugstore. Thoughts raced through my head—*suicide? Why? How did I blow it? Why didn't he call? Didn't he understand my daughter* was crying? *I didn't see that coming. How could I not see it? How could I miss it?* I was twenty-eight years old.

That weekend at Marco's funeral, I was the only Mott staff member in attendance and the only one who knew about Marco's secret. I wept for his wife and small children as I sat in the back of the Catholic church, eyes fixed on the crucifix hanging high above the altar in front. Christ's arms were stretched wide in love to a world that unmercifully drove a spear in His side.

I was still in shock. *I had no idea Marco would take such a drastic measure. I didn't see it coming. I lost my only chance to help him. What could I have done differently?* I carried the hurt and pain from Marco's death with me for years.

It wasn't until several years later that I realized what that something I could have done differently was. In my postgraduate masters in counseling studies, one of the first course electives was a class on recognizing the signs of someone at risk of committing suicide.

I learned the differences in behavior between a person just thinking about following through and someone who actually has a plan in place. I realized that instead of trying to console and redirect Marco, I should have been asking the right questions, finding out if he was thinking of hurting himself, discerning if he had a plan. I realize now I was too young and inexperienced to see these signs and engage him with the right questions.

Since my experience with Marco, I hope I have been able to give more reasons to live to those who sought my counsel rather than attempt to hurt or kill themselves. I am so thankful and blessed that God has afforded me the mercy to have never lost an individual since Marco over the last thirty years. That's not to toot my own horn or to say it will never happen. I sincerely hope it never does. But if I can help others learn about my errors made with Marco and help them see that life is a gift, help them discover the plethora of reasons they have to live, laugh, and love each day, then maybe his loss can someday and in some way be a redemptive life mark for others to realize there is hope.

Navigating Your Story

According to the Center of Disease Control (CDC), the statistics in the United States regarding suicide is that there are nearly over 45,000 persons who take their lives annually. Better put, an average of 123 kill themselves daily, or five human beings commit suicide every hour. Of that group, it's estimated that ninety percent or better suffer from major depression or mental illness and use either alcohol or drugs or combine them and create a dangerous cocktail.

Unfortunately, due to the Opioid crisis, another staggering 130 people not classified as suicide have cut their lives short due to the overuse of prescription or illegal drugs.

But according to research from the CDC and SAMHSA, the primary department in the U.S. for mental health and substance abuse recovery programs, more people struggle with alcoholism nationally and internationally than any other substance addiction. A 2015, study by the National Institute on Alcohol Abuse and Alcoholism reveals a significant correlation between depression and mental illness and alcohol, which is called co-occurring disorders. This means that people are binge drinking instead of using psychotropic medication or using the deadly cocktail by combining these together.

Addiction is an unfortunate reality for many, many families, including mine. I can almost guarantee that someone in your family, or someone close to you, is struggling with addiction. Whether it's alcohol or another substance, the problem is widespread and very real, and few of us live unimpacted by it.

The reality of addiction and suicide is often a shameful family secret. From the outside, everything looks fine. To your friends, your family may seem like the Norman Rockwell paintings: picture-perfect, put together, but on the inside, your reality is more often a home full of secrets. It looks more like drywall holes and peeling paint, an unhealthy place that feels emotionally, mentally, and physically out of order most of the time.

On the inside for many families, although the stigma of treatment is improving, still too often the secrets and the taboo subject are often not discussed. Few know where or to whom to turn to talk about it. Family gatherings come and go, and the problem is often avoided or covered up, especially if that individual is the patriarch or matriarch of the family. The floor is littered with eggshells that everyone is trying not to step on.

I've been there with my own family. I know the awkward discomfort.

So how does one navigate the storm of alcoholism and drugs?

Healing the Wounds

First, by admitting the truth.

Here's the honest way to approach someone when it comes to addiction and those it touches: In reality, we are all the walking wounded. We have to embrace that truth and admit recovery comes from one recognizing their need for help. Scripture reminds us there are two things whereby God can connect with and start helping us. For example, John 8:32 tells us that "the truth will set you free." Then Psalms 51:17 reminds us that God never ignores a contrite (broken, no more excuses) heart.

Psalm 147:3 says, "He heals the brokenhearted And binds up their wounds" (NASB).

Twelve-step programs refer to a "higher power" in the process of finding healing. For me, there is no higher power than the Almighty God, the Great Physician. Thankfully, we find the pathway to wholeness in Him. No two pathways will look exactly the same because no two people are created exactly alike. No two life experiences are exactly alike. Some have addictions; some are the collateral damage of addictions, and some have been hurt in other ways.

... *He heals the brokenhearted* ...

I find hope in the fact that no matter how our wounds came to be, no matter what our wounds are, when surrendered to our Father, He can and will heal them. He will heal your broken heart. He will make it whole again. He will make a way. He will lead you where you need to go through prayer, the guidance of the Holy Spirit, the Godly counsel and encouragement of others, and for those who need it, professional help.

... *and binds up their wounds* ...

Binding a wound is a several-step process: Assessing the seriousness of the wound to determine your plan of treatment; cleaning the wound with fresh, clean water; applying pressure to stop the bleeding; applying ointment to prevent infection; and wrapping the wound in a clean, sterile bandage.

The same process applies to wounds of the heart, mind, and soul. The inspired words in this Psalm were not carelessly chosen, quite the opposite. I believe He is showing us that there is a process to healing: coming to Him so He can guide you, letting His love, grace, and peace wash over you, and assuring you of His presence and sovereignty in your process. Here is where you crawl into His loving arms in preparation for the rest of the process.

Applying pressure to stop the bleeding. Wait, what? Not exactly a pretty picture, but this is where the work happens. *The beginning imprint of healing has to start with pressure against our deep wounds.*

When we submit our hurts to the Father, His goal is to make us more into His image, to "apply pressure" to those areas where work needs to be done, to apply positive pressure, life-giving pressure, cleansing pressure, purposeful pressure, transformative pressure.

Consider a diamond. Before it is that beautiful, precious stone every girl wants on her ring finger, it's an ugly, dirty, chalky piece of black coal. Only through a process of time, heat, and pressure does it become something beautiful. God wants you to be a diamond no matter what your wound is, no matter which side of addiction you may be on.

Whether addiction is even the issue or not, He desires to carry you through a process, to hold you when it gets difficult, and cheer you on in your victory. Does He choose to miraculously and suddenly heal some from the grip of addiction and deep wounds? Yes, He does! The how and why of whom that happens to is completely in His hands.

I wish I could spout a formula we could all use to make it happen for everyone, a formula that would take away any work that needed to be done. Because we live in a fallen world, this is not the case. If His path for you is not immediate healing, know that you are no less significant or loved by Him. As I said, no two paths to healing are completely alike just like no two fingerprints are alike. He created each of us wonderfully and uniquely. Why would we expect our healing journeys to be any different?

Depending on the severity of the wound or the cause of it, more care may be required. To keep the wound from becoming infected, protection is needed. In some cases, this means the help of a professional to give you the tools you need to move forward in your healing process.

The people you "wrap around" yourself are protection, people who will encourage you, who have walked your road before, who have become better despite their wounding instead of bitter because of it.

Charted Steps

This process applies to any kind of wounding. Is a professional always needed? No, not always. However, is pressure always required? Most likely, yes.

You may be asking yourself, "Why would anyone want to go through all that? Isn't it just easier, safer, to stay where I am, to live in what I know, even if it's not optimal?"

I would answer with a question: Is the legacy imprint you're leaving right now the one you really want to leave behind?

Let's get to work.

IMPRINT–Addictions and Deep Wounds

If you've been searching through your family history, is there any evidence of substance abuse? If yes, then with which family member? What effects did they have on your family through past generations leading up to your own?

Is there an addiction that you or other loved ones might be currently experiencing? Have you (or your loved one) sought the support of outside help? If not, start inquiring and do your own research to find a reputable place that has good outcomes, and if possible, a good faith-based approach of care as part of the treatment. Success stories are an important indication of the effectiveness of any program.

Have you or a loved one ever planned or thought of hurting yourselves? If so, seek a competent mental health provider immediately, one who combines helping the individual assess their current medications and usage and whether it's actually helping or hindering care. Look for signs of drug use in combination with other drugs with a trained professional, especially if weapons are involved. Don't try and deal with this alone.

As you come before our Heavenly Father in prayer, journal those prayers and the answers you are given. Hearing from the Lord could be as simple as an impression on your heart or a phone call from a friend that lines up with what you believe He is telling you. Remember this: chaos, negativity, isolation, and anything that is not in line with Scripture is not of the Lord.

In my twenty-five-plus years of experience as a counselor, I've learned that depression and hopelessness that lead to one seeking to harm oneself can come from a very self-focused, dark-centered place, a locked prison filled with lies and traps set by the father of all deception. His plan is clear—he seeks to kill, steal, and destroy us and take away all of one's hope and worth in living. Jesus made it clear that in order to remove these chains of darkness, we cannot find life without the provision of Christ, who is willing and waiting with the key to unlock the jailhouse door. His very words move us from darkness into His marvelous light.

He provides a transporting view of hopelessness to hope in Matthew 10:39 when He takes the key and swings open the door with these words: "He who has found his life ...."

In summary, I cannot impress upon you enough that if you're the only one in your family who sees addiction or family members hiding or experiencing suicidal ideation, make the professional contacts necessary and get them help as soon as possible. Once you let go and support them in prayer, you're giving God and those who are specifically trained to deal with your loved ones the opportunity that will hopefully help set them toward the journey of freedom from the dark place they have been living.

CHAPTER 5

Wade in the Water

"The real voyage of discovery consists not in seeking new landscapes, but in having new eyes."

— MARCEL PROUST

THE SUN IS HOVERING HIGH OVERHEAD. In the background, I hear the steading humming of multiple lawnmowers. The smell of fresh cut grass passes by and awakens my senses from a warm breeze. Doesn't that aroma just take you back?

I don't mow my own grass anymore, but the memories remain like yesterday. Responsibilities of managing three businesses leave little time for any kind of yardwork.

Watching the lawn service guys go row by row, meticulously creating a pattern and covering every inch of my property reminds me of all the conversations I had with the Lord when I had time for that seemingly monotonous task. I kind of miss those talks. Epiphany moments I had while pushing the mower around my little yard in Flint, Michigan, eventually changed my family's course.

I am not the first Mauck to have that experience. My great-grandfather Thomas Mauk had his own epiphany moments. The providential hand of God was revealed in my family line through Tom, who allowed himself to be redirected, opening the door for my family to choose another path.

William "Tom" Mauk: 1879–1966
(My Great-Grandfather)

William "Tom" Mauk was the first male child of William "Wild Bill" Mauk and America's eight children. America had learned that if she kept the children under her watchful care, Tom would be spared some, but not all of the beatings.

Tom was her favorite, and America... and America had a soft spot of protection... had a soft spot of protection for him. The two had a close, special bond. America limited Wild Bill's access to Tom growing up and kept him with her in the fields, on errands, and around the house. Even though Tom was spared the brunt of his father's abusive ways, he witnessed more than his fair share of abuse as a child. The drunken rages of his father were a shameful secret of the family to which he was privy. Although not to the extent of his older siblings, he probably nonetheless endured a bit of physical and emotional abuse himself despite America's efforts to shield him.

In his late teens and early twenties, Tom was known to enjoy a good party, but nothing like his father and uncles before him. I have a feeling America was a positive influence in that area as well.

When Tom was a young man, he didn't let any grass grow under his feet as evidenced in 1898, when he married his first wife Louverna Parsons. It's interesting, they married the same year she became pregnant, making one wonder if the marriage was prompted due to her pregnancy, something more common in that day. Tom and Louverna had three children: Myrtle Mae (born 1898), Molly (born 1901), and Walter Ernest (born 1903). Then Louverna passed away unexpectedly in 1904, leaving Tom a young, sad, widowed, single father, which forced him to grow up quickly.

A third-generation farmer, Tom did the only thing he knew how to do. He quickly left the party life behind and threw himself into working his land. His children were his driving purpose, and he wanted to provide for their future in a way that had not been done for him.

Fortunately, his mother America was able to come and care for the three children during the day, leaving Tom able to work the long, hard hours needed. As his farm grew, so did his reputation as a man of integrity in the community, which attracted the attention of a young Dutch English woman named Mary Holbrook. Tom and Mary wed in 1905. She took Tom's three children from his previous marriage and treated them as her children, and they would have plenty more of their own, twelve to be exact. In all, Tom and May raised fifteen children.

Another reason Mary and Tom may have wanted to leave Kentucky, was to put distance between Tom and his old partying friends from his late teens, as well as his father. Tom had told the story that illustrated why Kentucky, was not the best place for the Mauk boys. A few years prior to Tom leaving Ohio, a young lad spotted him in a country store and stopped him in the aisle. "Sir, my mother claims you are my biological father." Taken aback, Tom asked, "Son, who is your mother?" He told him her name. Tom scratched his chin. "Well, son, that very well could be, but then again, after close recollection, it's just as likely or more that I'm not."

Wild Bill died when Tom was twenty-nine. He made what I consider a smart move. He sold his share of the 144 acres in Olive Hill, Kentucky, purchased a twenty-acre farm in Scioto County, and moved the family to Ohio. The discrepancy in price was understood to be that the land in Ohio, was much better land and great for farming, whereas the acres in Kentucky, were full of ground holes, and a good portion of the land was on unlevel ground.

I find this decision symbolic on many levels that goes beyond him purchasing a better piece of land. Somehow, Tom must have had some knowledge of Grandfather Joseph's story and his Great-Uncle Peter's attempt to reconcile the family in some way. It's quite possible during his grandfather's sober moments, he heard bits and pieces of the stories of his great-grandfather Samuel and great-great-grandfather Frederick as well as stories from Peter about Hans Joseph.

The property he purchased was in the very same county where his great-great-grandfather Frederick had chosen as his new settlement for the entire Mauk family, the same place his great-grandfather Samuel had died, and the same place his grandfather Joseph had started such a painful life journey. Tom made it his business to lay to rest the anger and grief that had impacted them, and to a moderate extent, himself. Whether he realized it or not, Tom was reclaiming territory that had been lost physically, emotionally, and spiritually for the Mauk family.

All of this points to Tom being a peacemaker. He desired to bring peace not to just his immediate family but the entire Mauk family. He knew most of the family story, had seen his own father's agony, and was ready to start over. Tom was providentially moving back to a place where God would in time create a redemptive story.

Why did he wait until after his father's death? Death brought a new perspective as it does for so many of us. Perhaps he waited out of respect. Maybe it was to stay close to his mother and potentially protect her from any harm. Whatever the reason, Tom and the Mauk family now had a clean slate, a fresh start, and it would change the direction of our family legacy.

Life on the Farm

Upon arriving in Ohio, Tom and Mary got right to work establishing a farm and their family. There were plenty of hands to help with the work, and everyone did. My grandfather William "Lewis" Mauck, the first child from Tom's second wife Mary Holbrook-Mauk, and his siblings worked from daylight to dusk every single day. Chores included but were by no means limited to feeding the horses, cows, and chickens; mucking the stalls; milking the cows before breakfast, and working the vast garden. Eventually, the garden became the responsibility of the children and after that, the grandchildren would pitch in as well.

Several changes began to happen though in the 40s and 50s for the Mauk family. For example, the grandchildren were encouraged for the first time to complete and graduate from high school. In addition, my grandfather Lewis Mauk met a professor on the road who shared with him how the name "Mauk" had been misspelled all these years. It should include a "c" if it were to have the correct English spelling. Thus, in the early 50s, our family's last name was changed by Lewis Mauk to Lewis L. Mauck. For the last sixty-seven years, the name has been spelled as "Mauck."

Anyone who lived on my great grandfather Tom's farm was required to work. Even sons and daughters who left and then came back as adults had to contribute. If they had a family, they were also expected to do their part. No one got a free ride on Tom Mauck's farm. In fact, my own father vividly remembers inviting his friends over for dinner and on weekends, hearing "Grandpa Tom's" speech each time saying, "Everyone is welcome to eat around the Mauck table, but everyone is expected to work here as well." There were no lazy kids, grandkids, or even friends on Grandpa Tom's farm, and that probably added to its success.

When it came to correcting the children and even grandchildren, Grandpa Tom was a disciplinarian and could show his anger from time to time. However, his discipline was tempered with love and grace.

My father told me the story of one run-in with his grandpa's discipline. My father had not done what Grandpa Tom had requested in a timely manner, so Grandpa Tom gave my dad a knife and told him to go cut a switch. My dad knew exactly what that meant—he was getting a whipping.

So, my dad went outside and returned with the littlest limb of a tree branch with which he thought he could get away. Grandpa Tom gave him his licking, but I have to wonder if he wasn't a bit humored by my dad's choice of switches. Ten minutes later, Grandpa Tom gave five cents to my dad and his other cousins so they could go buy ice cream at the nearby country store.

I believe Grandpa Tom grew up observing his father Wild Bill's behavior over the years and recognized it as something he did not want to repeat with his own family. My dad remembers Grandpa Tom as a likeable man and a natural when it came to marketing his farm's homegrown fruits, vegetables, wheat, and pork. As part of their duties around the farm, his kids and grandkids put together a wagonful of goods, and he showed them just where to hang the signs and how to sell their produce and goods. If not enough items sold where they chose to set up, Grandpa Tom would hitch up the wagon to the old tractor and tow them down the road closer to town.

My father said that Grandpa Tom was one of the hardest working men he had ever known. He understood how to motivate his young grandsons to be up and at 'em every day to work on the farm alongside him.

Revival!

In the early 1920s, a wonderful black evangelist traveled to the Portsmouth area to preach. The town was abuzz with excitement about the Reverend William J. Seymour from Los Angeles holding meetings. Reverend Seymour was part of one of the greatest American revivals, the Azusa Street Revival. This revival started on the West Coast and spread like wildfire across the country as Reverend Seymour went from town to town holding tent revivals and preaching to the masses. He spoke of surrendering one's life to Jesus, accepting the power of the Holy Spirit, and the joy found in making Christ the Lord of one's life.

Many experienced God's presence in their lives for the first time and were brought to true repentance. Thousands were filled with the Spirit of God as a result of his anointed sermons. (Reverend Seymour is also credited as one of the pioneers of the Charismatic movement.)

Reverend Seymour had come to Ohio, to preach in a Brush Arbor meeting. That night after some singing, the conviction of the Holy Spirit was heavy on almost everyone in the room, including the entire Mauck family who Tom had invited.

Reverend Seymour started to preach under the anointing of God, and it wasn't long before people were streaming down the aisles to the front altar, not just for forgiveness, but to turn away from their sin and confess their need for true repentance and a right relationship with God. Conviction swept the entire congregation that night, leading to some major repentance and tears from Tom. Later, they described what it was like to be in the presence of God's love for each one of those nights. The entire family had never felt like this. An outpouring of God's Spirit infilled most of the family attending that night, an epiphany moment of true repentance and service to God. From that night on and until his death, Grandpa Tom asked all his family to come to the living room to pray before going to bed. Every meal was a time of giving thanks to God. Prayer and thanksgiving filled the Mauck home.

William "Tom" Mauk had finally answered the prayers of Hans Peter Mauk all those years, and even those of Hans' parents, prayers for a legacy of faith, freedom, and prosperity. The Mauck family was now firmly back under the grace and mercy of God's Son Jesus Christ, whom on that night became Tom, Mary, and many of the Mauck family's Savior and Lord.

More of My Story: Life's Utopia and Reality Clash!

"Man, I am so ready for this," my friend Greg said before taking a huge bite out of the best hamburgers either of us had ever eaten. It seemed everything tasted better today. Colors were brighter, the air was cleaner... the world was good. Yes, this was the life.

Greg was one of the few childhood friends I had. We played in the church pews—or more accurately, wrestled under the church pews at the age of four as little boys. Family connections had kept us in proximity to each other over the years.

After daydreaming about the awesomeness of finally becoming adults and the adventures that might lay ahead, I said, "Yeah, this is gonna be great," and slathered my fries with ketchup.

Of course, we had no real idea back then what becoming an adult really meant, but life would teach us some things here.

Life in the Fast Lane

Greg and I were headed to Huntington to live with my Uncle Roland and Aunt Jo. I recently discovered we were only about an hour from Portsmouth, Ohio, the city where my fourth-generational great-grandfather Samuel had passed away.

We planned to take the remainder of the summer to get settled. Then I planned to attend Marshall University of *We Are Marshall* fame. The sting of that fateful plane crash was still palpable around the campus, giving a defining resilience that only added to the charm of a college town.

I couldn't wait to run for the track team as a "walk-on" in the fall. We plugged into the youth group at my uncle's church and started looking for jobs. To us, we were living the dream, working men living on our own (with my uncle and aunt) and surrounded by beautiful ladies (the youth from church). We had reached the pinnacle of adulting in our fresh-out-of-high-school minds.

Tradewell Grocery had a couple of job openings, and both Greg and I were hired on as baggers. Working with Greg was an adventure. He was just downright funny, and he made working the third shift more than enjoyable with our high-speed dolly runs down the aisles, shopping cart races, riding the conveyor belts, and midnight cooking experiments in the breakroom once all the work was done. We would always have things shipshape by morning, but oh, we had fun.

On the home front, as much as we appreciated the generosity of my aunt and uncle (and living rent-free), staying with them kept the freedom we truly longed for at bay. Being on our best behavior was, frankly, exhausting. So as soon as we could, we found our own place in town, closer to work life and Marshall. Many plans and schemes came to life while we laughed until we cried into the wee hours of the morning on the balcony of that apartment.

We had a simple domestic agreement. Greg agreed to cook if I handled the cleanup. Sounded good to me; I hated cooking anyway. Since Greg was in charge of the cooking, I let him guide the grocery shopping. To keep an eye on expenses, Greg suggested we take full advantage of the specials at Tradewell. Again, sounded good to me. That first month, Tradewell's ran a special on the all-American favorite Kraft Macaroni & Cheese. Who doesn't love macaroni and cheese? It's the meal that pleases everyone from toddlers to baby boomers, right? As much as I loved that comfort food (still do!), after three straight macaroni-and-cheese dinners—one with ham, one with sausage, and one with SPAM—I began to second-guess the goodness of going along with Greg's food choices. Apparently, his cooking skills were better since he had more practice than me, but I couldn't imagine one more dinner with any cheese or noodles of any kind at that point. We both agreed it was time to eat out again. So, we became well-acquainted with another American classic, the McDonald's down the street, and when we had enough money, Dewight's, a little hometown restaurant in Huntington.

Great memories were made that summer hanging out, eating terribly unhealthy food, staying up as late as we wanted, and just being two young, naive, single guys in that downtown apartment. However, our dreams of extended independence after three months of living together were suddenly cut short one night. After a long day at work, I headed home, but Greg had a date and said he would be home later. Exhausted and facing an early shift the next morning, I went straight for my bed. Around two in the morning, a loud pounding at the door woke me up. Who in the world could it be this early in the morning? I opened the door quickly to see my Aunt Jo and cousin Ronda standing in front of me, eyes wide in a panic.

As soon as they saw I was fine, their tensed facial muscles relaxed, and they let out a sigh of relief. "Kenny," Ronda said, "You're okay. We thought you were with Greg tonight. He's been in a serious car accident involving a drunk driver and is in critical condition." I hadn't even realized Greg wasn't home yet.

The unconfirmed story was that Greg and I were coming back from a double date, and we were both in the hospital. I put on my clothes and went to the hospital only to find out he was in intensive care and couldn't take any visitors due to the severity of his injuries. What a wake-up call in life, to realize my best friend was in such bad shape. To make matters worse, I couldn't do anything to help. I wished I could have been allowed to support him with a prayer or word of encouragement. That night, I couldn't sleep as a result of my concern for Greg.

The next day, the gravity of the situation became clear. Greg's car was a mangled ball of metal and was completely totaled. I went to the crash site. Skid marks led to the spot where the drunk driver ran off the road into the ravine and revealed Greg's attempt to swerve out of his way. Broken glass was scattered everywhere. After reviewing the accident scene, I was amazed that Greg was still alive. I was thankful God had spared him. I looked up in the tree above us, and about twenty feet in the air were some debris, including part of Greg's windshield wipers hanging on some limbs. The impact had to be tremendous. Looking later at the picture of his car, it looked more like a crushed empty can, totally smashed. Here was another miracle. I said a small prayer of thanks while overlooking this scene, knowing without a doubt that God had kept him alive.

It would take weeks, and more likely months, for Greg to recuperate fully from his injuries. His parents decided to move him back home to Indiana. I could not afford our apartment on my own, and I had missed registering at Marshal. Instead of enjoying my newfound freedom with Greg, I felt God's direction may be for me to go home and regroup for what He really had in store for my life.

Crossroads

My parents had moved to a much older part of Flint over the summer of 1978. Then about two years later, in 1980, while I attended college at Mott for my associate's degree, we moved again to an older established college area. When I pulled onto the street of our new house, I immediately fell in love with the neighborhood. It was lined with beautiful tall trees and stately, well-kept Cape Cod style houses. My parents' was a tri-level home with a screened-in porch. Dad's store, Genesee Fabrics, owned for eight years, was just around the corner from our street, and the local community college was only a short bike ride by way of beautiful winding backroads.

After graduating with my associate's degree, I was no closer to knowing what I wanted to do with my life until I took a college interest inventory. I saw that my career path was firmly in the area of working with and helping people, including children and families. It pointed out career paths of elementary teacher, counselor, singer or musician, and YMCA director. Interesting, most of these areas were what I have spent the majority of my life doing.

Although finding some career options was helpful, I also discovered during this time that I was at a crossroads regarding my faith. I had grown up in church and had studied the Bible, but I began questioning a lot of things in life. Like many young people during their college years, I was being taught by too many agnostic and atheist college instructors. I wanted to make sure I was not living off my parents' faith, and I wanted to find God's purpose and direction in and through my life. So instead of going to the University of Michigan, I took a big detour to a small private seminary, Jackson College of Ministries in Jackson, Mississippi. I had given a secular school two years of indoctrination. It was time to give at least some equal time to the hard questions of my faith as a Christian as well. Fortunately, my parents supported me in my decision.

While travelling to Jackson, other logical questions surfaced. Would I be staying one semester? Two? Did I want to consider music, something I really loved, as a career choice? In some ways, I can see now that I was a young man searching for significance. By not having a serious young lady in my life now made my decision easier. I began to embrace the idea of building my own independence, washing my own clothes, learning to cook my own food. This somewhat fly-by-the-seat-of-my-pants decision would fortunately become a very significant time in my life, one I would deeply appreciate someday.

When God Shows Up

Musically, I began to learn a lot. My piano instructor Wayne Goodine was and remains an exceptional pianist. He took my understanding of piano and playing it to a whole new level. I was beginning to learn how to play the piano by rote instead of just by note. Wayne not only helped hone my piano skills, he showed me how to really enjoy playing an instrument with better thought and precision. I began writing songs on the piano and sometimes played the drums in church. I'm a better musician today because of his influence. I met many other great musicians and singers, some of whom became well-known artists in both the church and gospel music industry.

More importantly, my spiritual life took a huge leap forward. While in Jackson, my prayers were pleas for my life to make sense. I needed direction. I didn't just want a degree; I wanted to know who I was. I wanted purpose. I wanted God to show up and reveal Himself in my life. I needed to know God was real.

No longer was it enough to merely know the God of my parents; I wanted and needed my own undeniable personal encounter with

Jesus Christ. I was on a journey to discover my faith, one that was for real and for myself.

One night toward the end of the semester, my goal of becoming independent was coming true. Many of the deep-seeded questions I was inquiring about regarding God and Scripture were starting to be resolved in terms of real answers. I was finding peace within His Word.

Finally, I had one more hurdle yet to clear. It came when the rest of the college students decided to sleep. My roommate had gone home for the weekend, and I was all alone in my room. I decided to take a walk. Eventually, I found an empty classroom with carpeted floors. I sat down and whispered my prayer, thanking God for all of the answers He provided to me through others that semester. Kneeling with my arms lifted toward heaven, weeping, I cried out and then internalized these words, "God, if You're real, I now need to know and feel you're here with me. I need to actually feel Your presence and arms wrapped around me like my Heavenly Father would do. Just, please, show me that You're there. I want You not just to be the Savior and Lord over my family but Savior and Lord of my life as well and over the choices and decisions I make in all I ultimately do."

Well, after being vulnerable with a short prayer, God did meet me that night. I felt something come over me. It was the presence of a warm embrace that a father would give to one of his cherished children. I began to sing songs I had learned about Him and lifted my arms to my Heavenly Father, so much so, I became lost in the presence of Jesus. I must have been there several hours because when I awoke, I was lying on my back with dried tears on my face. I was at such peace that I had fallen asleep. Never had I felt more content in my life than at that moment, realizing God was truly real, and He had visited me personally.

Upon getting up, I knew then that not only did God exist, but He also existed as a supernatural supreme being that loved me, not because of my goodness, but because of His mercy and grace at the cross at Calvary. I realized that like me, He desired for us to walk with and talk to each other every day. I had a similar experience at the age of twelve that I had nearly forgotten about, but tonight was much deeper and with more understanding as a twenty-one-year-old young man. I was overwhelmed knowing I had just encountered the God of all creation, of Abraham, Isaac, and Jacob, and the presence of Jesus Christ was with me.

After getting up and walking back to my dorm, I realized at that moment it was time to go back home. This move back to Michigan, confirmed that my faith was true. I would have no problem debating any of my professors about why I believed in God, my faith, and that the assuredness of my salvation was safely found not in anything from what I had done, but from what He had done.

Once back in Flint, my hometown of ten years, I was accepted at the University of Michigan-Flint to obtain my bachelor's degree in elementary education. Instead of continuing to arrange and direct the 60 Voice Choir at Faith Tabernacle Church during my last two years at the university, I started a contemporary Christian band and wrote and arranged songs and played the keyboard.

I will forever be thankful for my years at Faith Tabernacle in Flint, Michigan, and to have met so many awesome people like Ken Tucker, Tim Pierson, Scott Frost (brother of Craig Frost of the famous band Grand Funk Railroad), Reverend Berniece and Dave Matejeck, the Whittakers, Evans, Avants, and so many other great individuals and families, too many to name. Little did I realize how important that night at Jackson College of Ministries would mean to me. That epiphany prayer in the classroom would cause me to listen to God along my life's journey and run to His calling. It cured me from the temptation of running away like that of my fifth-generational great-grandfather Frederick.

Navigating Your Story

I have to wonder about Grandpa Tom's process in making the decision to move to Ohio. Exactly when did he first have the thought? How long did he wrestle with doubts, excuses, and reasons not to go? Did he even have doubts?

How much input and influence did his wife Mary have in the decision to relocate? What was the final deciding factor? What confirmations did he see along the way? What fears and apprehensions did his children have?

I wonder about these things because I look back on my own epiphany moments and see the process I went through. I see how long it took for me to actually step out in obedience and go, and I see the confirmations and providential hand of God along the way.

Be a Chain Breaker

While I don't know his exact thinking process, Grandpa Tom's actions are evidence enough in understanding the damaging role the past had played in his family. At some point, somehow, Tom realized a chain needed to be broken. To not take action would be a detriment to his family. Staying in the same place, not just physically but emotionally and spiritually, was not an option.

When we don't realize the important role our past has in understanding who we are today, we potentially leave ourselves open to generational curses of fear and shame. Tom knew that if his family was to break free from the past, present action was required. He decided to be the chain breaker.

Deciding to take action is a first step. More importantly, we need God to assist us in healing from the past. We must be willing not only to confront those issues head on, but also to surrender ourselves to the Lord and take the risk as my great-grandfather did for his family.

John 8:36 says, "If the Son sets you free, you will be free indeed" (NIV). *We are promised freedom through Jesus.* When our hearts are surrendered to Him, one providential epiphany moment can and will lead us to the road less traveled, a place where God in His mercy leads us out from the shadows of the past. Taking us by the hand, He draws us out of the darkness of loss and victimhood into the light of His grace. In that light, God's ultimate desire for His children is revealed: to see His children, you and I, live in true freedom.

Charted Steps

Epiphany moments are life changers. Imprinted changes. Trajectory corrections. It's never too late to change your family's direction. To identify those moments in your generational family's life and your own is to unveil the thread of God's providence, His guiding hand and purposes.

IMPRINT: Epiphany Moments
IMPRINT: God's Providence
IMPRINT: Surrender

As you think through these questions, thank God for the moments He shows you. Thank Him for the revelations He gives, whether they reveal a positive direction or the need for change. Both are positive discoveries when surrendered to His purposes.

1. Has there been an epiphany moment that changed your family's direction? Were you or someone in your generational family the person who turned things around?

2. Was faith a definite factor in the decision to change? Briefly identify that electrical life-changing spiritual or monumental moment(s).
3. Like myself, can you look back and see how your plans were suddenly changed by events and circumstances that ended up being the main catalyst of growth and change into becoming an adult?
4. Perhaps as you were reading this chapter, the need for a new chapter in your family's story was revealed to you. Are you ready to hear and respond to Him? Why or why not?

I encourage you to spend time in prayer, laying any hesitations, questions, and fears of change or unknowns at the feet of the ultimate Chain Breaker, so that you and your family can experience the freedom that is waiting for you!

CHAPTER 6

Course Corrections

"Forgiveness is the fragrance that the violet sheds on the heel that has crushed it."

— MARK TWAIN

THE EVENING SUN SLOWLY MELTS into the horizon, painting the sky above me from a palette of soft blues, beautiful purples, and brilliant oranges. I wonder when the sun sets on my life, will it be this brilliant? Will what I leave behind be beautiful, enriching, and a blessing to my family like the scene I am observing?

My thoughts shift to other men in my family and land on my grandfathers, my mother's father and my father's father. So far, I have focused solely on the Mauck side of the family, but my Grandfather Nichols actually had a greater impact on my life than any of my grandparents. My life story would not be complete without including him. His imprint will most definitely be reflected in mine as will that of my grandfather Lewis. The sunsets of each grandfather's life could not have been more different.

A Tale of Two Grandfathers

William "Lewis" Mauck: 1907–1985
(My Paternal Grandfather)

My grandfather William Lewis Mauck, the fourth child of Tom and Mary, attended the tent revival led by the Reverend William Joseph Seymour of Azusa Street fame with Grandpa Tom and the family when he was sixteen years old. Lewis was among those who met the Lord that day and was saved.

The Frazier family also attended that night and gave their hearts to the Lord as well. Lewis and young Victor Frazier became good friends over the next few years, and that's how Lewis got to know Elizabeth, Victor's little sister, one who would eventually become his wife and my grandmother.

I often wonder what transpired over the next six years between Elizabeth (better known as Tessa) and my grandfather. What started out as a buddy's kid sister eventually turned into a friendship and then love. Elizabeth and Lewis were married in July 1927. They were seventeen and twenty, respectively.

After his conversion, Lewis dove into Scripture, studying the Word intensely. He came to believe the Bible was the divinely inspired Word of God, in supernatural healing, and in the power of the Holy Spirit to change people's lives.

Two years after marrying Elizabeth, Lewis began traveling and preaching as a Pentecostal evangelist. In speaking with several ministers who knew of him while he was alive, I've learned much about his career as a traveling evangelist. Lewis, along with his good friend and now the Reverend Victor Frazier, began ministering at various

United Pentecostal Churches throughout West Virginia, Southern Ohio, and Kentucky. Between the two of them, hundreds were baptized in lakes, ponds, and even the Ohio River. Lewis was instrumental in developing and growing churches in the Kanawha City area, just outside of Charleston, West Virginia, and then traveled extensively throughout the tri-state area of West Virginia, Ohio, and parts of Kentucky.

In the early years, many recognized Reverend Lewis Mauck's anointed speaking when he preached. Pastors and other evangelists saw him as a minister with an auspicious future. A highly charismatic individual who sincerely cared for people and had an extensive knowledge of the Bible, Lewis led many to accept Jesus Christ over the next ten years.

How I wish the story ended there... in the good years... in the years of saving souls and living a godly life under His anointing. Unfortunately, this story would end up having many twists and wrong turns as well.

Grandfather Lewis was known to be a very good-looking man, full of charisma and charm. He grew up on a farm, and despite the fact that he only had a seventh-grade education, his preaching and evangelistic abilities were quite impressive and garnered him much attention. Eventually, pride began to creep in.

At the height of my grandfather's quick rise to local evangelistic stardom came a historical and sobering event for our country. On December 7, 1941, Japan bombed Pearl Harbor, and the United States entered the frenzy of World War II. As over sixteen million Americans, mostly young men, went off to Europe to fight Hitler, many young American women were left home to hold down the fort, to work while taking care of the children.

The war presented our country with many issues, such as the rationing of gasoline, women working men's jobs, and women also working several jobs on top of single parenting and keeping the household running.

Besides being a young, charismatic preacher, sometimes full of himself, traveling without his wife, and preaching to girlfriends, fiancés, and mothers whose men were at war, my grandfather was also a pretty good handyman. Spending much time alone in homes without the head of the household present while fixing things around the house and comforting distraught women was a recipe for disaster. Lewis succumbed to temptation and would end up having multiple affairs. In time, they eventually ended his days as a minister.

The Truth Comes Out

When my grandmother Elizabeth finally confronted my grandfather about his affairs, he confessed every detail she wanted to know. Although she tried to forgive, forgetting was another level of trust she would never be able get past.

Around 1945, after two years of coming in and out of the home, my grandparents had a fight over the past that was the tipping point. My grandfather packed all his things, and the next morning he left.

My dad remembers that last morning after an evening of continual loud exchanges, his father kissing him and his sister, my Aunt Jo, goodbye, but no words were exchanged between them as they could recall. Dad was twelve years old. As his father was opening the door to leave, my dad pleaded, begged him to stay. But Grandpa Mauck walked out of the house, threw his things in the car, got in, and started down the long drive out to the main road.

My dad got on his bike and rode as fast and as hard as he could, pedaling feverishly. He chased his father's car down the long driveway, crying out, pleading, "Dad, please don't leave me! Dad, come back. Please don't leave us again!"

No matter how fast he pedaled, the car never stopped; it just kept going. In fact, the car began to pick up speed until my dad realized his bike was no match.

Finally, my grandfather disappeared out of sight. My dad was still yelling through sobs all the way home, "Dad, please don't leave me. Please don't leave me!" That would be the last time his father would live with them as a family, even though later in years he and Tessa, who would become known to her grandchildren as "Ma Ma Tess," attempted to reconcile only to fail each time. Too many things said or left unsaid.

Grandfather Lewis continued to run, not only in and out of the lives of his children but that of his grandchildren as well. Without exception, I remember how he would ride up with a flashy new car and a new top hat and be off again within twenty-four hours to see another friend or acquaintance. His visits were always very short with a dramatic flair and gaps of years in between. Other than those sporadic, brief visits, my grandfather was MIA in his children's and grandchildren's lives. One of his means to survive was to marry women who had land, money, or had obtained wealth as to afford him the time to travel and not be as concerned about his finances.

Family Secrets

The truth is my grandfather did not divulge everything to his children, grandchildren, or ex-wives. It wasn't until later when his adult children, my father, Aunt Jo, Lynn, and Laane, began to learn more about each other. In fact, while writing this book, we found out he fathered several other children we never knew existed outside of all three of three marriages we knew about. Once I found out about them, I wondered if their experience was anything like my father's.

Once in 1974, my father took me up north in Michigan, to visit two of my father's step-siblings Laane and Lynn. Both were wonderful people, with Laane having a wonderful family of her own and Lynn becoming a male nurse. Amazingly, most of the children Lewis fathered would have been glad to look beyond his indiscretions, but it was his own internal shame and guilt that was the stumbling block whereby he could not forgive himself.

I have found most all the family suffered from the same malady of loss. They wanted a father who could spend some time with them and would have embraced each other a long time ago if he could have reconciled these indiscretions within his own life.

In 2017, after he had passed, Lewis' other two adult children Cindy and Jerry found my father (who was eighty-five at the time), my aunt, Lynn, and Laane. A man who had so much going for him early in his life also had significant issues with which he needed to deal. Unfortunately, he had no counselors or ministers to whom he could go to. He left a trail of tears, but all his children, once lost from each other, ended up finding each other.

My Grandpa Mauck's running and life secrets would end in 1985, not far from where his second-generational great-grandfather Samuel had passed away in Scioto, Ohio. His imprinted life history story that began in Southern Ohio, would also be where his life would end.

To my knowledge, Lewis never asked for forgiveness from my dad or my aunt or any of the other family members. His unwillingness to seek forgiveness for the hurt he caused left insecurity in my father for years to come. Each child coped in their own way, and most all found the grace about which their father so reverently spoke. All wished Lewis could have found it by making amends for himself as well.

Ma Ma Tess, Always Room in Her Heart and at Her Kitchen Table

I would be remiss if I didn't share the tremendous respect I have for my father's mother, my grandmother, who we affectionately called Ma Ma Tess. As Grandpa Lewis' first wife, she was a delight to all of us as her grandchildren—myself, Candy, Tammy, and my cousin Landy and twin first cousins Ronda and Jonda.

My grandparents lived throughout the Great Depression, but they always had enough food for everyone and anyone who found themselves around Ma Ma Tess's table. But even in the worst of times, she could be found standing for hours if needed in the food lines to make sure her family and friends had enough to eat. Quality time was a priority, and she was sure to spend it with everyone who came to visit her.

Ma Ma Tess made sure everyone in the family attended church. She made sure the family knew proper etiquette, including how to properly set up a dining room and the proper placement of the silverware on a place setting. She danced with us, sang songs with us, played games with us, rode her bike right next to us, always had a spoon handy to give us a taste of her latest concoction, which was always amazing. She lived her whole life to love God, her family, and children. Ma Ma Tess was a mom to all.

She never stopped loving Lewis nor her family. Even after their divorce and numerous failed attempts to reconcile, she still showed him kindness. The last time she took care of him was during his final months of life. What a gracious, loving woman she was.

I think I speak on behalf of all of my siblings and cousins when I say Ma Ma Tess was and always will remain one of the most loving, special relatives we have ever known.

Marcus "Pa Paw" Nichols: 1900–1999
(My Maternal Grandfather)

My mother's father, Pa Paw Nichols from Louisiana, couldn't have been more different than my Grandpa Lewis. Marcus "Mark" Nichols stood at only five foot seven inches tall, but to me, he stood eight feet tall. Pa Paw was one of the most significant individuals of my life as a child and through memories he left imprinted on me as an adult.

He represented to me all that a grandpa should be, what a grandfather looks like, smells like, and acts like. His gentle nature, demeanor, and love for the underdog were unmatched. He was laid back, funny as all get out, and loved his grandkids. He was the grandpa every kid wanted to have and the grandpa I strive to be. To me, Mark Nichols was and remains a man among men.

My grandmother, Mertie Mae Nichols, was one of the toughest women I had ever met. Her outlook on life was relatively black and white. Not many gray areas existed in the world for Ma Maw, and that made for some entertaining conversations over the years. Both my Ma Maw and Pa Paw were two of the greatest examples of faith I have ever seen.

Every minute of the nearly twenty-hour drive from Michigan, to their home in DeRidder, Louisiana, was soon forgotten as we entered their home. Pa Paw and Ma Maw always had dinner planned and spent hours preparing for our arrival at the table. Tired and starving, we raced to the front door, clamoring to be the first to savor the tantalizing aromas of bona fide southern cooking. The beautiful buffet of pot roast, ham, fresh sweet potatoes, green beans, black-eyed peas, greens, mashed potatoes and gravy, corn on the cob, and scrumptious fresh banana creme and hot pecan pies were some of the most momentous smells of my life. The feast continued all week with peach cobbler, banana pudding (a Southern staple), and the best homemade jam and homemade ice cream you ever put in your mouth. Oh, yeah! The long day that started in the wee hours and all those hours of driving was always worth every minute once we hit Roberts Street.

As good as all that food was, after dinner was my favorite time. I would shadow my Pa Paw every moment I could, following him out to his impressive garden that grew bigger each time we visited. His homegrown tomatoes were the best in the world. We would walk through the garden, and he would tell me all the different vegetables he was growing each year.

The weather was about one hundred degrees in the shade in the summer, which was when our school was out, so Ma Maw always had fresh-squeezed lemonade waiting for us and a fan right on our faces.

Pa Paw would sit me down and fill me in on everything he had done to his old '57 Plymouth since our last visit. Paid off some twenty years earlier, the car still looked brand-spanking new with white-walled tires and the same hard-plastic covers on the seats to keep them clean. It ran like a champion race car. An oil change was never missed and always happened at 3,000 miles on the dot. I'm still amazed at just how neat and clean that car remained his whole life, but that was my Pa Paw. He did everything with excellence and was the hardest working man I would ever meet.

Looking back over my time with Pa Paw, I realize his main influence on my life came from watching how he lived his life. You see, he was the neighborhood social worker and handyman for a widow or single mom. He fixed broken windows and doors that jammed at the bottom, or he would cut down a stubborn tree after a windy storm. There was no fanfare, and he was always respectful and honorable, never out of line with anyone. He never once told me why he had to go down the street for a while, but my mom and grandmother would.

I'll never forget watching my grandfather lovingly care for my Ma Maw as best as he could when she was diagnosed with dementia in her late sixties. She eventually passed away in 1982. I was twenty-three. After going to her funeral, I thought that my grandfather would finally have some time to rest and what relief he must be feeling. But that night, he demanded my parents remain in his full-size bed. Then right before he crawled into the other twin bed in the guest room where I was staying, I overheard his prayer. It will forever be etched in my mind.

His voice broke and was thick with emotion as he prayed: *"Dear Lord, thank You for all the wonderful years You gave me and Mertie Mae together, for those have been some of the best years of my life."*

Lying silently in the dark in the other twin bed, I couldn't stop the tears. We had buried his sweetheart of sixty-two years, the last thirteen of which had been some of the hardest of his life. He had cared for Ma Maw and watched her illness progress to the point of not recognizing him or any of her family anymore.

My grandfather's prayer spoke volumes to me. He loved Ma Maw in sickness and in health and continued to love her until his death ten years later, a few weeks before his ninety-ninth birthday. He always remained committed in love and faithful to his one and only wife.

More of My Story

My two grandfathers have both left lasting imprints on my life, albeit very different ones. With God's help, I hope both are passed down through me as positive imprints on my own family.

Looking back, I hurt for my father. Many times, he has told me how painful it was to never see his father reconcile with the family. Because of the emotional hurt he experienced growing up, going to bed at night with an absent father, Dad vowed never to do the same to us as his children. At least fifty times, if not more throughout my lifetime, my dad told us that mom could kick him out of the bedroom but never out of the home. He never wanted his children to feel the pain he had in a broken home.

Immediate and extended family, myself included, have continued to struggle with forgiving my grandfather for the damage he caused. He never could come to terms with his own past and never asked those whom he harmed for forgiveness.

Just as importantly, I do not believe he ever did truly forgive himself. Instead of facing his issues, he ran. My Grandpa Mauck (Lewis), ran from place to place, from woman to woman, from distraction to distraction, never really stopping to ask himself why. His running left a trail of heartache and brokenness for most of his children.

Grandpa Mauck would die in Southern Ohio, from prostate cancer on April 26, 1985, at the age of seventy-eight. It's my understanding that just a mere handful of family members were present at his gravesite. Here he was finally put to rest in a small cemetery in the little town of Friendship, Ohio, near Scioto. Here lay a man with high visibility at one major point in his life but never realizing the great positive impact his life could have made on so many had he just sought reconciliation.

I love both my grandfathers, but my Grandpa Mauck chose the lonely road to grief and pain similar to that of Frederick over the loss of Samuel. The tendency to run from loss and pain unfortunately causes us more pain and hurt. Our redemptive story needs people and God to help us heal and become whole again.

In contrast, at my Pa Paw Nichols' funeral held in De Ridder, Louisiana, I was asked to share a few words. In front of a semi-packed church auditorium, I shared stories I had heard of him seeing the first Ford Model T car ever to come down the streets of

DeRidder, of racing through town on his horse, letting everyone know we were at war and as well when it ended. I told of his service in World War II working in the shipyards to get another ship out to war, slaving deep in the hulls of our navy ships as a welder, nailing down and making sure the massive ship engines were secure while living on little sleep. Then in the Korean and Vietnam Wars, he drove supplies while troops were being trained.

Here lay a man of honor who had little visibility in terms of public service or speaking. However, he had made huge impacts on the lives of his children, grandchildren, and their children demonstrated by the crowd that day honoring my ninety-nine-year-old grandfather, born in 1900, and passing away in 1999.

At the end of my eulogy, I looked out at all those in the audience who had taken time off from work, even traveled great distances to be there to honor my Pa Paw, the majority of whom I did not know. I thanked them for coming.

As I stepped down from the stage, I kissed my grandfather on his forehead as he had done to me so many times when I was a young boy about to go to sleep.

On my long ride back to Michigan, I thought about my two grandfathers. I couldn't help but compare their passings. One of my grandfathers preached and baptized hundreds, maybe more in his young life, a man who had a very public ministry. Yet few, if any, came to see him when he was ill in South Point, Ohio, or when he was buried there in the Friendship, Ohio, cemetery. Conversely, Pa Paw Nichols cared for those in the church few knew about. He had touched the lives of entire families by fixing a door for a single parent or widow. He cut someone's grass, worked at a shipyard, yet he left such a huge life-changing imprint on me and so many others. Even though most of those he actually helped were gone years before him, their families came to honor Pa Paw Nichols.

Navigating Your Story

On a recent trip to New York for writers, I experienced Uber for the first time. I had some interesting conversations with three of my eight drivers. Once these drivers found out I was a counselor, they began pouring out their hearts, sharing their stories.

One was struggling with his wife's over-commitment and lack of investment in their relationship that led to divorce. The second man was missing his children now that he and his wife were separated, and the third spoke of past unresolved issues with his family.

I listened intently to each one, reading between the lines of what they were saying. Each story was completely different, yet all had a common thread. Each needed resolution to make amends or seek forgiveness with a family member.

I let them know that life can change, but it usually starts with our willingness to take the first step by reconciling with God first, then seeking it with those with whom we are estranged.

Forgive Me

A few months ago while laboring over Grandfather Lewis Mauck's past indiscretions, I realized I needed to make some amends myself. It was time for me to finally come to grips with the family secret. Years of guilt and shame hovered over my father, my aunt, and Lewis' grandchildren: Landy, Ronda, Jonda, Candy, Tammy, and myself. My turn had come to face down my family's generational curses and the iniquities passed down from the Mauck men who had caused so much pain in their lives and those within our family linage.

As I prepared myself, I thought, *I'm going to forgive each of these men in my family* (Joseph, William "Wild Bill," and now Grandfather Lewis). In my mind, I was going to right all the wrongs through my prayer and devotional time and finally rid myself of all this stuff and junk left over that needed closure.

When I was about to pray, God's presence overwhelmed me, and I felt a sincere sense of conviction. The words that came out of my mouth and the stirring in my heart were completely different from what I had thought! As I started to quietly pray, Christ gently yet powerfully showed me that I had other steps I personally needed to take prior to seeking to make true amends with my forefathers.

He spoke to my heart and said, "Kenny, trying to reconcile all the wrongs your grandfathers committed is not what I am asking of you." As a result, my prayer actually began directed at my own heart; it needed to be cleaned out first. So I started with my own brokenness.

Father in Heaven,

Forgive me. I must first make amends with You and ask that You forgive me for such arrogance and help me realize I need to ask You with a humble heart to see how far I am from whom I need to be. I can't confront another person in our family or anyone else who has wronged me or my family without first asking You to forgive me for my greed, lust, pride, and false sense of control. I have hurt my relationship with You due to my own selfish actions, inactions, things needed to be said, or things left unsaid, and I ask Your forgiveness.

Lord, I also know my lack of true repentance has caused my wife, children, grandchildren, and friends pain as a result of my not being totally broken about my own sin and failures. Because I have not come to you sooner, my actions have more than likely caused unnecessary pain in those I love. So please forgive me for the frustration, anger, and hurt caused by my own pride. I ask You to give me the opportunity to make it right. If there is anyone I may have hurt as a result of my own unresolved loss, hurt, or pain, please reveal it to me so that I may seek forgiveness from them personally.

As I began to pray, tears streamed down my face. I realized God would not allow me to minimize my own offenses and sins. Just because I may not have fathered a child out of wedlock or had sex outside of marriage, God was having none of my self-righteousness, He sought from me a contrite heart of brokenness over my own sin.

The Lord reminded me of a phrase I had learned while training with Steven Covey. "Seek first to understand, then to be understood." This phrase accentuated the steps I needed to walk through, so first I began to seek true forgiveness in my own heart. It was vital that I first embrace the grace of God for myself before ever thinking about addressing the sins and weaknesses left from my generational family.

Isn't that just like our God, to get right to the heart of the matter and be more concerned about what we need from Him prior to considering what might be needed to make things right with others.

Letter Writing and the "Empty Chair"

My greatest hurt regarding Grandpa Lewis still needed to be confronted, but not from a place of anger. After some thought, I wrote a letter and planned to read it out loud to my deceased grandfather. Letter writing is something I have asked others in counseling to do, to make amends with one of their relatives with whom they needed closure and resolution. It could be from a relative who had passed away or had left significant emotional scars on their family.

To facilitate the process, I decided to use another exercise I have taken others through when confronting an unresolved loss, a therapeutic healing approach titled the "Empty Chair." The empty chair represents the person removed from your life in some way or for some reason, but their actions continue to have a hold on them. This might include one's raw feelings as a result of a horrible divorce, abuse, neglect, death, or a separation.

I placed an older picture of my grandfather in the empty chair and sat there staring at it for a few moments. Then I took a deep breath and began:

> Grandpa Mauck, I realize you are not physically here, but this is the only way I can create a sense of connection between us now. I remember seeing you once at my pee-wee football practice in Mobile, Alabama. You wore your fedora hat. As I recall, your visits with my dad, mom, and us as grandchildren were always very short. I wanted to get to know you, but it seemed like you were constantly on the run, coming in around time for lunch and gone by evening or before we got up the next morning.
>
> Because you needed to work the fields on your dad's farm in Scioto, Ohio, I now realize this only allowed you to complete school through the seventh grade. That had to be tough to work the farm as a young boy. Being the oldest male of your father Tom and mother Mary probably meant more was required of you. I do know early on, you were taught how to build and fix things. At the age of twenty, you married my grandma Ma Ma Tess and felt called to ministry as a result of Reverend Seymour's tent revival. In the early years, your ministry actually flourished as evidenced by the number of people saved and baptized. You did some wonderful things, but somewhere your charisma and good looks gave way to pride, ego, and a lust for women.
>
> I'm not trying to judge you, but my dad tearfully revealed to me an incident that happened when he was twelve years old. You were leaving this family, and as you drove down the long driveway, Dad followed you on his bike, pleading as hard as he could for you to stop. He just wanted to say goodbye to the only father he knew and wanted you to know how much he loved you.
>
> Just this last year around Dad's eighty-fifth birthday, news of two additional children you fathered came to light. My dad, while very

surprised, took the news well and wanted to make contact with his newly discovered siblings. My sister Candy and I also wanted to reach out to these newly found relatives. Fortunately, we were able to connect with them. I wish you could have seen the great reunion of all your children. We were denied getting to know them all these years due to a secret none of us knew about. We got to speak with your daughter, Cynthia, whom we found was raised in West Virginia. Candy and Dad got to speak with Jerry, your son from Michigan. We had never met them all these years. It's my hope this scene makes you happy, not sad.

My desire in sharing these things is to free all our family and yourself from the cave of guilt, shame, and anger. I watched my own father suffer emotionally, seeking affirmation and attention from people as a result of your absence throughout most of his life. I know from being a counselor that an absent father combined with a broken home is one of the hardest things for a child to overcome. Without God's grace, all of your children could have grown up with hardened feelings of unresolved loss. Each family member has had to come to terms in their own way and find their own path to forgive, knowing each of us needs our own forgiveness from Christ. We have no other right but to forgive and love you and others that hurt us intentionally or unintentionally.

In summarizing, I don't want there to be anymore untold secrets in our family, and I have to believe you would not want that as well. So I am breaking the curse of secrets this afternoon by addressing this on behalf of your children, grandchildren, great-grandchildren, and generations to follow. Today is a new Mauck family declaration, one that involves transparency, forgiveness, and mercy, a day of celebration and a new journey full of imprints of love that will impact the Mauck family for generations to come, proclaiming that all dark things must end by the bright light of truth and the freedom that follows by exposing it. You can be known as one we can point to that lived too long in the shadows of fear, unresolved hurt like your grandfather Joseph. So my prayer is that you finally find freedom from any remaining secrets the enemy of your and my souls has leveled against us.

I am declaring a new day of recognizing we all can celebrate knowing we are made whole by realizing Christ has redeemed our individual and family story. I hope that before you left this earth, you reconciled with God, knowing and understanding His grace paid it all! When all is said and done, I pray you have found peace for your soul like we as your children and grandchildren have had to find peace for our own lives as well.

Grandpa Mauck, you were forgiven by Christ long ago at the cross. I love you and want you to know you have an amazing family and that you can rest now in the fact that you have and are unconditionally loved as well.

Love and prayers!

Your grandson, Kenny

God has been so faithful in this process of acknowledging my own need for forgiveness. I am finding in my heart that love requires action, and a great part of that means actively forgiving those family and friends close to us who may have hurt us. If we don't, then Christ cannot forgive us. God's faithfulness to me causes me to want to walk as a believer, praying my desires become more like His for my own family. This act of forgiveness I have found is a daily process and one that's an ongoing treasured imprint I am learning from as part of my journey.

Know Your Enemy

I recognize the enemy of our soul is Satan himself. He desires to keep us bound with lies and deception meant to kill, steal, and destroy. Unforgiveness and secrets are his two key weapons.

But Scripture reminds us how to defeat him. In 1 Peter 5:8, we're told, "Be alert and of sober mind. Your enemy the devil prowls around like a roaring lion looking for someone to devour" (NIV). Also, here are the victory verses that Jesus gives us to counteract against our enemy. In John 14:6 and John 8:32, Jesus states, the important benefits we have in Christ "I am the way, the truth, and the life. ....." And "Then you will know the truth [Jesus], and the truth will set you free."

Through this verse, I realized that no one in my family is the enemy. I'm not saying that dealing with relationships, boundaries, and offenses don't happen, nor am I brushing aside the fact that there are consequences of negative behavior, abuse, and actions of those we trust.

However, we are called to a place of reconciliation so our hearts are not left full of bitterness and anger. In light of that, I'm saying that in the process of seeking personal restoration, healing, and reconciliation with family, we need to realize that we are not actually and ultimately fighting against the person who offended us, but the evil one who continually uses hurt and pain to haunt and attack us. We are ultimately fighting against one whose sole purpose is to destroy anything and everything that remotely points to our Heavenly Father's desire to heal and redeem our story.

When you see your family members and ancestors through the lens of Scripture, at some point, you won't be able to help but have some level of empathy and compassion.

This realization has helped me make great strides in the area of forgiveness. It has spurred me to pray even more fervently to be free of the things that have plagued our entire generational family line. I pray for angel armies of God to surround every one of my children and keep the devouring lion of lies and deception at bay. It motivates me to learn more about my family history so that I am fully aware of the potential arrows and darts that had derailed and detoured my family generationally. That's why Grandfather Tom's tent revival was so necessary. It was a turning-back point to the God of my sixth-generational great-grandfather Hans Peter Mock (Mauck).

Charted Steps
Making Amends Requires Intentional Grace

Forgiveness and making amends are not easy subjects. Admitting you and I have hurt someone or confronting someone who has hurt us are both uncomfortable, vulnerable acts that go straight to the heart and soul of living a redemptive life Yet, both forgiveness and making amends are necessary parts of the charted progressive steps of living a godly life and creating the legacy imprint that will bless your and my own families.

IMPRINT: Making Amends

Use wisdom, and prayerfully plan to make amends with someone you have hurt overtly or covertly. When I go to the dentist, I don't like the awkward and painful sights and sounds I have to go through to repair a cavity-laden tooth or an abscess that impacts the nerve. Yet when it's done and over, I feel wonderful again.

So too is the process of forgiveness or making amends. Initially it's painful, but the end result is one of feeling clean and healed again. Here's an important first step: Go before the Lord in private and ask Him for His guidance when seeking to reconcile with another family member or friend. Ask Him to show you what is in your heart before you take any other action. Remember this essential act of *forgiveness* is meant primarily to free you and me, yet the act can be so impactful. Its residual effect can result in healing to the recipient as well.

If the person you need to make amends with is no longer living, use my letter as an example. Or work with a professional who has training who can assist with an Empty Chair or related process to help you heal your emotions and spirit. Write out the words you would say to them if they were here. Write about your experience afterwards that may support generational healing for your family members as well.

In closing this chapter, while writing this book, I took the difficult journey and decision to seek out anyone I may have hurt or with whom had not made amends. It was not an easy process; in fact, it initially was one of the most painful and awkward things to do. Yet conversely, looking at the end result, I now realize it was one of the most freeing things I have ever done as well.

Life is way too short to hold onto anger, resentment, or bitterness. Let love, mercy, and kindness become the central place of your healing nature. Find words of comfort and contriteness to those who have felt wronged, then embrace them to show that the love of God is the only thing that truly heals the soul completely. Even though two people didn't allow reconciliation between us, I found the very effort mended the hurt inside me by honoring God though the process He asks of us. In closing, forgiveness is ultimately for our own benefit. It frees us to be who God intended us to be, more like Him.

Making amends with others is an eternal imprinted gift from God. Watch your wings fly freely with the winds of God's grace always intended for you!

Questions that need answering:

1. Ask yourself if you there is any unforgiveness in your heart toward someone and if it's still causing you problems with moving on in your life.
2. Is there someone you need to ask for forgiveness as to something you have said or done? Consider and pray about making amends in regards to this through a letter, or if amiable, meeting them in person to make it right.

CHAPTER 7

Finding Your Sea Legs

> "For in every adult there dwells the child that was, and in every child there lies the adult that will be."
>
> — JOHN CONNOLY

'VE SPENT A LOT OF TIME walking through the countryside lately. I'm reminded of the long journey my parents have traveled and all that I have learned from them. The long-term imprints in each of my ancestor's story makes me realize that I have become the "keeper of the story" and opens a new dimension.

I feel as if a spotlight is shining down on me and that I am in the eye of the storm. A multitude of events swirling all around me have come together to bring me to exactly where I am in this moment. I must now take on the role of weaving all the storylines together, including the overlapping moments from my parents' and my own—

the major events, the ones that have shaped me and made me who I am. I must include those childhood moments that stand out as defining moments that imprinted my life, that shifted perspective, defined the fears, the hopes, and the dreams, the humor and the tragedy, the safe places, and the risks.

I could share many stories about my childhood years. In light of the legacy and imprints we carry, a few stand taller than the rest. Childhood is the time of our voyage when we get our sea legs. We learn the good and the bad about the world around us and develop our own ways of responding. When we are kids, our stories are intertwined with those who raise us. Out of all our generational lines, the impact of parental imprints can have the most direct inscription on our own.

For the Mauck family, the actual story of my parents' courtship and marriage brings to life some drama, and now in hindsight, plenty of humor in telling their true-to-life story. However, I need to first set up this story back to the time of my father's life and his service in the Korean War.

William "Louie" Mauck: 1932–Present and Melonee D. Nichols-Mauck: 1935–Present
My Parents

William Louis Mauck, better known as "Louie," served as an Army corpsman. The childhood accident that had left my father blind in one eye ruled out a combat assignment, so he was trained to serve as a field hospital nurse's assistant in the Korean War. The following led up to his enlistment and training in the Army and is an important part of understanding my dad's story.

Shortly before enlisting, Louie met a girl at a church in Gary, Indiana, and married her shortly afterward. He would soon realize the natural consequences of making such a huge life decision so quickly.

The young couple had little time together before he left for basic training. Communication was sparse, and the distance in miles mirrored the gap that gradually grew between them relationally. Unfortunately, Louie found out from his mother Tessa that his first wife was living in their trailer with another man.

He returned home on special leave from basic training, but he was not welcomed at the door of the trailer. In fact, when he knocked on the trailer door, his wife would not even open it. She hoped he would just go away, so she decided to ignore his knocks. He wouldn't leave and instead baited her by stating he knew there was a man inside with her. She then confirmed his suspicions when he overheard her telling someone else, "You just stay in here."

Coming from a divorced home, Louie didn't want to fail in marriage as he felt his parents had. However, she ignored every attempt he made that night to reconcile. A neighbor ended up calling the police because of the loud voices and the late hour. When the police arrived, Louie reluctantly accepted the fact that he had to file for divorce. Before leaving, he told her, "I don't want to ever see you again." Those were his last words to her.

Louie felt despondent on his return to his basic training base in North Carolina. As he drove on the mountains' winding roads, the thought occurred to him of how easy it would be to end all this pain and misery by driving off one of the cliffs. But within a few miles, God's' peace that surpasses our feelings and emotions came upon him. His hope in Christ was all He had left.

Serving at Tripler Hospital in Honolulu

When basic training ended, and the Korean War came closer to ending, thousands of wounded soldiers were being shipped back to the States. In the early 1950s, Louie received orders to transfer to Tripler Hospital in Honolulu, Hawaii. Instead of field triage, he assisted the nurses in caring for the soldiers with the worst combat injuries. These soldiers were unable to perform the most basic of daily tasks independently. Louie bathed them, clothed them, emptied their bedpans, changed their wound dressings, and fed those who could not feed themselves. The work was physically, emotionally, and mentally taxing.

This experience in a large Army hospital would be one of the most difficult assignments he would ever experience as a young man. The scars these wounded soldiers bore ran deep. The new reality that some of them faced was so daunting that many could not cope. If their injuries didn't send them home, the thought of going back to what many considered hell on earth was unfathomable. Many attempted suicide, and some were successful. Day after day, from sunup to sundown, Louie cared for these men.

A Fresh Start

By the age of twenty-three, Louie had grown up significantly, having just experienced and observed the worst of pain and hopelessness in his life and in the lives of others. Still reeling from the loss of his marriage, he chose not to renew his enlistment in the Army. He wanted a fresh start, a do-over of sorts. Needing a change of scenery, Louie left Hawaii, and moved to be closer to his sister Jolene and her husband Roland.

It was 1954, and Jolene and Roland Gardner lived in the small town of DeRidder Louisiana, where Roland pastored the First Pentecostal Church. DeRidder was like a Sherriff Andy Taylor Mayberry-esque kind of town, the kind of place where everyone knew each other, and everyone knew each other's business.

Louie immediately jumped into life in DeRidder, and the First Pentecostal Church was one of the main life events of town. The first week, he began studying music at McNeese State University in

The Nichols gather together for this picture, with (left to right) Marce, Melonee, Marcus (Kenny's grandfather), Casiel, Merta Mae, and Wanda (DeRidder, Louisiana, 1943).

Kenny's great-great-grandparents, Jospeph and Sarah Mauck, have their picture taken in Moccasin Ben, Kentucky, in 1850.

Kenny's sixth-generational great-grandfather Hans Peter Mauk (1707–1771) traveled from Germany to America in 1733. (Portrait sketch by Joshua Toholsky)

Frederick Mauk, Kenny's fifth-generational great-grandfather, was an adventurer.

Samuel Mauk, Kenny's fourth-generational great-grandfather (1785–1819), was named after the ship *Samuel* that brought his grandfather to America.

"William 'Bill' Mauck, Kenny's second-generational great-grandfather (top left), poses with wife America Harper (3rd from left) and Tom Mauk (3rd from right), Kenny's great-grandfather.

Tom Mauk, Kenny's great-grandfather, was a man who turned his life around by accepting Christ at a tent revival. The Mauk family would finally turn back to God, not perfect yet one of honoring God and family again. (Photo: ca. 1907)

Rev. William "Lewis" Mauck (Kenny's grandfather) and his family pose for a picture. They are (left to right) his wife Tessa Elizabeth and his children William (Lou) Mauck and daughter Jolene (Portsmouth, Ohio; ca. 1939).

The LifeCare Family Services staff is what makes it one of the premier children and family organizations in Tennessee.

(Left) Kenny would establish a high school record at Kearsley High School, with the assistance of Coach Marsh, in the 330-yard low hurdles event (1977). (Right) Kenny's high school track coach, Don Marsh, hall of famer and national high school runner-up coach, watches his athletes compete.

Louie and Melonee will be celebrating 64 years of marriage in 2019.

The family gathers to celebrate Louie and Melonee's 60th wedding anniversary.

Kenny's sisters Candy (left) and Tammy (right) have been an inspiration that God has used to teach him about His love and grace.

Our three grandchildren—Easton, Gracelyn, and Cooper—have made huge imprints on Raye Ann's and Kenny's lives!

Kelsey

Kenny and Raye's children as youngsters are here with their godchild Aleeya, who they agreed as a family to live with them during a time her family needed support.

Aleeya Landon Megan

Here are the three grown Mauck children, Landon, Megan, and Kelsey. Each has left a lifetime of impressions that neither words nor pictures could ever do justice.

Pastor L.H. Hardwick (center), his sermon, and his sons Steven (left) and Mike (right), helped LifeCare become successful due to their early support.

Ernie and Ann Robertson, Kenny's father-in-law and mother-in-law, are shown here. Ernie was a significant help in starting LifeCare and was on its board.

Kenny's family enjoys a day at their Florida beach favorite vacation spot: (left to right) Kelsey, Michael, Megan's husband, Cooper, Megan, baby Gracelyn, Easton, Landon, Raye, and Kenny

Kenny and Raye's daughter Kelsey and her fiancé Jon will get married 2020.

Landon and Brittany Mauck married September 2019.

Kenny's sister-in-law Dina and brother-in-law Brent pose for a picture. Brent helped significantly in building out projects for Kenny's nonprofits.

This Bible represents God speaking and branding Kenny's soul with His hand of favor and direction. Deuteronomy 11:18 says, "Imprint these words of mine on your hearts and minds, bind them as a sign on your hands, and let them be a symbol on your foreheads."

The Mauck family sitting on a tree represents lasting reflective imprints. (Left to right: Landon, Kenny, Raye Ann, Kelsey, and Megan)

Many got together at Mertie Mae's funeral in 1981, including (left to right) Don Evans, Chairman of the Board, life mentor, and family friend for 48 years, who poses with his family (left to right), Kerri, Barb, Don, and Kim.

The LifeCare Foundation Board of Directors, (left to right) Bill Campbell, Jeff Parris, Bruce Boder, Chairman Don Evan, Dan Finley, and Jim Carter, pose together with Raye and Kenny (center) for this group picture.

Kenny and Raye Ann (left) enjoy an afternoon with Butch and Melanie Leix (right), long-time friends from Michigan.

Family members attend Mertie Mae Nichol's funeral in 1981. (Left to right: Rebecca, Karen, Mark, Greg, Tammy, Paw Pa Nichols, Kenny, Rusty, Candy, and Ron)

Life-long friends (left to right) Pat and Kim Campbell and Brenda and Dave Ross return from a cruise with Raye Ann and Kenny.

The Maucks and friends from Tennessee, attend a Bunco marriage party.

Kenny's first cousin Landy, who passed away in 2017, poses for a picture with his family in Colorado.
(Left to right: Joy, Lauren, Dyson, Dionne, Scott, and Landy—center back row)

Family members gather to honor and pay their last respects to Landy Gardner at his funeral.
(Left to right: Mike Berner, Tom Gardner, Candy, Raye Ann, Kenny, and Greg Gardner)

Raye Ann and Kenny celebrated their 35th wedding anniversary in Venice, Italy.

On their way to Italy, Raye and Kenny visited Giessen Germany where Hans Peter Mauck left for America in the 1700s. It was an emotional day as they reflected on the fact that the Mauck story began in this very location.

The Mauck family believes in everyone leaving his life imprints—"handing off" legacy stories to future generations.

Kenny loves to play hide-and-go-seek with his grandchildren. Life is not all about meeting goals, but rather living in the moment and having fun with loved ones.

Manny, Kenny's dog, has been a constant companion to him throughout the writing of this book.

Lake Charles and immersing himself in church life at First Pentecostal Church, where he played trumpet.

One night while finishing up the dishes at Joleen and Roland's, he glanced out the parsonage kitchen window and saw folks arriving for Wednesday night service. About that time, two girls strolled by. One in particular caught his eye. Louie didn't know it then, but these were part of the Nichols Sisters. They sang on the radio and in churches. Many considered the group to be local Christian celebrities, comparable to The Andrews Sisters.

When he saw the youngest young lady, Melonee Nichols, he blurted out to himself, "I've just got to meet that girl!"

Later that week, Louie arrived for orchestra rehearsal and made his way to the horn section. He looked up from his seat to see none other than Melonee Nichols, the sister who caught his eye on Wednesday. She also sat in the horn section next to an open chair and was holding a trumpet, same as Louie.

And so it began. Louie and Melonee saw each other every week at rehearsal, spent time together chatting before, during, and afterward about life, school, and really about everything. Any time they were at church, Louie and Melonee were together, talking and laughing.

"Pediddle!"

Over the next couple of months, Louie and Melonee continued to spend time together at church. Louie thought about asking Melonee out several times, but a flood of painful memories from his failed marriage rushed in when he tried and drowned his courage. So, for now, he remained content with a growing friendship.

A church in a nearby town held a camp meeting in late fall each year, and a group of young adults from First Pentecostal Church decided to go. Louie volunteered to be the driver for the evening, seeing the perfect opportunity to spend time with Melonee outside of church without actually asking her out.

On the way back to DeRidder, Louie suggested a game of pediddle to pass the time. In case you aren't familiar with the game, a "pediddle" is a car with only one working headlight. The first one to see it yells, "Pediddle!" and earns a point. At the end of the game, the person with the most points wins.

However, this game of pediddle involved all the passengers hitting Louie if he wasn't the first to see a missing headlight. But if he did see it first, he got to kiss one of the girls in the car.

The game was quite intense with everyone leaning forward, straining to be the first to see what was coming in the distance and exclaiming, "Pediddle!" before anyone else. Then they would playfully argue over who actually did see it first. All of a sudden, Louie had a brilliant yet slightly terrifying idea.

"All right, all. How about this? If I get a pediddle, I get to kiss Melonee."

After a very short awkward moment, Melonee, who was sitting next to him, smiled slowly and said, "All right because that's *not* going to happen!"

The game kicked back in, every eye focused on the dark horizon, kibitzing back and forth about who was going to win. The girls banded together to help Melonee see the next one first.

"Pediddle!" Louie shouted, pointing and causing the car to swerve and everyone to jump in their seat.

Quickly regaining his composure and control of the car, a triumphant grin spread across his face. That night, even though he didn't score the most points in the game, Louie still won. He did indeed get to kiss Melonee, a little peck on the lips.

After church the next Sunday, Louie finally worked up the nerve to ask Melonee out on an official date for lunch and golfing, to which she enthusiastically agreed. Another small kiss at the end of that date before parting ways sealed the deal.

Both knew they were meant to be together, but neither understood the opposition they would soon be facing.

A Line in the Sand

Roland didn't keep his brother-in-law Louie's recent divorce a secret from his congregation. He had done his best to balance rigid church doctrine with Christ-like compassion and family loyalty. The church's doctrine regarding divorce, however, was clear-cut and strict. Divorce was an invisible scarlet letter Louie unwillingly bore. His presence was allowed, even embraced by the congregation, but some lines were not to be crossed.

Melonee's mother Mertie Mae Nichols seemingly welcomed Louie's presence and involvement in the church. Even if she had an opinion about his situation, Mertie Mae didn't want to be unwelcoming, that is until she got wind of Louie and Melonee's date.

Marching straight into Roland's office, Mertie Mae's mama bear emerged. "Pastor Gardner, I cannot believe you invited that, that, divorced brother-in-law of yours into our church; worse yet, that you allowed him to date my daughter. Related or not, you should have seen the trouble coming."

Remaining calm, Roland gestured toward the chair opposite his desk. "Now Mertie Mae, have a seat, and let's talk about this."

Undeterred, Mertie Mae continued, "You should have made it perfectly clear that he was not to get involved with any of the girls in this church after being divorced just a year. How could you let this happen?"

Roland made another attempt. "Mertie Mae, please, let's be reasona..."

Mertie Mae interrupted, yelling and red-faced. "My Melonee will not be a casualty of that man's wayward path. Shame on you, Pastor Gardner! Shame on you!"

Mertie Mae ranted on for what felt like an eternity to Roland. In reality, just a few minutes had passed. He had just about heard all he could take. Slowly, he stood and drew in a deep breath. Before he could utter a word of a verbal throwback, Mertie Mae drew a line in the sand. "You tell that brother-in-law of yours that I forbid him to see or speak to my Melonee again. I want Louie Mauck to leave this town immediately. Period. End of discussion."

Roland's eyebrows rose in surprise at such a bold demand. "Mertie Mae, I can't do that since he has been part of fighting for our country. Plus, he's my brother-in-law."

Mertie Mae turned to quickly storm out of the office. She grabbed the doorknob, intending to slam the door for emphasis, but checked herself, regained her composure, and instead quietly pulled the door closed behind her. She was, after all, a lady.

Pastor Roland slowly sank back into the leather of his chair, incredulous, not quite knowing what to do next. That night, he relayed Mertie Mae's ultimatum to Louie, insisting that the relationship end for the benefit of all involved, including him.

Breaking Up with the One You Love

In spite of the hard line taken by Mertie Mae and Roland's discussion with Louie, Melonee and Louie still managed to see each other over the ensuing months, mostly at church. Every time Mertie Mae learned of a rendezvous, even a simple conversation after services, explosive objections reverberated around town and in the church community, which especially concerned Roland. Dissention among church members over his own family did not promote healthy church life or job security for Roland.

After being apprised one too many times of Mertie Mae's unsettling public tirades, Roland knew he had no choice. He needed to set up a meet with Louie and Melonee together to address the situation head on.

The meeting was short and did not go well. Roland quickly realized that lecturing and logical reasoning were not winning. So, he switched tactics. Leaning on family loyalty, he said, "I know you two care for each other, but there are some, including your mom, Melonee, who have problems with a recently divorced man dating within our church." He looked at his brother-in-law. "Because you're family, I was hoping there would be more acceptance, Louie."

Louie knew their relationship was putting Melonee, himself, and his brother-in-law in a very difficult place.

Leaning forward in his chair, Roland folded his hands on the desk, pensively staring down at the open Bible in front of him, silently pleading to God to give him wisdom. The atmosphere in the room was thick. He looked across the desk at his brother-in-law.

At last he broke the silence, gently yet resolutely stating, "I am sorry. Please understand the difficult situation I'm in. The conflict you two are creating, not only with Melonee's mother but also within the church, must stop. I see only one solution. If you're going to stay here in this church and live in this town, Louie, it's best for all involved, including the both of you, if you break off your relationship. Completely. Immediately. Please. I'm asking…"

Louie and Melonee sat silently staring at the floor. Roland felt for them both. It was the saddest he had ever seen his brother-in-law. After a long pause, Louie took Melonee by the hand, and the couple left the office deeply disheartened.

When they reached the church parking lot, Louie said, "I wish there was another way then ending it like this…."

"If there is, I don't see it," Melonee softly replied.

The truth was hard. Melonee loved her parents and hated seeing her mother so distraught. Louie loved his brother-in-law and his sister and didn't want to be the cause of strife between them or the reason Roland lost his job.

Both wanted to do the right thing, and the right thing right now seemed to be to break up for all concerned.

Let's Get Hitched

Soon after the breakup, classes at McNeese let out for Christmas break, and Louie headed to Indiana, with Jolene and Roland where they all used to live to spend the holidays with Roland's parents. He hoped the time away might take his mind off life in DeRidder and Melonee.

Back on his old stomping grounds, he easily busied himself with family, festivities, and friends. But every celebration and happy moment brought a twinge of sadness and only solidified the truth that life without Melonee was no option. These were the memories, the times, the future he wanted to share with her. He even bought a suit while there, hoping that someday he would marry Melonee with him wearing it.

Returning to DeRidder after the holidays, Louie wasted no time. He called on Melonee's close girlfriend Billy Jack to arrange a meeting with Melonee on the Texas-Louisiana, border. She was one of Melonee's closet friends, and if anyone could make that happen, it would be her.

Billy Jack drove Melonee to the meeting spot. Once Melonee saw Louie waiting, she got out of the car and into his.

Wasting no time, Louie laid it all on the line. He grabbed both of her hands in his. "Melonee, these past four months with you have been the best of my life. The last few weeks without you have been the worst. Every time I laughed, my first thought was wanting to share the joy with you. Every gathering, I found myself wishing you were there. You were my last thought at night and my first thought in the morning. I want that to be true for the rest of our lives. I want to spend the rest of my life making you happy. I love you now and forever."

Gazing into her eyes, he asked, "Melonee Nichols, will you marry me?"

Melonee's eye filled with tears as she wrapped her arms around him and breathed, "Yes!"

Louie wanted to elope right then, but Melonee needed a little time. Absolutely, spending the rest of her life with Louie was what she wanted. However, she was not yet quite ready to so boldly go against her parents' wishes.

Grabbing her hands, Louie reassured her, "Don't worry. I have a plan. Don't give up; just wait to hear from me.

"Man and Wife"

The young couple endured two more weeks apart before Louie called on Bama Colton, an older yet loyal friend from the church who knew Melonee growing up. He also asked Billy Jack and his dear friend Sidney Mercantel to help put his plan in motion.

Around noon on Saturday, February 19, 1955, as the bank where Melonee worked was closing, Bama Colton pulled up to her job to pick her up. Melonee acted like all was well as they strolled out to her car, not expecting anything more than a ride home.

As she opened the car door, a white flash from the back seat caught her eye. Sliding into the front seat, she closed the door and turned to see what it was. Two of her outfits were folded in the back seat of the car. Her heart skipped a beat.

She glanced over at Bama, who sat there smiling. They gave each other a quick hug, cried and laughed together. Bama gave Melonee some of the details, but words were few thereafter as Bama and Melonee drove down Main Street and out of town.

Louie and Mama Tess waited in his car at the designated secret hideout off a road near U.S. Highway 171 for what seemed to be the longest hour of Louie's life. They figured it was the perfect rendezvous location in DeRidder, Louisiana, to meet and elope. However, that didn't keep questions and doubts from bouncing around inside Louie's head. *What if she doesn't show up? She thinks Bama is picking her up for lunch. What if she feels blindsided and backs out?* He was plagued with past disappointments of having his dad leave and promising at times to return and then feeling letdown when it didn't happen.

Just as he was about to drive himself crazy, Bama's car pulled up with Melonee beaming in the passenger seat. Before the car came to a complete stop, Louie and Melonee flew out of their vehicles and embraced.

Louie quickly put Melonee's bags and clothing into his trunk, and the four of them excitedly headed about thirty-five miles south to DeQuincy where Sidney attended the United Pentecostal Church. Sidney had persuaded his pastor to marry Louie and Melonee, and he handled all the arrangements.

Louie, Melonee, and the small group of four others met at the church in DeQuincy. Young Pastor H.L. Bennett was expecting them and hastily ushered them inside. Fifteen minutes later, the young couple stood at the altar with Sidney as the best man and Billy Jack as the maid of honor. Finally, Louie and Melonee said, "I do."

Prior to and during the short service, phones across the town and county blew up with Mertie Mae feverishly searching for clues as to why her daughter hadn't come home from work and where she was now. She grew more worried, alerting the local police, questioning several local ministers, and interrogating all of Louie's and Melonee's friends in an attempt to track down her daughter.

Just as the pastor pronounced, "Husband and wife," the phone rang in his study off the side of the sanctuary. Everyone froze. Knowing, panicked glances flashed between the members of the wedding party. Excusing himself, Pastor Bennett left and answered the phone.

"Good afternoon, DeQuincy United Pentecostal Church. This is Pastor Bennett. How may I help you today?"

As Mertie Mae bombarded Pastor Bennett with question after question, trying to ascertain the whereabouts of her daughter, he leaned out of the office door, motioning for a quick exit through the foyer doors out front. As soon as the newlyweds were out of sight, he politely interrupted, "Why, yes, Sister Nichols, we just completed their marriage ceremony, and unfortunately, the couple has already left the church."

The Wrath of Mertie Mae

"Still on the warpath" is a mild phrase for Mertie Mae's state of mind after that call. By early evening, Mertie Mae had alerted everyone she had known since birth to be on the lookout for Louie and Melonee. Exhausted and heartbroken, she sank onto the couch knowing the couple would now forever be known as Mr. and Mrs. William L. Mauck.

Realizing how worried Mertie Mae must be and how protective she was when it came to her girls, Louie and Melonee had no doubt that the police had been recruited by her mother to bring them home. Instead of returning to DeRidder, the couple continued west on the back roads of Louisiana, avoiding main roads and highways whenever possible.

After driving several hours, they arrived in Baton Rouge for the night. They stayed a few days, splurging the first night on a nice hotel, and then moving to something less expensive afterward to save money.

Back home in DeRidder, Mertie Mae struggled to sort out her mixed feelings. She was angry at Louie for taking her baby girl. She was mad at Melonee for agreeing to go. "How could Melonee do this to our family? If I ever get my hands on that Louie Mauck...," she ranted and then worried, "Where on Earth could they be?"

Ranting and raving eventually gave way to pacing and fretting, and in the end, resignation. "What's done is done," she said stiffly. "And I warned her. I told her if she left, it would end her relationship with the family."

Melonee's father Mark Nichols was more concerned about his daughter's safety and happiness. Although disappointed that his daughter had eloped, he was not given to bouts of emotions as that of his wife.

A few days passed with no sightings, leads, or any word from Melonee. So as a mother, Mertie Mae did the only logical thing to do under the circumstances. She invited friends and family to join her at the church that evening to pray.

When everyone arrived, Mertie Mae did not seem to be praying like the others but lamenting the loss of her young daughter. Most described it as more of a wake for Melonee than a prayer meeting. The evening ended with Mertie Mae still shaken and confused, thanking everyone for coming.

Word got back to Melonee and Louie about how emotional Mertie Mae appeared at the prayer meeting. They knew they had upset her horribly but hoped she was beginning to accept the fact that they were married. Instead, they were told that family in DeRidder would not be welcoming them home. With no money and no home to return to, honeymoon bliss faded, and harsh reality set it.

Louie made a few calls and finally found some older family friends in the church who had a small apartment behind their home. They were willing to take the newlyweds in until they got on their feet and could get a place on their own.

Going back to the Nichols' home could not be avoided entirely. Melonee needed her personal belongings from her parents' house. Louie had packed up all of his belongings the day of the elopement, but without advanced notice, Melonee had nothing but the two outfits and a small overnight bag Billy Jack had pulled together for the occasion. Not wanting to owe her parents anything, they agreed to retrieve only those things that Melonee had paid for with her own money, which was most of her closet.

The couple arrived at the Nichols' home the next morning with mixed emotions. Mertie Mae greeted Louie very coolly at the door. Before stepping out of the way, Mertie Mae made sure it was understood: Louie was not welcome in her home, never, and once Melonee walked out that front door, there was no coming back.

Melonee took her mother at her literal word, carrying her things from the bedroom to the front door, making a handoff to Louie, who then hauled the loads from the porch to the car. After several trips, Melonee gathered the last load and fought back the tears as she walked to the front door and stepped out onto the porch. Mertie Mae closed the door behind her.

The temporary housing Louie arranged didn't last long. Once word got out about where they were staying, Mertie Mae made feelings known. Trying to avoid any added pressure for the host family, Melonee and Louie felt it best to leave and put some distance between themselves and DeRidder after that day.

Landing in Lake Charles, Louisiana, Louie continued pursuing his music studies, and Melonee found a job at the local bank. Lake Charles was close enough to keep a finger on the pulse of DeRidder, yet far enough away to not deal with icy rejection on a daily basis.

Icebreaker

It's been said that two things bring a family together—weddings and funerals. Well, not always weddings in my family's case! I add to that list as a general rule—grandbabies.

My parents Louie and Melonee had been married about eighteen months when my older sister Canda Lou Mauck was born. Mertie Mae heard of the birth of her first grandchild secondhand through the grapevine, and her heart for the first time began to soften. Having several grandchildren of my own, I can attest to the fact that grandbabies have the power to melt the hardest of hearts. With that softening eventually came forgiveness, followed by acceptance.

Realizing Louie and Melonee's love was not just some fleeting young romance destined to fade away, my Ma Maw and Pa Paw finally chose to end the standoff.

As soon as Ma Maw Mertie Mae cradled Candy in her arms, the miracle of love surrounded everyone in the room, and my parents and grandparents were never estranged again. In fact, my Ma Maw once considered my father as one of her favorite sons-in-law.

When my parents celebrated their sixty-third anniversary on February 19, 2018, I retold their story to my children and grandchildren. We showed pictures of their wedding, laughed at the funny parts, cried at the hard things, and ate great food while celebrating my parents', their grandparents' and great-grandparents' story, soon to be sixty-five years and counting after one official date and a controversial and highly protested elopement. Their real-life story is full of imperfections with joy and laughter, hurt and sadness, but woven with love and a theme of redemption. I wouldn't trade it for the most perfect love story in the world.

Robin Kent Mauck: 1958–Present
(More of My Story)

Two years after my sister Candy's birth melted the ice between my parents and grandparents, I came along. My legal given name is Robin Kent Mauck. My father named me "Robin" after the famed tale "Robin Hood," and my mom chose my middle name "Kent." It was defined as an English Scandinavian name, meaning "unconquered and/or a bright white light." Maybe that's why I am so competitive in nature and love the white sand on a beautiful day. It seems I was the only other Mauck, other than Samuel, named after something that originated from the British and Celtic region.

My ancestral story began with Hans, moved through Frederick, Samuel, Joseph, "Wild Bill," my great-grandfather Tom, my grandfather Lewis, my father Louie, and now mine where my father's and my storylines intertwine. I carry with me not only the generational life imprints passed down from those who had gone before me, but also imprints made on me throughout my life, all of which I will pass down to the next generation of the Mauck family.

A Matter of Life and Breath

As a youngster, I had severe asthma. The first three years of my life, I had to sleep sitting up so that I could breathe more easily.

My parents took shifts throughout the night, one getting a few hours of sleep while the other sat up with me, then trading off. Not to get too scientific, but inhalers as we know them today did not become a standard treatment for asthma sufferers until the mid-1960s. Even if they were available, they would not have been an affordable option. Nebulizers were not nearly as effective, so unfortunately for my parents and for me, I had little relief as a baby and into my toddler years.

While my asthma was no joke, we all laugh now at the funny stories Mom and Dad share from those years, like the time Dad's cousin Paul and his friend Buddy, who were around twenty years old, had come for a short visit. We were playing, and they started tossing me back and forth through the air, unaware that I suffered from asthma.

The three of us were having a grand ole' time until I started turning blue, which kind of freaked out the two young, single guys. My parents quickly intervened, reassuring everyone that I would be okay but also admonishing all to be more careful in the future.

For me, asthma attacks were like clockwork, a not-so-fun part of the evening routine for my family. Each one included an intense episode of croupy coughing and ended with me finally passing out to the hum of a large, oversized house fan and the aroma of Vicks VapoRub generously spread all over my chest.

Good times.

When I was about two, my family moved to South Bend, Indiana, where my Uncle Roland pastored a church at the time. After the events surrounding Mom and Dad's elopement, he resigned from First Pentecostal Church in DeRidder and accepted a pastorate in South Bend. My dad's parents had separated, and my grandmother was now living in South Bend as well. So when my father's employer opened a new branch in the area, it made sense for us to transfer.

By then, my asthma had landed me in the hospital more than a few times and caused my mom to miss too many Wednesday and Sunday night services. One Sunday night in particular, I was having one of my worst episodes. My mother's concern grew as each breath became shallower, and the wheezing increased.

She was considering calling an ambulance, but in the meantime, she called for my uncle at the church right before the start of service to ask for prayer. By the time he hung up the phone, the music minister had already started, but my uncle was so alarmed by my mother's call that he walked in, went straight to the podium, and raised his hand to stop the singing. He shared the conversation he had with my mother and asked everyone to stand with him and pray for me.

At the same time at home, my mom began praying for God to touch my lungs and open my airways. What happened next was nothing short of a miracle. Within five minutes of those prayers, I drew in a long, deep sustained breath. And then another. And another. The wheezing subsided. My breathing calmed, and the asthma attack suddenly ended.

I rested in my mother's arms as she held me and cried, thanking God for His mercies and goodness with each unhindered breath. When I finally fell asleep, she gently laid me down in my bed.

For the first night since my birth, my parents received the gift of a full night's rest. I slept through the night until morning, and I have not had one episode of asthma since that evening.

Skeptics may attempt to explain my miracle in terms of scientific or medical reasoning, but I have searched and found little medical evidence to support the sudden curing of asthma. Some may call it coincidence, saying I just finally grew out of it, but for me, there really is no other explanation. As a believer in Jesus Christ, I know I was healed. I experienced a real miracle.

Now, I don't understand why some people are healed, and some are not. That's a theological question I'll let someone else tackle. What I do know is up until that night, I was a very sick little boy, and since that night, I have had no attacks with asthma.

While I no longer live with asthma, I still have emotional scars. I have dealt with an enormous imprint of fear growing up, especially when it came to heights, deep water, and being alone. As a result of losing my breath due to asthma, I was told that inadvertently sometimes I would tighten up and become fearful when it came to swimming in a pool, riding a Ferris wheel, or anything whereby I was suddenly thrust in the air or placed in water over my head.

Demo, a True Friend of "Mind"

An active imagination is essential to being a kid. Like a lot of kids, I had an exceptionally great one. Remember those little green Army men? I had a ton of them, and I'd set up battles and barracks all over the living room. The battles my armies fought were epic—full of large walls, bombs exploding everywhere, paratroopers floating through the air, cannons blasting enemy strongholds. My props included books, connecting logs, rubber bands, and marbles if available.

As a high-ranking general, I led my men into battle, chest out, knees high as I marched—BOOM! I would dive over the back of the couch in the wake of a massive detonation. Nothing made me angrier than one of my sisters destroying rows of my Army men as she shuffled her way through the midst of my units ready to fight or a call notifying me it was time to eat, ruthlessly pulling me back from the battlefields of my mind and into reality.

My imagination also comforted my fears. One of my many fears was being alone in my room. My sisters shared a room and had each other. Mom and Dad shared a room. I couldn't understand why I had no one.

One day when I was about three years old, I met Demo. He was loyal, brave, fun, and a little mischievous and quickly became my best friend. We were inseparable. Whenever I needed someone to play with, Demo was available. If I needed someone to talk to, Demo dropped by. In fact, Demo did everything with me—played with me, sat with me when I didn't feel like playing, sang with me, blew up enemy soldiers with me, hunted game with me, ate meals with me, and slept next to me at night.

One morning at breakfast, I asked my mom for toast with my eggs and if my friend could have a piece of toast too. Without missing a beat, she asked, "What's your friend's name, Kenny?"

"My friend's name is Demo, and he wants toast too, Momma," I stated proudly.

Mom just smiled and tried to hold back her laughter. She then nodded Demo's way and said, "Nice to meet you, Demo," and placed two pieces of toast on the table.

Demo moved with me from our trailer to our new home in South Bend, but I finally lost touch with him somewhere around the age of four, somewhere between Portland, Oregon, and Vancouver, Washington. My imagination stayed with me because over the years, my creative energies shifted from imaginary friends and make-believe war zones to writing songs, crafting articles for magazines, journaling inspirational ideas for two nonprofit companies, and now writing my first book.

I give my dad and mother a good part of the credit for the creative thread of my life. Mom became the inspiration holder of my childhood dreams. Never once did she correct me or try to weaken my intensely imaginative mind, including my imaginary friend. At any point, she could have corrected me and let me know that was not reality. Instead, she saw it as a beginning point of something special leading to early steps of creativity and development, something she believed God would one day use for His purposes. She somehow found a way to nurture and empower and see all the good in it. For that I will be forever appreciative and indebted to my mom.

Bottoms Up

In 1964, our family moved from Vancouver to Joplin, Missouri. Joplin was where I learned to ride bikes and horses. As a hunter of great fame, I built my own hunting lodge in our backyard out of cardboard boxes and scrap wood and hunted the most magnificent birds of prey with my trusty Red Ryder BB Gun. I didn't just see black and white; I saw good and evil. Yes, some of my fondest memories and one of my most valuable life lessons came from Joplin.

My first attempt at friendship didn't go well. The boy's name was Mike. We had just moved to Joplin, the seventh move since I was born in Lake Charles. I was six, and he was eight. I was flattered to hang with someone older than me.

Those first few days, Mike and I played fine at our house. We rode our bikes all over the neighborhood. He introduced me to the other kids on the block.

One afternoon, we pulled up into his driveway, and he invited me inside his parents' home. Seemingly, they had divorced, and his mother was now a single parent, so Mike spent a few hours alone each day prior to his mom getting home from work. He developed friends in the neighborhood, most older than me. I didn't think it was a big deal to go into his house since mine was right across the street, and my mom was home.

Mike's front door opened and revealed something I'd never seen, at least not in my home. His parents had built a huge wet bar right in the middle of their living room, complete with glass shelves loaded with every kind of liquor known to man.

It was a hot summer day, and we were in desperate need of a drink. Bouncing inside, Mike pointed to one of the modern, sleek, smooth leather barstools and said, "Have a seat!"

I hopped up, admiring the shiny, colorful display of bottles—short, fat liquor bottles, tall skinny wine bottles, beveled decanters—bottles of all sizes, shapes, and colors.

Mike slid behind the counter and grabbed some glasses. I was mesmerized by a shiny blue bottle at the far end of the shelf as I heard the glug of our refreshment filling the glasses.

"Wanna taste something?" Mike asked.

"Sure. Do you have a cola?" I mumbled, still riveted on the blue bottle.

"Okay. Well, it's not coke, but I think you might like it." Mike laughed and slid a really teeny glass full of what did not look like a dark substance in front of me.

I looked down and thought, *Wow, glasses sure are small in Missouri.* "What is it?" I asked.

"Just try it," he said, scooting the glass even closer.

I hesitated and picked up the glass. This didn't smell like any soda I had ever drank. A little alarm went off somewhere in my six-year-old brain, but I unfortunately ignored it.

"Come on, just take a sip. It's not gonna hurt 'ya," Mike urged.

I raised my glass, eyeing the golden liquid inside. Deep down, I knew I shouldn't, but I really wanted to impress my new friend and was thirsty. The alarm in my brain was fully audible now, but I quickly closed my eyes and tossed the small amount of golden liquid down the hatch before I lost my nerve. As it hit my stomach, nostrils, and throat all at the same time, I could hear my body and brain suddenly screaming out, *"Fire, Fire! You're on fire!"*

Instantaneously, I felt a searing pain in my throat a hundred times worse than any sore throat I ever had. The inside of my nose was on fire. To add insult to injury, Mike was bent over laughing hysterically. My eyes were still on fire. Even my ears were on fire. I felt flames scorching my innards all the way down to my stomach. I looked down and then at the mirror over the bar and looked at my face, half expecting to see myself actually burst into flames.

Letting out a sick piercing sound like wanting to throw up, I sprinted for the door. I left as quickly as I had thrown that shot down. I could hear Mike still laughing at me.

Right then and there, I vowed never to drink straight whisky again (and I haven't to this day), and my friendship with Mike abruptly ended.

Mr. Oliver's Horses

When you moved as much as I did growing up (ten times by the time I was ten years old), lasting friendships were a bit of an anomaly. Uprooting and relocating during formative years can leave a child at a real relational disadvantage.

Even if friendships were few and far between, my dad made sure we had plenty of great experiences growing up. We got acquainted with Mike's next-door neighbor, Mr. Oliver, who became a great friend of our family. Mr. Oliver was a sweet man. In the afternoons, he came out and talked to us when we came home from school and also when my dad got home from work each evening. Dad and Mr. Oliver chatted about everything from the weather to the economy, but Mr. Oliver's face lit up when Dad talked about his own horse Brownie and about life on Grandpa Tom's farm. Mr. Oliver owned a horse ranch near the Missouri-Arkansas, border, and his favorite thing to talk about was his horses.

One evening, Mr. Oliver made Dad an offer he couldn't resist. If Dad would bring us kids out a couple of weekends a month to care for the horses, muck the stalls, and make sure they had water and hay, Dad could teach us how to ride for free. His handler would be there to make sure we got in okay.

Dad jumped at the opportunity to pass on to his kids a way of life he had known and loved. So, one or two weekends each month, my father drove us to spend Saturdays at the old farm. True to his word, in exchange for working on the farm, Mr. Oliver let us ride his horses for free.

My horse was a lovable stinker named Lady, whose goal with every ride was to return back to the barn as fast as possible for food and water. Lady knew that once back at the barn, riding was done for the day. She looked for any opportunity to hightail it back. So *my* goal every Saturday was to get her out of the barn and keep her headed in the right direction on the trail.

I now live in an area surrounded by horse farms, much like Mr. Oliver's ranch and Grandpa Tom's farm. Daily as I drive home, I'm reminded of those horseback-riding days. I look back on Mr. Oliver as an angel of sorts for opening up his heart and sharing his resources with my dad, allowing him to create such amazing memories for my family, passing on a piece of family history.

Those childhood memories are precious to me. The work, the fun, the adventures, and the time spent with family are some of my fondest remembrances, memories that I, in turn, have passed down to my own family. If there was horseback riding where we went on vacations with my kids, we were on the trail. More recently, I've taken my twin grandsons riding with me. I hope to instill a love and enjoyment of riding in them as my father did for me, passing on a family tradition that goes back generations.

My dad worked hard to provide experiences such as Mr. Oliver's horse farm for us. We also went on great family vacations, which were a big deal in the Mauck family, lasting more than a week. They usually involved extended family. I remember one such vacation, not as much for the warm fuzzy memories, but the life lesson learned while playing with my cousins in the pool.

Fighting for My Life

When I was about ten years old, the entire family, including extended family, went tent camping at Carter Caves State Resort Park Campground, not far from an area where Joseph Mauck lived with his family.

Being in the water at this young age was still not my favorite thing to do. But it was the summer of 1968, so I decided to venture into the deep end of the pool near the roped area. Feet touching the bottom at all times was just fine, thank you very much. On the other hand, my twin eleven-year-old cousins, Ronda and Jonda, swam like fish.

One day, I watched my cousins splash each other in the camp's pool, bobbing up and down in the water with ease. I decided to carefully venture to the other side of the rope that marks the slope down to the deep end. I grabbed the pool rope, gave myself a good pep talk, and bobbed under to the other side, death grip on the rope.

When I came up for air, I thought, *Hey, that wasn't half-bad*, and bobbed back to the shallow side, never letting go of the rope. I did this a few times, not noticing my cousins stealthily approaching. Ronda and Jonda were two preacher's kids that were looking for a good time to play with their cousin. They probably knew I was a little fearful, but later they would find out how petrified I was swimming in water over my head.

I surfaced on the deep side one last time. That's when I noticed them approaching, heads low to the water like sharks, sneaking toward their prey, one on one side and one on the other, closing in for the "kill." Then in horror, I realized I had let go of the rope, which was now floating just out of reach. Before I could open my mouth in protest, I was jerked under the water. Fighting to break free, I struggled to the surface attempting to gasp for air only to have my cousins acting as hungry sharks pulling me under again.

Instead of sucking in air, I was sucking in water. In what seemed like slow motion, I could feel their hands holding me under the water and hear them laughing above me, while the taste of chlorine in my mouth and nose overwhelmed me.

It all happened so fast. I couldn't breathe, so I began to panic. I knew I was drowning. I was taking in too much water without air, and yet somehow, I knew I had one last bit of energy. I shot straight up from the bottom and out of the water. I began swinging wildly and landed a big right hook square on Jonda's face and eye. I also landed a body blow on Ronda. As she backed away, I noticed Jonda leaving the pool in tears after I had hit her. The rope was now available to help me get out of the pool. When I was finally able to get to the side, I climbed out as the angry words flew between us.

At first, our parents didn't realize what had happened. To them, it was simply about kids being kids in a pool. I don't think for a minute they truly realized the level of panic nor the depths of the imprint of fear those early years of asthma struggles had left. Honestly, I couldn't have articulated all of that as a ten-year-old either.

We all got a good "talking to," and I was punished for hitting my cousins. I don't blame my cousins at all; they were having fun. I was experimenting in water over my head. For me, I counted that day as a watermark moment in my life. I learned that sometimes, you have to defend yourself when you're in danger. That summer, I also learned how important it was to know how to swim. In fact, as a result of that event, I now give credit to my twin cousins for making me learn how to become an *excellent* swimmer.

We now laugh about the pool incident and many other escapades from our childhood. We reminisce about the good old days and about the shenanigans we would get into at their dad's church when my family came for a visit. So many great memories were made together.

The pool incident stands out because after it happened, I was different. I stood up for myself more after that day, and eventually, that developed into standing up for others. I also live with less fear. For that, I can thank my dear first cousins Ronda and Jonda again!

Home Sweet Home... Finally

My father's line of work impacted my childhood greatly. Working in the department store industry, my father made frequent trips to New York, sometimes as a buyer, sometimes for networking purposes.

I often dreaded his return from those trips because if we were moving again, that's when we found out. Too many times to count, he would come back with a new promotion, and more often than not, that meant a new city. The thought of packing up, leaving our friends, starting all over at a new school, and making new ones did not appeal to me at all. By the time I was eleven, we had lived in West Lake, Louisiana; South Bend, Indiana; Portland, Oregon; Vancouver, Washington; Joplin, Missouri; Mobile, Alabama; and Flint, Michigan. Sometimes, we moved twice in the same city.

When I was eleven years old, my father once again was offered a job with a better salary, and the family moved to Flint. I remember my mother's first impressions of that city. Driving through town for the first time, we all commented that Flint was not pretty. In fact, to us, it was ugly.

Turning to my dad, Mom said flatly, "Well, after this lovely tour of Flint, I have to say it's not the most beautiful place we've lived, which is probably why we'll end up staying here."

We all laughed, inwardly hoping Mom's words might come true. Why? We were all sick of moving. We were ready to stay in one place and put some real roots down.

My mother's words were prophetic. When the company my father worked for closed its doors, instead of traveling to New York as he always did, my father teamed up with investors and opened his own store, Genesee Fabrics. I think he sensed a mutiny in the works if he attempted to uproot us again.

So, from fifth grade at Buffey Elementary until graduation from Kearsley High School, I went through more than one school year with the same group of friends and settled into a community. I called Flint home for more than twenty years.

Discovering My Calling

You've probably been asked which teacher you remembered the most? I would ask, "What teacher left the greatest imprint on you?"

In fifth grade, I met one such teacher, Mr. Walton. Every day at recess, Mr. Walton supervised us and somehow found the time to speak positive things into each one of our lives. He commended sharing and good choices and recognized the strengths he saw in each child.

One specific time while I was running with some of my friends, he called me over. "Hey, Kenny," he said, "you have a great stride. Have you ever thought about running track and doing field events for the school?"

The look on my face must have given away that I wasn't even sure what field events were, so he explained. "At the end of the year, we have field events that include relay races, sack races, sprints, and the long jump."

Well, that sounded great to me, so I signed up for all four events. I took home three blue ribbons.

Not only did Mr. Walton give me the confidence to try something new by seeing something in me that I couldn't see myself, but memories of his influence in my life also helped me decide to become a teacher. I didn't want to be just any teacher, but the kind who found something affirming and encouraging in every student. I've carried that calling, modeled so well by Mr. Walton, into every career path I've been blessed to follow.

The influence of Mr. Walton was truly an early life-gift moment to me. He not only taught me to believe in myself and my abilities, he believed in me as well. He could see me doing great things, and running would be a part of it.

Even to this day, I realize we all need a Mr. Walton in our lives to remind us what makes us unique and point us toward our purpose.

Hurdles on and off the Track

Elementary school was just the beginning of my career in track.

Kearsley High School had one of the best track coaches around. Coach Don Marsh inspired those who ran for him to do more than just attempt to be good; he expected and demanded the best from us.

Coach also had the gift of encouragement, and he had a knack for finding talent for his track program. Kearsley assistant coaches would attend middle school to scout out the next generation of runners. After one meet, one of the assistants, Coach Thiel, came up to me and told me to keep up the good work because Coach Marsh thought I had the potential to make a great addition to the Kearsley team one day. Those words motivated me all through junior high.

In my sophomore year, which back then was the first official year at my high school, I finally began running for Coach Marsh. My main event was hurdles. Initially, I wasn't that good at it, continually knocking over too many of them. Coach always encouraged and believed in me, and I gradually improved. My junior year, I started participating in more track meets but still struggled with knocking over that last hurdle. It wasn't until my senior year that I really found my stride.

We were undefeated in our meets that year and made it to the Big Nine Championship Meet. The movie *Chariots of Fire* would be how I would describe that day.

I prayed similarly to that of Eric Liddell from the movie, that this would be the day the Lord had made, and for me to glorify Him for the gift of running He had given me. Throughout that Friday afternoon heading to the Big Nine Conference Championship, I hummed the chorus, "This is the day that the Lord hath made; I will rejoice and be glad in it." I ended up racing my all-time best in the 120-yard high hurdles that afternoon and set a new Kearsley High School record in the 330 low hurdles at 39.2 seconds.

While basking in the glory of my record-setting run and feeling pretty good after the race, Coach Marsh walked up to me. He put his arm around my shoulders and said, "Kenny, nobody will ever beat that record."

Wow, I thought. *Coach is really proud of me!* A huge grin spread across my face.

With a twinkle in his eye, Coach continued. "You see, after this year, races will be measured in meters. So, technically, no one will ever beat your record because it's in yards." He always knew just the right way to remind one that they should remain humble in victory.

Looking back, it wasn't about setting a record as much as it was about contributing to my team and winning a championship. My own personal accomplishment would have meant little had it not led to our team's mutual goal of winning the Big Nine Championship. More importantly, it meant doing something that honored God by using the gifts and talents He had given to me with which to praise Him.

I can only explain that day as feeling God's joy as I ran, comparable to that of the famous movie *Chariots of Fire*. The curse of falling on the last hurdle that had weakened my confidence and dampened my morale over the past few races was crushed that day. I knew He was with me as I sprinted that race in an almost out-of-body experience, feeling as if I was soaring over each hurdle.

Navigating Your Story

Just as it has been for me, the process of discovering your ancestral stories and recognizing the imprints made in your life can give you a new perspective. Maybe they already have as you read through the previous chapters and started completing the guided questions I have provided for you. For me, I look back on these moments—my parents' story and the childhood memories that stand out in my mind with new clarity.

Time gives us the gift of hindsight, a chance to look back on situations with a bigger-picture perspective and hopefully greater wisdom. We are able to find the humor, such as in the story of my parents' courtship and elopement. Living it, I'm quite sure was not fun, but since then, my parents and grandparents were able to chuckle when they shared their story.

We are better able to see patterns and themes, not just in our own lives but within the context of stories passed down from generation to generation when we take the time to look back. The overlaps of faith, risk, fear, forgiveness, loss, and lessons learned rise up from the pages so much more. They strengthen our understanding of the whys of our makeup.

Running

One theme weaving its way through my family story is that of running, running from, running to, and actual running in my own story. Hans ran from persecution; Frederick ran in search of significance; William "Bill" Mauck ran to alcohol to escape his own personal demons; Uncle Tom ran to God for healing; Grandpa Lewis ran away from responsibility; and my father ran from the pain of an absent father and failed marriage, also in search of significance.

The imprint of my father's running is one of the most compelling to me. Bouncing around from town to town, between several states made it virtually impossible to develop deep friendships in my formative elementary school years. I was always "the new kid," the last one picked for team sports, the one trying to fit into the established clicks and hierarchy. It's probably a good explanation as to why I now root for the underdog. I don't like anyone to be left out because I can empathize.

A mobile childhood also impacted my life in that I made a decision early on that I would do things differently for my family. I committed to giving my children the opportunity to grow up in one place and establish deep roots, the kind I didn't get a chance to grow until junior high school.

One way of life is not right and the other wrong. That's not at all my point, but both make an imprint on those who live it. My point is that whether you stay or leave a home or place can simply impact the future and influences in our lives.

Victory

Running left another imprint in my life. Reflecting on my track days and influences of Coach Marsh, I've drawn inspiration from these experiences when facing hurdles in my business and personal lives. Having the experience of competing and meeting goals has made me more confidant to run over or through the next obstacle.

I'm reminded that just like that championship day in high school, God still challenges me, picking me up, dusting me off when I fall, and carrying me over each hurdle and over the finish line. Only now, I realize more than ever the race before us is an eternal one, just as Philippians 3:14 says, "I press toward the mark for the prize of the high calling of God in Christ Jesus" (KJV).

Your calling, my promise, the path He has laid out before you and me is the race we run. Any obstacle that stands in our way ultimately stands in the way of the Almighty. This means that if we let Him carry us, let Him steady us, the obstacle really doesn't stand a chance. When I attended Kearsley High School, I sang in several different performing choirs and ensembles in addition to running track. I loved music, but I initially loved the world of track even more. But now, music, writing, and sharing through speaking is just as much a passion as well. But I have no regrets as to the progression and journey I have taken. Through it all, God has been faithful and mercifully shown favor in my life.

Romans 5:8 promises us that all things will work for good for those called according to His purposes. No matter what the obstacle is—no matter what the imprint is—ultimately, it will be worked for our good and for His purposes. We overcome in victory because our God will have nothing less. You may not be able to understand this due to what you're going through right now, but know that what God promises, He will eventually use it for our good, including those heartaches we encounter.

For me, Psalm 119:32 says it well. "I run in the path of your commands, for you have broadened my understanding" (NIV).

I am grateful for the new and deeper understanding I have of myself and my God through what He is revealing to me through this study of my and my family's story.

Charted Steps

When you think of the standout moments from your childhood, what word comes to mind? What lifelong impact was made? Those would be your imprint experiences.

Just a few of mine would be:

IMPRINT—Miracles—Hearing the Story of My Healing from Asthma
IMPRINT—Fear—Perfect Love from family and friends caused me to build confidence and overcome my fears
IMPRINT—Overcoming Fear—such as learning how to swim and fly an airplane, riding roller coasters, etc.
IMPRINT—Overcoming Obstacles—I risked losing my entire savings to start nonprofits that ended up serving thousands of kids and providing millions of dollars of care for them.

IMPRINT—Searching for Significance—Affirmation from my parents and Paw Pa.

IMPRINT—Lack of Opportunity to Plant Real Roots in Formative Years from Multiple Moves—I love to travel now and have created roots here in Nashville for my own children and grandchildren.

I could list so many more imprints from my own life, like living down the street from a railroad track in Mobile, Alabama, hearing that Martin Luther King was shot, and knowing that the street where my seven-year-old African-American friend lived was being littered and looted. I watched as forced busing caused us to move from Mobile, and I felt bad having to say goodbye to my first African-American friend Leon from my elementary school, one whom I had just got acquainted with the previous year. Would I ever see him again? No, but I would never forget him. My parents would move us to Michigan, that summer. My days of innocence were challenged as I watched real anger and fear during the riots after the loss of Dr. King. These were the kinds of events and imprints that shape us and can form how we respond as adults. It's important that each one of us recall our formative roots and imprints.

1. Think of your childhood and those memories that stand out the most—the funny, the not-so-funny, both good and bad. What about those memories stick with you? What word associations do you make with them? Take some time to write these thoughts down.
2. What adult figure, child, or friend helped mold, influence, or affirm you growing up?
3. Looking at your answers to the above, what imprints from childhood do you need to overcome that have stifled, hampered, or held you back from living life to the fullest?

4. What imprints do you need to fully embrace and move forward in your life as you pursue your God-given calling and mission? Journal your declarations. How will you move forward in this new knowledge?

CHAPTER

Discovery

> "I pray because I can't help myself. I pray because I'm helpless. I pray because the need flows out of me all the time, waking and sleeping. It (prayer) doesn't change God. It changes me!
>
> —C. S. LEWIS

God's Call Comes in Twos: Prayer and Timing

IN THE SUMMER OF 1982, DURING MY SENIOR year at the University of Michigan, my parents relocated to Nashville. In the meantime, a friend of mine helped me secure a summer job in a hospital in Lexington, Kentucky, and we had planned to lease a room together.

However, upon arriving in Lexington, I was notified by my parents that my sister was going through a very difficult time, probably her toughest yet, one that could end her marriage. My dad and mom expressed deep concern. As the big brother, I felt she needed me. So, I notified my friend that I couldn't accept that position. I instead found a summer job at Kroger's in Nashville and lived with my parents.

My father did offer me an incentive that gave me that extra push to live in Nashville as I approached my twenty-fourth birthday. It came in the form of a motorcycle he knew I loved to ride. He made a promise that I could ride it once I got to Nashville. Well, the lure of a motorcycle coupled with the love and devotion to family won me over. I was all in!

All was good, and I began to pray and think about my life and in what direction I was heading. My devotional time and listening to music created a time of sanctuary. I followed that up with attending Christ Church and realizing the pull of God on my life. I loved Nashville and spent time with my sister. We worked out together as I encouraged her to get back to good emotional and physical health.

I also enjoyed my motorcycle, but it kept stalling out on the beautiful but busy road called Old Hickory. During this time, some road construction was occurring. So one day while heading to work, I got behind a line of backed-up cars, and my motorcycle stalled yet again. I quickly pulled my bike off the road and glanced across the street at the hills lined up behind what looked like a small mansion. It was as if God spoke in that still small voice and said, "Nashville is where you will live someday and raise your family."

I was single, so I tucked those words in to my spirit, got the bike running again, and hit the gears to get to work fast. I thought, *I have to head back in the fall to Flint to finish my student teaching, but I want to come right back here as soon as I'm done.*

I then made a proclamation to my parents. "Mom and Dad, after graduation, I'm coming back here to live."

Although this epiphany moment and time in prayer was drawing me closer to God, I was lonely and wanted a relationship with a special young lady, but only if God and His timing allowed for it. Boy! God surely, in short order, would be teaching me about His timing.

Kenny Mauck: 1958–Present
Raye Ann Hill-Mauck: 1960–Present

I seem to fall into that category of people where nothing goes smoothly, and often for someone looking in, my life can at times look initially like a sitcom. Meeting my wife Raye Ann for the first time would, unfortunately, follow suit. Maybe "unfortunate" is too harsh a word because I look back on that time with a sense of humor and gratitude.

My style of dating was spur of the moment. For example, if I wanted to get to know someone, I was spontaneous rather than call them a few days in advance. I would normally ask a young lady if she'd like to grab a bite to eat on the spur of the moment, like right after church or during a break in school. I didn't plan much beyond that when it came to dating. For the most part, this approach had worked pretty well for me, until I met Raye Ann Hill.

A Beautiful Young Lady, Inside and Out!

It was the end of the summer of 1982. Instead of majoring in music, I decided to become a teacher. I moved from Nashville back to Flint, Michigan, to complete my required student teaching assignment so I could officially become an elementary school teacher. I intended to graduate that fall from the University of Michigan and return to Nashville. I had about $700 saved up to cover expenses while I completed my degree. It was not a lot of money to stretch over five months of expenses, even for a twenty-four-year-old who would be living on ramen noodles and peanut butter. (When you finally get to the student teaching part of earning your degree, you still aren't getting paid. You're free labor to a teacher for an entire semester.) Fortunately, some dear friends offered me a rent-free bedroom in their home, which would really help make the most of the money I had.

My friend Tim and I picked up right where we had left off when I arrived back in Flint. I knew Tim from Faith Tabernacle Church where we both attended for years before I left for Nashville. Getting back up to speed after my absence, I asked Tim what was new since I had left. Had anything changed? Anything interesting happen?

A huge smile spread across his face, and he said, "Oh, yeah, there are three new great-looking young ladies who are attending the church. Really good-looking babes."

Well, what young man wouldn't be glad to hear that news? Even though I wanted a relationship, I had to stay focused on my plan, and that was returning to Nashville after graduation and getting a job. If I didn't find a job right away, my fallback was to pursue finding a job in the Peace Corps.

Sitting in my first service back at Faith Tabernacle, Tim plopped down next to me and said, "Guess what? All the new girls I was telling you about? They're singing in the choir today. I'll point them out to you."

After praise and worship and during the offering, Tim leaned over and pointed out the three new girls. The first was a pastor's daughter and very pretty. The second had a sweet smile and radiated joy. The third? She was the most beautiful young lady I had ever seen. I couldn't take my eyes off of her. Believe me, I tried two or three times, but she had captivated me.

Finally, I gathered my wits enough to ask Tim, "*Who is that?*" Seeing an opportunity to mess with me a little, Tim smiled mischievously and said, "Oh, that's Raye Ann, and you can't like her because I do!"

That broke my gaze. I turned and looked at Tim. He stared back with a twinkle in his eye. He was actually much younger than Raye Ann, so I was pretty sure he wasn't interested in her and was pulling my leg. I said, "Well, I would like to meet her after church anyway."

Tim shrugged and replied, "Okay, yeah, I think I can arrange that."

After the service, Tim motioned to Raye Ann, and she headed in our direction. I thought, *She's even more stunning up close than from a distance.*

As she drew nearer, I realized I was staring and quickly averted my eyes, pretending to be looking for someone else. When I looked back, there she was, right in front of me. I was standing face to face with one of the most beautiful creatures I had ever seen.

"Raye Ann," Tim said, "This is my friend Kenny. He just moved back home from Nashville."

Trying to keep my composure, I held out my hand cordially to shake hers and thought, *I definitely need to get to know Raye Ann while I'm here.*

Strike One! Strike Two!

The next time I saw Raye Ann was Wednesday night after church. I had been working up the nerve to ask her if she would like to go and grab something to eat afterward. Shaking inside, I finally took the plunge and asked her as confidently and as coolly as I could muster.

She looked at me sadly and said, "You know, I would consider it, but my clothes need to be washed for work, and I wouldn't want you to just sit there, watching me work."

I felt my face get hot. "Okay, well we can do a rain check and meet another time."

As she walked away, I shook my head trying to sort out my thoughts. *My clothes need to be washed? That's actually worse than I need to wash my hair. Have I ever been turned down for a date because of dirty clothes?* The answer was an unequivocal no. Strike one.

I needed a little time to regroup, so I waited a week until the following Sunday to take another swing at it. Pumping myself up, I thought, *It's Sunday. She's single. So am I. We both have to eat. I'll just ask her to dinner, and we can get to know each other. Simple. Easy.*

I waited until after the service, and my face lit up when I saw her. Again, I forced myself to act casual. "Hey, would you like to go to dinner with me this afternoon?" *Perfect*, I thought. *This is going to be great.*

No. Not perfect.

Sweetly, she responded, "Well, I would, but I promised my grandmother I would have Sunday dinner with her this afternoon."

I was stunned.

She continued, "I really want to, but I need to keep my commitment to her."

I recovered enough to get her phone number at least so that I could call her later that week. This was definitely not a good sign, though. First, trumped by the laundry. Now sidelined by her grandmother. I was more than a little leery, and yet perhaps, it *was* short notice. Maybe she really did have plans with her grandmother. If that really was true, I was impressed, and it potentially spoke volumes about her character.

Always the optimist, I left the church that day thinking, *Wow, she's a young lady who keeps her commitments.* By this time, I realized that if this was ever going to happen, I had better step up my game. I couldn't remember being turned down for a date twice in a row by the same girl who seemed to connect with me. It was truly a very humbling place for me to be, for sure.

My thoughts continued to swirl. *Maybe she just doesn't want to go out with me.* My ego limped just a bit, and a few weeks went by before I attempted again. Mulling the whole situation over one day, I thought, *You know, Kenny, you have never really tried to plan something in advance with her. She does have a full-time job as an executive secretary at General Motors, so her schedule is already pretty full. So, this time, maybe give her at least a few-days' notice.* Light bulb!

As luck would have it, a group called the Second Chapter of Acts, a Christian rock group from California, was playing on the Michigan State Campus. I had heard the lead singer sounded like Stevie Wonder, and that intrigued me. With both Raye Ann and I being musicians in the church, I thought I had found the perfect opportunity.

I thought, *I'm going to give this one last shot. Come on, Kenny, let's go for it. If she says no again, no more calls, no more attempts. At least you tried. If it doesn't work this time, then it probably really wasn't meant to be.*

After picking up the phone and hanging it back up three or four times, I finally went for it.

Full Count with Bases Loaded

The phone rang a couple of times, and I was quickly losing my nerve until I heard, "Hello?" on the other end. My mind momentarily went blank, and I all could say was, "Raye Ann, this is Kenny Mauck from church." I waited, holding my breath, bracing myself.

"Well, hello there. I know your voice. I'm glad you called!"

Relief! I wound up for the final pitch, "Well, good. I have some tickets to what I think will be a wonderful concert with a great Christian rock group from California this weekend, and I'd love to take you. If you say no, just know I'll bring a guitar outside your apartment window and sing all night." *Yes, way to go, Kenny. Good one!* I thought.

To my utter delight, she responded, "Well, actually, I was just thinking about you, and yes, I would be very happy to go with you this weekend."

Yes, hit it out of the park!

God's Love Is True Love

That first date with Raye Ann went well. The concert was great. On the way home, we talked about the show, music in general, and even sang a few songs from church together. Leading up to our second date, God had been impressing a specific Scripture on my heart. I kept repeating it over and over in my thoughts throughout that evening.

The Scripture was Matthew 6:33, "But seek ye first the kingdom of God, and his righteousness; and all these things shall be added to you." *What were "these things"?* I wondered.

When I went to call Raye Ann the next day, the same Scripture came to mind. I felt the Lord guiding me, *Do this the right way, Kenny, My way, not yours.*

Instead of telling her on that call all the reasons we should be together, all the things we had in common, I listened. I shared with her how much I had enjoyed the evening with her, and I found out she had a great time as well.

After a few more dates, the relationship seemed to be growing, but I had to be sure we were on the same page about God's direction in our lives. One night while talking on the phone, I told her I was open to being really good friends if that's what God's intent was for us.

We talked a little more. Before hanging up, I said, "Hey, I have a Scripture I want to share with you. It's something that's been on my heart for a while. It's from Matthew 6:33, 'Seek ye first the kingdom of God, and his righteousness ...'"

Before I could finish, she interrupted, "'... and all these things shall be added unto you.' I was just reading the same passage before you called. I have it right here in front of me."

That call put God first in the relationship. Our friendship turned from just two people dating into two people committing to a more serious and deeper relationship. We were married a year later on August 13, 1983. Now some thirty-five years later, it's obvious to me that God was seeking to knit our hearts together with Him first for the long haul. Our relationship has been tied to a much deeper anchor and purpose than we ever could have imagined back then.

To this day, Matthew 6:33 has been the mantel over our lives. Like all marriages, we have been tested. In those times, we realized just how important those marital vows were that we had made to each other so many years ago. For example, some of these other things were our three children, Landon, Megan, and Kelsey, a daughter-in-law named Brittany, two sons-in-law, Michael and Jonathan, and three grandchildren, Easton and Cooper, age eight, and Gracelyn Hope, age two.

The feelings meter of marriage can change, but love ultimately is a decision. When times get tough, and believe me they have, we have reminded each other of this Scripture that the Lord gave us so many years ago. It's helped us get our priorities back in order.

Looking back, I can see God truly wanted our relationship to initially blossom as friends by putting Christ Jesus first in our hearts and lives.

Getting My Real Education

That same year, I graduated from the University of Michigan with my bachelor of science degree in elementary education and started substitute teaching to get my foot in the door of the school system in Flint. I was fortunate to be able to work with my lifetime mentor Don Evans, who was a principal at one of the schools in town. I had known Don since I was ten years old, and since I had no experience, substituting at his school was a valuable opportunity. One day I would be the math teacher, the next day the kindergarten teacher playing on the floor, the next day the music teacher, the gym teacher, you name it, I taught it.

In one of the larger schools in a low-income inner-city neighborhood, the teachers and students faced overwhelming issues. Behavioral problems, drugs, lack of respect, even gang activity was the daily norm. It's a little humorous to me that so much time is spent learning and studying in preparation for a career when the real education begins once all that knowledge is actually put to work. There are just some things for which no class can adequately prepare you. I had heard the term "combat pay" bouncing around the halls regarding inner-city schools but didn't fully understand what it meant until I was in one.

For over two years, I found myself in every situation you can think of—from confiscating a knife brought to school by a student to sitting on my seat littered with tacks to dealing with constant disrespectful attitudes and behavior in the classroom from students who were twice my size. What struck me most was that usually time after time, the perpetrators and initiators were the same group of kids, and most of them came from less-than-favorable home situations.

My heart grieved to see these students learning such poor behavior patterns at such young ages. Now, I see how the imprints they received at home directed their entire outlook on life and heavily impacted how they responded to everything.

Don ran his school differently from many of the other schools in that district. His teachers, students, and parents were taught respect, which was paramount and essential to the learning process and environment. He trained his teachers well, making sure we had good manipulative and tactical skills to help children with learning disabilities excel. Teachers in Don's school also learned positive and assertive classroom discipline techniques to foster a peaceful, productive atmosphere.

On a personal level, Don showed me what it would take to become a "master teacher" and encouraged me on that path. Although I did not substitute exclusively at his school, I was continually under his guidance. I not only gained valuable teaching experience, but looking back, I can also see how exponentially I matured under his mentorship.

After being a substitute teacher for a year, I ran into the Director of the Career Development Center of Mott College in a grocery store in Flint, Michigan. He asked if I might be interested in applying for a temporary position at Mott College. It was a providential meeting for sure since I really wanted to get back into a college position.

The providential part was that a few months after starting that position, at twenty-six-years old, I was given the opportunity to get a much better long-term position with the Academic Development Center at Mott. I would serve as a college program advisor, which would be one of my most rewarding jobs. It would serve me well later in that it involved both single parents and veterans seeking to attend college to acquire a technical, nursing, or social work skill. I would end up serving this population again for most of my career.

The Revolving Dollar

While working in the Academic Development Center, a grant program titled "College Survival Skills" gave me the opportunity to help students who struggled to succeed academically for a variety of reasons. They were given a second chance to obtain their two-year degree. Many of these parents fought to stay above the poverty level.

The academic development skills were solvable for the most part through government-aided programs like we had at Mott. But there were two obstacles that proved to be the most difficult: childcare and transportation. Eventually, we got the childcare monies to assist and find good caregivers, but the transportation bus fare seemed to always be a big issue. Some of these single parents just did not have the one-dollar bus fare each way left in the budget after covering everything else, and transportation was not covered by the grant.

My heart broke for these parents who were working so hard to make a better life for themselves and their children, only to be stopped dead in their tracks for want of a dollar. At first, I pulled money out of my own wallet to help out, but working with so many students, I began to feel the pinch in my own budget. These students didn't want to have to borrow money from me, and I wasn't sure if I could financially continue doing this over the long road either.

Laboring over this issue one day, it came to me. I contacted my caseload of single parents with my idea of the "Revolving Dollar." I would start by hanging up the first one-dollar bill on my billboard in my office. If someone needed bus fare and took it down, it had to be replaced the next day by them or a fellow classmate. If you took the dollar, it was your responsibility to reciprocate with a dollar as soon as possible. If you noticed the dollar was missing and had a dollar to give, pin it up there.

Being a part of empowering someone to achieve their dreams without doing it for them is something everyone needs to experience. A day never passed where the dollar wasn't used, nor did a day ever pass where the dollar wasn't replaced. Sometimes, more than one-dollar bill was on the board. To me, single parents are heroes, especially these. They worked so hard and took advantage not of a handout, but of a solution to a problem and an opportunity to give and receive. They ran with it in pursuit of their dreams of finishing college.

I carry that revolving-dollar mentality with me still into other areas of my life. It's why I always had money in my pocket when I said goodbye to Carlos and bought him a snack from the vending machine. I make sure I have a dollar or at least change in my pocket whenever I go to one of our centers.

I've seen the impact that a single dollar or a simple act of kindness can make, the empowerment it can give, like showing love in the most practical ways, like feeding the hungry, or driving one to get proper care.

Leaving the Mauck Name Imprint
Life's Greatest Gifts!

My grandfather Tom Mauck started a new trend. He had only one son, my father Lewis, who would carry on the Mauck name. Then my father had one son—me. So when my wife and I finally had our first male child Landon, I have to admit I felt some relief.

After Landon was born in April 1985, two years later, our dream of having a little girl came true as our daughter Megan was born in July 1987. I felt our family seemed complete having a boy and girl. We owned a little home on a little street called Dakota, and right across from our house was a park. The memories of teaching my little boy and girl how to ride their bikes, taking them to church and to the park, and being able to become a kid again by wrestling with Landon and helping both children get on and off all the playground slides and swings has and remains some the richer imprints of my life.

Lawnmower Moments with God

I never gave up on God's call about me eventually raising my family in Nashville, but I couldn't help but wonder, maybe He had other plans.

I was thirty-two years old now. Being this long in Flint caused me to wonder if I would ever be returning to Nashville. Would it even be feasible at this point? I was beginning to question myself and God if that was just wishful thinking on my part. Yet any time I would just about settle in and get comfortable, God would speak to me in the most interesting places, such as mowing the lawn while singing or thinking about His call on my life. Funny thing, cutting grass created lots of time to think... listen... and pray silently.

God used that weekly ritual as an opportunity talk with me in the quietness of my heart. He was somehow keeping the dream alive, assuring me that He had not forgotten me or His promises to me. The Lord used this time to brand thoughts and impressions upon my heart.

Sometimes I would just stop the lawnmower and ask quietly, "Is this really You, God?" Now that I think about it, the neighbors must have wondered who I was talking to as I stood in my yard. Raye Ann once asked me, "Are you talking to yourself when you cut the grass?"

I too would have wondered the same thing. So, I decided to wait and explain later that it was actually God and me having some private time to figure things out.

Nonetheless, the longer I stayed in Flint, the more entrenched and rooted I became. I realized it would take a miracle to get me to Nashville, Tennessee. I convinced myself I was good with the idea of staying in Michigan, and that it would probably be best with my current circumstances.

Finally, it came to a head after eight years of wrestling with God and my own doubts and fears. I got to the point where I didn't want to mow the lawn anymore. In those "lawnmower-moment" conversations with God, it was becoming more and more difficult to justify my inaction and my list of why nots.

Finally, in the spring of 1990, having graduated with my degree in counseling from Eastern Michigan University, I realized I had to do something to figure this out. So, I finally sought advice from a man in Nashville for whom I had acquired the greatest respect and confidence when it came to spiritual matters. I put in a call to Pastor L. H. Hardwick. Now, I had not spoken with the Hardwicks since I left Nashville eight years ago. I coached myself as the phone rang. If no one answered, that would be my sign.

After a few rings, much to my surprise, Pastor Hardwick's wife Montelle answered. When I heard her voice, I felt a peace come over me. I dove right in and shared my story, my promise from God, my dilemma regarding returning to Nashville, and all the reasons I had come up with for staying where I was, and my concerns about leaving a good job and finding another in Nashville. I told her I just didn't understand why, after eight years of creating a life in Michigan, God was still knocking on my heart about moving to Nashville.

Her answer was as kind as it was wise. She simply said, "Kenny, if God wants you in Nashville, you shouldn't worry. He'll make it happen. As for a job, there are plenty of opportunities, and He'll lead you to the right one."

About a month after that conversation, I was cutting the grass again. The internal dialogue between God and me was so loud, at least in my heart and mind, I couldn't even concentrate on mowing at all. If this was truly God, I had to at least give it a shot. Not even getting through the first couple of rows, I turned off the lawnmower and went inside.

Raye Ann looked at me quizzically. All I could tell her was that I didn't think the voices in my head were going to stop. I confided that I hadn't been talking to myself; God and I had been having quiet conversations in my head about Nashville for a while. I felt after all this time, at least I needed to try to be obedient and send my resume somewhere in Nashville.

I told her about the peace I felt in my conversation with Pastor Hardwick's wife. I also shared with her my reservations about moving her away from the only place she had ever lived and away from her support system.

She said, "Let's just pray, and like Sister Montelle said, 'If it's meant to be, it will happen.'"

I began exploring the Nashville job market, focusing on elementary and secondary schools. Honestly, I think that was my way of trying to sabotage the whole thing by not focusing on the colleges in the area. However, God's ways are not our own, are they? Sure enough, four new schools were being built in the Williamson County area just south of Nashville, which meant opportunities for a job. The catch? Only sixty-five to seventy-five applicants were being hired, and over one thousand had applied.

Well, there it was. How was I going to get that lucky?

Oh, I love my wife. She knows me well. When I shared this with her, rather than allowing me to accept defeat so readily and stay in my comfort zone, her response was, "Well, you won't know if you don't try, so quit thinking about it and at least try."

Inside, I'm pretty sure she was thinking, *Time to put up or shut up!*

That was the wind in my sails I needed. I put in my resume along with the other thousand-plus applicants for a job with Williamson County Schools. I remember telling Raye Ann that it was going to take a miracle to get hired, that the chances were less than ten percent statistically, but I was going for it!

Confirmations

Even though I had my eyes on a counselor position, the next step in the process was passing the National Teachers Exam (NTE). I traveled to Detroit to take the exam and waited for a call for an interview. Honestly, I wasn't holding my breath. With a thousand applicants to sort through, my resume could likely become white noise. To my surprise, though, I got my answer. I got a call from Williamson County Human Resources to come interview, so I made plans the next week to travel to Nashville. That call was the first of several confirmations of faith the Lord would give me to move.

At my initial interview, I found out the position I had wanted in counseling had already been filled. But Mr. Ford, the principal who conducted the first interview, liked my background and experience and did have an open position as a fifth-grade teacher. I was supposed to also have an interview with Ms. Gamble, the new principal. If she liked my resume as much as he did, he thought I might be a strong candidate for the job.

Before leaving the room, he made a quick call to Ms. Gamble to set up the interview with her, but she stated it wasn't necessary. If Mr. Ford felt right about hiring me, she would agree to it as well. So, his next few words stopped me in my tracks. "Kenny, I think you would do a good job for us. Do you want the position?"

I don't exactly remember everything I said due to the shock, but I do remember saying, "Yes, sir, I would" while thinking, *Did I just get offered a fifth-grade teaching position?*

I thanked him, and before I left the room, Mr. Ford said, "Well, it's yours. When can you move down?"

My second confirmation.

I asked, "Mr. Ford, by the way, what is the name of the school where I'll be teaching?"

He smiled. "Well, it's a brand-new school called 'Trinity.'"

I couldn't believe my ears. Trinity? As in the Father-Son-and-Holy-Spirit Trinity? The very essence of God was the name of my new school. At that point, I thought, *How much more confirmation does one need?*

I walked to my vehicle and looked up toward heaven with reverence in my heart. Eight very long years, and I was finally moving back to Nashville. *You have such a great sense of humor, Lord. Trinity Elementary!*

As I sat in my car, tears of joy streamed down my face. The years ticked off in my mind: 1983. 1984. 1985. 1986. 1987. 1988. 1989. Now in 1990, eight years after I heard God speak to me, I knew this had not happened by chance. All those years, I had pushed back, reasoned away, made excuses, gotten comfortable, but God had this door waiting for me all along. He knew all those years I was not yet ready. Patiently, lovingly, and consistently He was calling, waiting for me to answer in obedience and wade into the water. I remembered what Montelle Hardwick last said to me: "Kenny, if it's God's will, He will make a way."

Within a week of returning home after my interview, the final hurdle to move came in a letter from the National Teaching Exam I had taken. Nervously, I took my score sheet out of its envelope, knowing that if I didn't pass, there would be no teaching position. I then read my results.

I met Raye Ann with a big smile that spread across my entire face. I had passed! That was the other important confirmation check-off item. I was now officially a Tennessee teacher!

The Big Move

With only a month to go before the move, I put in my notice at Mott Community College and got to work preparing for the big day. What I wasn't expecting was my five-year-old son Landon's reaction to the news. If it meant leaving his treehouse, he was not going. Now, this wasn't just any treehouse; it was a true one, the kind that wrapped around a tree high above the ground, the kind you see in movies. Landon and his friends played there just about every day.

I joined Landon in his treehouse one day. He seemed sad.

"Son," I said, "if this treehouse means that much to you, we'll build another one once we find a new home."

Trying to play it cool and hide his excitement, he finally looked at me sideways and said, "Okay. I'll go." I won him over. He was now onboard. Time to hit the road.

We listed the house through a realtor friend, but it didn't sell right away. I couldn't wait any longer. I had to leave to begin preparing myself and my classroom for the school year.

Raye Ann had to stay until the house sold. In the meantime, I quickly got my classroom ready and then had to wrap up my old job at Mott College in Michigan, as well. We asked Raye Ann's parents to watch the kids so she could make a quick trip to Nashville and find us a place to rent. I sent her off with a few guidelines. We needed to live near Christ Church, which was on Old Hickory Boulevard and near the interstate.

To my delight, Raye Ann quickly found us a very nice condo and took care of the lease before school started. When I asked her where it was, she couldn't remember what part of the city it was located, but said she had followed my instructions, and our place was near Old Hickory. I didn't think much about her response and was excited to go and see our new home.

If you're from Nashville, one knows about Old Hickory that usually loops around a good portion of the entire city. When I told a colleague that my wife had found us a place near Old Hickory, he looked at me, smiled, and asked, "Which Old Hickory? Old Hickory is everywhere."

Suddenly, my face fell flat. Oh no. Had I been specific enough? What if Raye Ann had gotten us a place all the way on the other side of town, thirty miles away?

I ran to the nearest phone in a panic and called Raye Ann. She gave me the address, and I quickly looked it up on the map and became overjoyed. It was within a half-mile of Christ Church and not far from the interstate. I breathed a huge sigh of relief and thankfulness for God's direction. For me, it was another confirmation that we were on the right track, and He was in the details.

Our house finally sold, and I travelled to Michigan the weekend before school started to move my family to Nashville. Our friend Don Evans, his wife Barbara, and Raye Ann's parents helped me load up the truck, and we were off. Raye Ann, the kids, and I drove in the car, and my father-in-law followed us in the moving van.

When we arrived at our place, more confirmation awaited us. Our new neighbors, one from Mississippi, and one a Nashville native, were out front with food and arms ready to help us move in. For the next two hours, they stayed and helped us unload, and they fed us since we had been on the road for twelve hours. This was a confirmation from God. Here we were, meeting these two families, who just happened to be outside in the middle of the night. We were tired and hungry, and they brought us food. They had no idea we were arriving, and I don't ever remember them being out front that late again. What angels! But God wasn't finished yet; He had a few more confirmations left.

On my first day at Trinity Elementary, I met a man named Dan Finley, who for the last twenty-three years, I have counted among my best friends. Dan was the only other teacher specializing in children with special learning needs. And bonus—he attended Christ Church and sang in the choir that my cousin Landy directed.

I love how God just knows, affirms, and shows up in our lives. I didn't realize it then, but God knew that Dan would be a trusted advisor to both of our two companies and would also become one of my dearest friends in Nashville.

Perspective!

Although I truly believed God had His hand in our move, and I was just glad to once again feel His peace in my life, we did have challenges. One of the biggest was finances. The move was expensive, and we were adjusting to one income instead of two since Ray Ann had taken her golden handshake by being a ten-year employee of General Motors. While on paper we appeared to have made a slightly better-than-lateral movement with my job, Williamson County was in the top fifteen wealthiest counties in the nation. The cost of living went right along with that statistic. Our dollars did not stretch quite as far in Nashville as they did in Michigan.

Life has a way of piling things on whether we're ready for it or not. As if financial challenges were not enough, about a month into the first school year, my wife met me at the door after work with "that look." Guys, you know, *the look*. Then your wife asks you to sit down for a minute; she has something to tell you...

Raye Ann looked at me and said, "I'm pregnant."

The words hung heavy in the air for more than a few seconds. She smiled, waiting for me to respond. I sat there, unmoving, a deer caught in the headlights.

I knew I should be excited, but all I could say was, "Wow."

Not, "Wow!"

Just, "Wow."

Sensing my apprehension due to our limited finances, Raye Ann attempted to smooth things over, saying she felt the same way initially. No, we had not been anticipating having another baby, but she believed this baby was meant to be. Of course, down deep, I'm *sure* I was excited, but my thoughts were consumed with the practicality of a third child. I was already having a little difficulty feeding two children and paying the bills, so how was this going to work out?

Still living in my stunned state the next day, I drove down the interstate through a heavy rainstorm. My thoughts were anywhere but on the road until a semi suddenly stopped dead in front of me and caused me to slam on my brakes. My brain was fully alert now as I snapped back to reality and found the semi's headlights and high bumper hovering right over the top of my little Geo Metro's hood.

Moments like these are perspective changers. How quickly I went from a stunned deer caught in the headlights to a father finding solutions. I thought about this precious little life, this baby growing inside my beautiful wife, and realized I had not even come to God in the last twenty-four hours with my concerns.

Upon pulling into the school, I parked and said a small prayer. "God, You have given us a precious new baby. I'm trusting You will provide the room and resources for this special life gift as well." He had brought us this far. How could I ever doubt him after all He had done for us.

Before our new baby was born, our two other children, Landon and Megan, were confident the baby was going to be another boy. At first, they were a bit disappointed to learn it was not a brother. But once they held their baby sister, she had them and us all wrapped around her little finger. My wife and I could never imagine our family without our little "Kelsey girl" in it. She was the period to our sentence, the last piece of the puzzle that completed us as a family.

God Is Good

As I am writing this, I can't help but be reminded of how good our Lord is. After spending our first year in Nashville in the condo, we had run out of room with a third child. We moved to Smyrna, a small suburban town south of Nashville in Rutherford County. I had to drive over thirty-five minutes one way to get to Trinity School each day, but I didn't mind. It was full of beautiful rolling hills and a place to turn up the music and enjoy the ride between my house and place to work.

Our new home was on a cul-de-sac that provided safety and room for our children to play games, shoot a basketball, learn to ride bikes, and of course, jump on the trampoline. Kelsey, our eight-month-old baby girl, would have her a brand-new room in which to sleep.

In fact, we had moved into the very home in which this book is being written twenty-seven years later. We had come full circle. Just down the road five minutes or so from where we currently live is the little Trinity Elementary School where I was hired to teach so many years ago. It reminds me of my own father who enjoyed living near Grandpa Tom's farm in Scioto for a while. Now my children and grandchildren can take comfort that God has truly called us to this great peace of heaven in Tennessee. Providence? Yes, I have no doubt.

Navigating Your Story

The time between childhood and adulthood—adolescence and young adulthood—is a beautiful, treacherous, gut-wrenching yet amazing season of becoming and discovery. We begin to explore and discover who we really are outside of our parents' influence. We find and develop our faith and beliefs for ourselves.

The search for purpose and the answer to the question, *Why am I here?* come to the forefront. This is the leg of the voyage when we begin to take ownership of our journey, make decisions on where our ship is going, try to figure out how it will get there, and determine who we want along for the ride.

Young adulthood is where blinders are removed. Rose-colored glasses fall off. As children, we are the center of our universe, and we filter life through that lens. As we move from childhood into our twenties and even thirties, we begin to see that we are part of something much bigger than ourselves. It's not the first time we've heard of the bigger picture, but for many, it's the first time we actually see a bigger picture.

A Matter of Trust

Eight years of waiting. Eight years of questioning. Eight years of arguing. Eight years of sometimes burying my head in the sand.

Doubt wasn't the issue. I didn't doubt that God existed or had spoken to me. I believed I was supposed to go to Nashville. I believed *He told me* I was supposed to go to Nashville. So, why didn't I just jump in headfirst right away and go?

Trust.

Believing I heard Him was not enough. Believing in Him was not enough. Believing He had it all figured out and had the answers, now that was another story.

Trusting that He was going to make it all happen, take care of me, have a job for me so that I could support my family? Trusting that friendships were waiting for me, that purpose was waiting for me? Giving up the life Raye and I were building in Flint, the friends and family, the security and comfort we had? Pulling up the roots we had set?

I couldn't actually see that part. Roots were a big deal to me now that I had control of my own life and movements. Pulling them up scared me. I had things figured out and under control in Flint, and I liked it that way. I firmly believe God's timing is perfect. I had taken baby trust steps along the way, but at this point in my life, this looked like a record-setting long jump of trust. It was a tremendous step for me, and His timing allowed for the waiting. Only in this instance, I wasn't waiting on God; He was waiting on me.

I'm reminded of Proverbs 3:5-6, "Trust in the LORD with all thine heart; and lean not unto thine own understanding. In all thy ways acknowledge him, and he shall direct thy paths" (KJV).

Today, I can say He did exactly what He promised in these verses. He directed my paths. He has been faithful in every area. I could not have imagined the life we have, the plans He had for me, the company He would give me to steward, or the people He would bring into my life when I finally chose to trust Him with our future.

Charted Steps

IMPRINT—God's Revelation
IMPRINT—Finding Love
IMPRINT—Trust

This season of discovering who I am, discovering God's path for my life and what He had planned for me would eventually take years of attempting to understand. It would be a journey of trust! To think it would take so long and many talks until He unequivocally confirmed to me that we were to move to Nashville is an amazing imprinted branding experience on my heart. I shall never forget it. After all these years, I can't imagine how different my life would have been had I not finally given up and began to just trust His promises. The great news is that to this day, He has never given up on His promises to you as well!

Trusting God is an issue for many of us. Not trusting Him with relationships, with finding love, with our future, with our finances, with... *you fill in the blank,* can put a roadblock in your journey to finding and fulfilling your God-called purpose. So stop, be still, and begin to prayerfully listen to His calling in your life, identifying and working through any trust issues so that you can freely walk confidently in God's purposes for your life.

1. When you hear the word "trust," what emotions surface? What areas of life come to mind? Finances? Relationships? Future occupation or a brand-new location to live?
2. Have you ever prayed and prayed about something, and it won't let you go or dismiss it? Have you considered that God is speaking to you, or are you still like me, thinking it can't be for me? Maybe it's time to test it out and see if it is God actually speaking to your heart about something.
3. Meditate and seek God's Word about your walk of faith and where you are at with His call and purpose for your life.
4. Spend some time praying and ask God to fulfill His calling and mission for your life. Let your faith, and not fear, confirm each present and future step in your life.

CHAPTER 9

Assembling Your Crew

> "Don't just find people. Find *your* people."
>
> — KENNY MAUCK

LEAVING A POWERFUL LIFE IMPRINT and legacy involves passion. Our founding company, LifeCare, will remain a tangible piece of that legacy imprint. But more importantly, it was my being still long enough to hear God despite the crazy noisy in this world and realizing it was His plan, not mine, that would work.

I say "our" company because I didn't do this alone. God graciously brought people into my life, both smarter and more talented than me. People like my wife, my son Landon, Sean McPherson,

Jim Carter, and so many more would fulfill a specific role and help me with this vision. I surrounded myself with men and women who share a similar passion and enthusiastically shared a vision. That's what made us successful!

The Crew

Choosing the right crew is important. Remember my original mission statement back in chapter 2, the one with all the positions I knew I'd need, the one with a blank space next to each job title? If I had just pulled that out, put together the standard job description, and started collecting and reviewing resumes and hiring based solely on that criteria, the LifeCare leadership in place today would most likely not have been chosen.

Even though I did post job listings and sort through many resumes, many times I did not hire the one most qualified on paper. Every one of my hires won me over during the interview or through a life lived before becoming an employee. Some are now dear friends and neighbors whose character and skills I had the opportunity to observe firsthand. All proved to be some of the most outstanding leaders and faithful workers with whom I have ever had the privilege to work.

Rule number one: Don't just find people. Find your people.

Don't exempt anyone based merely on a resume. Raw talent, gifting, chemistry, and passion are far more paramount to drive the mission. Be open to whomever the Lord puts in front of you. If you are hearing a yes in your spirit, even when the paper in front of you says no, listen to the voice. Don't just read the words.

My initial administrative and clinical staff consisted of a bus driver, a neighbor with triplets, a former college basketball player, a woman with a huge heart full of love for kids, a former music-industry employee, a conservative nurse from California, a community-oriented true-country gal, a spouse with great attention to detail, a son with good people skills, and an auditor from another company who impressed me so much as a person, I convinced him to come work for me.

One of the first employees I hired was a young, intelligent Christian man named Sean McPherson. When I interviewed Sean, I had three job openings I needed to fill. At the time, Sean drove buses for a company that took students on trips to Washington, D.C. He had worked with kids in the inner city and as a youth group leader at his church while earning his master's degree. Outside of that, he hadn't had much opportunity to gain experience.

By the end of his interview, even though his resume said otherwise, I realized he was actually qualified for all three open positions. So, rather than choose for him, I laid all three options out and let him decide.

Sean went for the job with the most responsibility, and that spoke volumes to me. Over the years, I've grown to respect Sean as a man of wisdom and character. He's someone I've come to think of as a second son. He has been with LifeCare for seventeen years, became our vice president in 2010, and is positioned to become the next President of LifeCare Family Services in the fall of 2019.

Another one of my key leaders is Jim Carter. To this day, I can say I have never really looked at Jim's resume. Prior to his hiring, I already knew exactly what he did. I was aware of his reputation for excellence in the fields of mental health and administration and of his experience caring for handicapped individuals.

Jim became one of our clinical and administrative auditors. His keen eye and attention to detail are impeccable. Quality control takes time to develop and maintain and was initially a problem for our company. Then Jim came onboard, and under his leadership, quality control is now a defining factor of our company. Jim brought in best practices techniques to better serve our families, children, seniors, and those in need of rehabilitative services.

Jim has faithfully served over a decade, becoming vice president in 2011, and now he oversees the daily operations of our sister company LifeCare Foundations. Foundations serves veterans, seniors, and people of all ages with a physical handicap or intellectual disability in need of 24-7 housing or adult daycare assistance.

I continued the unorthodox methods of hiring when I brought one of my neighbors onboard. I didn't notice her for an outstanding interview or stellar resume. No, she was hired based on her ability to multitask. You see, this neighbor is the mother of three children—triplets, who were babies at the time. I was always impressed with her ability to change three diapers and serve up three bottles all at once, utilizing only two hands and sometimes a foot. My decision to offer her a job was finalized one day while observing her through our living room window, putting the three boys into their car or baby carriage seats without shedding a single tear or showing significant frustration. I realized she would be a good multitasker.

There's something to be said for getting to know your neighbors. Mine were very instrumental in the initial staffing of Lifecare. In addition to my mother-of-three multi-tasking phenomenal neighbor, I also hired Christy Scruggs based on the referral of another neighbor.

Christy played point guard on the women's basketball team for Middle Tennessee State University. Her time-management skills and ability to know when to delegate or take the task on herself have been a considerable asset to LifeCare. Having little billing experience, Christy came onboard and has grown into a great leader and a specialist in every aspect of detailed claims and billing.

Christy is a multi-talented individual who can do (and has done) just about anything put in front of her. She has been with us for fifteen years and is now Director of Claims of both LifeCare and another subsidiary company of the management company 3LS, Omni Community Health.

Before any of these wonderful people came onboard, I hired Dominique Miller. Dominique's passion is at-risk children, and her contribution was essential, especially at the beginning of LifeCare. Dominique managed our first advocacy cases, tracking progress and ensuring that kids who were struggling in school due to a poor home environment were succeeding after our involvement. The situations these kids lived in ranged from parents who abused drugs to neglect to physical or sexual abuse. Part of Dominique's work was finding a safe home with a relative, or in cases other than abuse, working with the biological parents to ensure the child thrived and could remain in their home.

Dominique recently earned her master's in social work and will be leaving LifeCare after twenty years of service for a new ministry opportunity with her husband. The indelible imprint she leaves behind covers my family, our company, and the hundreds upon hundreds of families she served.

One of the greatest stories of her impact on others I can share comes from one of her cases she had managed for years. The teenager had become pregnant. When it came time to deliver, she asked Dominique to be the one at her side. Dominique, being the passionate caregiver she was, absolutely agreed. As the baby was born, through tears of joy, the teen mother whispered, "Meet your new godchild. Her name is *Dominique!*" Dominique, you will be greatly missed!

Our head coordinating nurse Rebecca Rahman has been with us for eight years. Rebecca is a hoot. A California transplant and converted Tennessee football fan, Rebecca is without a doubt a true lover of people from any and every walk of life. With a background in insurance, Rebecca oversees LifeCare's and Omni Community Health's medical coordination for the entire state of Tennessee. She's become a part of the family, even spending time looking in on and caring for my parents when they lived in Tennessee. A genuine person and faithful friend, Rebecca would be an asset to any company team.

One of our longest-standing medical providers is Tory Woodard. Tory exudes a genuine love for every person he comes in contact with regardless of status or background. An exemplary leader, Tory has been with us ten years and is one of the best prescribing nurse practitioners I have ever known.

Christal Wise hails from Lawrenceburg, Tennessee, a small city where the Amish still travel by horse and buggy to shop and where most of the town know each other. Her knowledge of the people, the schools, the criminal justice facilities, and local businesses in the area make Christal a perfect choice to be our advocate in her hometown. She is one of the most graciously kind individuals you will ever meet, making it easy for those with whom she works within the system and the families she assists to be at ease and trust her guidance.

Myrna Kemp is another excellent addition to our leadership team. Myrna was one of the exceptions to my unusual hire trend in that her resume and experience exactly matched her position. She brings a strong work ethic and top-notch listening skills, both as a therapist and as a leader in the company. But Myrna's smile is what wins us all over. When things aren't going as smoothly as we would like at one of our community mental health centers, her positive energy and leadership are refreshing to all involved.

Like the rest of us at LifeCare, no job is beneath her. She willingly rolls up her sleeves and gets to the business at hand, and that's why she is so respected by the team.

David Thomas rounds out our leadership staff. He began his career in Nashville in the music business but soon found his real passion and gifting were in counseling. David came to LifeCare from Cumberland Heights with experience in drug and alcohol recovery and has been with us for fourteen years. Starting in a licensed counselor capacity, David has grown with the company, finishing his doctorate in counseling psychology and becoming our clinical director a few years back.

More important than his impressive scholastic and postgraduate achievements, David is one of the most faithful, committed, and trusting individuals I know. His love for Christ is reflected in the way he treats his clients and employees. One of the most respected leaders in our organization, he illustrates with his life and work how a genuinely committed team member looks and acts at LifeCare.

The secret of LifeCare's success lies not solely within a visionary leader, but in the great people like those mentioned above, and others noted throughout the book or within the Acknowledgements section.

I'm grateful to each and every employee who has served over the last twenty-plus years. A vision can only go so far with one person. A vision carried by many has no limits.

Flying with Eagles

By mid-2001, LifeCare had completely overrun our dining area and our garage. After taking on our first few employees, we desperately needed more room. I began looking at options, but I wasn't sure our budget could handle the expense of outside office space.

At the same time, my friend Dave Ramsey was on the rise, shooting up the ladder with his book *Financial Peace*, and growing from local to national status and fame as one of America's favorite personal finance coach and expert, both on the radio and other selected media. Dave found out that we needed more space, so he graciously offered us space to sublease in his offices at the Ramsey Building. Raye Ann and I gladly took him up on his offer and reclaimed our home, and my wife, her parking spot.

Early every Wednesday morning, Dave met with a group called the Eagles. They consisted of ten to twelve men, all entrepreneur types, great thinkers and leaders in the community, including a builder, writer, music producer, minister, marriage ministry founder, podcaster, speaker, men's coach and facilitator, CPA, commercial real estate owner and businessman, and Dave. He invited me along one day, and I started attending regularly. Those men and our Wednesday morning meetings became an integral part of my development as a leader and as a man.

Throughout our years together, the Eagles became more than just a bunch of guys in a weekly meeting. We became friends. We did life together. Every man in that group experienced extreme business or personal hardship or loss, including me. We prayed for each other, encouraged each other, read and studied great books together, such as *Mere Christianity* by C.S. Lewis and *Soul Survivor* by Philip Yancey. Our families spent time together. We attended each other's kids' weddings.

When our friend and fellow Eagle, Pastor David Foster, suddenly passed away, we stood with and supported his family—our family. Looking down the aisle at his funeral, I was so proud to see all of us, his fellow Eagles, celebrating his life together.

As LifeCare continued to grow, so did the demands on my schedule. Staff meetings, board meetings, meetings with accountants, auditors, attorneys, contracting, and staffing filled my day to the brim, and one of my biggest disappointments was not being able to make every Eagles meeting each week. Along with that, we had since moved from the Ramsey building, and the longer drive only added to the stress.

Dave and the others were beginning to experience similar life and work demands pulling for their attention. Around 2012, the Eagles mutually decided it was time to disband, at least from weekly meetings. But that decade together bonded us deeply for life, and I know without a doubt, if I were to call any of these men today in need of real help, or if they called on me, we would be there for each other in a heartbeat.

Rule number two: Find your Eagles.

We need the accountability, encouragement, and support of each other more than we realize. For me, the Eagles became a tangible example of Proverbs 27:17, which says, "As iron sharpens iron, so one person sharpens another" (NIV).

We may convince ourselves that we are not relationally oriented or that we are fine with being a loner or "an island," but scripturally and practically, that doesn't hold water. For your ship to stay sound and seaworthy, you need a strong crew. You need people who will lift you up when you need it, challenge you, encourage you, and just do life with you. You need your own Eagles.

A Perfect Storm and a Perfect Gift

In 2009, the perfect storm hit our company. One of our contractors was beyond past due in payments, and we were bleeding over $100,000 a month.

After several months of trying to recoup the loss to no avail, we were forced to lay off one-third of our staff. Our little five loaves and two fish company had miraculously exploded to 200 employees with millions of dollars in contracts. Now, seven years later, to lose 1.75 million dollars and sixty great employees was extremely difficult to take.

We were broke, so broke that I asked all the remaining administrative staff, including myself, to take substantial salary cuts so that we could stay afloat. I put a freeze on purchase orders of any kind and cut everything else I could to the bone. Adding insult to injury, that same contractor, one of our largest, terminated our future contract. I went into a state of depression.

How bad really were things? Well, Dave and his wife Sharon had asked if I had any materials on losing a pet for kids. The family dog had died, and the kids were taking it hard. Of course, I did know of the perfect book, a therapeutic coloring book designed to help kids process loss.

When later that week, I went to get the book to give them, I discovered a child had already started coloring a couple of pages with a marker. I literally had that one copy left. Due to my own edict forbidding the ordering of any materials until we got our budget under control, I could not order additional copies.

I had no other option. Using liquid white out, I covered the two or three magic marker spots.

I met Dave later that day and gave him the little bereavement book and apologized all over myself for its horrible condition. Two weeks later, I received a package in the mail. I was a little surprised because, well, I hadn't approved any purchase orders.

When I opened the box, brand-new coloring books spilled out onto my desk and sat there staring me in the face, the exact same one I had given to Dave for his kids. My eyes filled with tears.

Dave and I have never spoken about his gift. Even now, I get a lump in my throat thinking of his genuine kindness. I'm still touched and humbled. Dave absolutely saw not only my need but my unspoken desperation and threw me a life preserver. What might look like a seemingly small act of generosity to others spoke volumes to me of his belief in me and the value of our friendship. It gave me more hope than I think he ever knew. (Thank you, my friend!)

The Ramseys remain great friends of ours. Our families have made some great memories together since our Eagle days, including many a summer on Tims Ford Lake here in Tennessee. Dave is quite the water skier and actually taught our kids how to ski out on Percy Priest Lake. In fact, Dave taught all of the Eagles' kids how to ski.

Heaven-Sized Impressions of True Friends Who Leave a Lifetime of Imprints

"One who has unreliable companions soon comes to ruin, but there is a friend that sticks, (regardless of the season, situation, or time), closer than any brother" (Proverbs 18:24).

The true wealth of one's life is not in how many material possessions they might acquire, but it's in having a handful of true close friends that are present with you throughout each season of life and willing to walk out life with you ("Mauckism").

Over the years I have been blessed with some amazing lifelong friends, ones who I can call on in a moment's notice, and I know they would be there for me and I as well for them.

Lifetimers—Those Cherished Old Friends Who Go Way Back!

Lifetimers are those lifelong friends who don't require a call from each other every day, but there is such a strong life connection with them that you think of them often. You pick right back up from the last time you spoke, regardless of the amount of time since you last saw each other. I have about ten or so dear lifelong friends like this, most (except one) around my same age, and some live very far from me. There's an inner bond between us that regardless of time, place, or position in life, we know nothing can separate us.

These longtime friends remind me of the classic gospel quartet song "Old Friends," sung by the Gaither Vocal Band. These old friends come in the form of a few first names like Greg, Ken, Dan, Pat, Don, and others etched throughout time. These are the people who God allowed me to build those lifelong connections whereby time, place, and circumstances could never break. These are the friends of mine who represent some of my most valued memories in that most have known me since I was just a child or adolescent. To have friends I have known most of my life, ranging from thirty to forty-five years, means more to me than hitting any lottery. They are invaluable to my life.

Recently, one of my lifetimer friends Greg Gardner had a challenging and difficult loss in his life. Greg's grandson Sabastian, a seven-year-old little boy, died while suffering from a rare intestinal disease called *Hirschsprung's disease*, which was a malfunction or dysfunction in the intestines since birth. Greg, his wife Raybecca, daughter Brittany, Sabastian's mom, and extended family learned to appreciate him over the last seven years. He learned to live his whole life being fed by a tube and had a bag that served as his colon. Other than this, he seemed to be like every other child seeking to play with his toys.

After giving Greg and the family a day or two to deal with their loss, I called Greg. He had been my lifetime friend since the age of three. I began to comfort him as best I could. I didn't say much at first, just listened to his heart. As he talked with me, I tried to hide my tears, but the more I tried, the more they came down my face like a waterfall. I realized I was feeling Greg's actual hurt and pain as he spoke.

Greg shared the emotional roller coaster. A week earlier, they were excited to take him to Nebraska for the transplant he needed from a donor. Afterward, they received the great news of how well the surgery went. But then a few days afterward, his brain would not wake up and accept the new intestinal organs.

He told me about the heart-warming "hero's walk." The entire hospital floor staff stood silently in honor against the walls as Sabastian's family walked behind his hospital bed for the last time prior to pulling out all the tubes. It would be the last goodbye from all who tried to help him.

I continued to struggle with my emotions so that I could simply hear the heart of this grandfather say goodbye to his only grandchild. I struggled to be strong for my dear friend who had fought so diligently, wishing so much that his grandson would live. Both the sorrow and joy of it all was evident.

I finally stopped the tears and began to joyfully share about Sabastian now facing another "Hero's Walk," a welcome in heaven. A new angel was being led to his new Heavenly home.

Greg's daughter Brittany had birthed a gift to their entire family, and the precious memories Sabastian, Greg, and his family experienced would forever be branded within their hearts. Sabastian's loss here on Earth would become heaven's gain. He left an everlasting imprint that Greg's family can one day eternally join as well.

As Greg completed sharing, I could envision his entire family lifting up their hands, giving back to the loving God this precious gift of life they were allowed to embrace, care for, and love for a season. In the midst of their loss, they could now find joy and solace in that Sabastian was now in the safe eternal arms of his Heavenly Father.

As dear friends, we both shared the reality and soberness that this earth is not our ultimate home. I have my dear friend Greg to thank for sharing one of his most amazing heaven-sized life imprints with me.

Brothers and Friends of Faith—The Inspirational Epiphany of Flying

I also have my band of brothers, folks who watch my back yet represent balance. They are the ones who sharpen iron upon iron. They encourage but also love me enough to challenge me, my worldview, beliefs, and round out my life by offering me a different perspective. These are the men who will acknowledge my most important life accomplishments yet keep me centered and humbled by not always agreeing with everything I say while respecting my right to my feelings.

Yes, some of these men represent the Eagles, but these brothers and friends of faith represent other men as well—business leaders, entrepreneurs, ministers, and other community leaders who own or understand what it takes to be a well-tested leader. These are guys who are no rubber-stamped friends, who are solid and walk and talk with a sound intentional mission, ones who will remind me of what's important and to pass on what really matters most to my children and grandchildren.

These are guys who love God and their fellow brothers of faith, men with first names like Dave, Mike, Tim, Ken, Jeff, Tom, Gene, Don, Dan, and Aaron. These are the kinds of friends who will remain faithful friends. They not only can challenge you but are open to being challenged as well.

Each of these men are invaluable friends in my life. We have shared our personal victories, losses, and what attributes lead to successful business opportunities. This group of men and the memories of Dave Ramsey opening up his entire boardroom next to his office all those years, despite being so busy, speaks volumes to me. I may no longer have all the Eagles to meet with, but the good news is I have other great men like Tim Clinton, Ken Abraham, and others like my successful cousin Mike. These men have inspired me to keep unearthing what God has birthed deep in my soul, even though I may only initially see these treasured dreams come true only through the eyes of my faith.

To this day, Dr. Tim Clinton is one of the most encouraging and futurist-thinking individuals I know, one who Dr. James Dobson has put in charge of his outreach radio ministries, and one who now inspires Ken Harrison, the Director of Promise Keepers, and hundreds of thousands of men all across our country. His personal affirmation and support are invaluable to men like myself—dads and husbands across America.

The same goes for Ken Abraham, an eighteen-time *New York Times* best-selling author and friend who helped me significantly while writing my book. In fact, Ken paced me several times to slow down and reflect, to realize a book of this topic and potential magnitude needed time to simmer. Like a good meal, it needed a lot of preparation, care, and reflection. I should ensure that all the savory juices of each page and chapter would whet the reader's appetite.

These great men spent time inspiring those like myself to seek life's highest watermark standard of excellence and stretch in order to reach greater heights in one's faith and walk with God. All these aforementioned men have helped me realize that God is not finished with any of us.

Now in reflection, looking behind me as to the vast great mountains and valleys I have crossed gives me a sense of humility and confidence and a clear view of the heavenly mountains and valleys yet still to fly.

Hang-Time Friends—Beloved Ones You and I Do Life With

Hang-time friends are those true beloved friends who unconditionally love us. These are the ones we seem to always find the time to do things with, folks who love to be with you. They're the ones with whom you like to attend ball games, go on a vacation, go to the movies, have picnics, play card games, golf, etc. These are the special couples with whom you attend and spend special occasions, such as your kid's graduation party, weddings, anniversaries, new grandbabies, and other special moments of celebration.

These are the kinds of friends and loved ones who will most likely be there when a loved one, such as a parent or a dear fellow friend or family member, passes away. They bake for you when you or your loved ones are sick, and they come to visit you at the hospital, buy your kids things, share in a special birthday, or put on a wedding shower for one of your daughters. They are the same ones who are the first to volunteer, and several, if not all of them, would be willing to carry your casket at your funeral.

These are the kinds of friends with last names like the Wilsons, Abernathys, Abrahams, Campbells, Rings, Sorbos, Sykes, Leixs, Robinsons, Harringtons, Rileys, and so many others, too many to name. They have and continue to leave imprints on me and those within my family. These are not just people who huddle and pray, but special ones who through their actions, walk through life with us. These are the endearing friends who came and served us dinners, cards, and called to show how much they really cared when Raye Ann was so ill with both her episodes of kidney stones surgery and more recently, a triangulated hernia. These are the cherished ones who become part of our extended family. They are considered invaluable parts of our life circle.

Speaking of extended loved ones' support, Brent, my brother-in-law, and his wife Dina remain so special to us. Brent's random acts of kindness to us and our immediate family this last year was very special and appreciated.

All these great friends and loved ones are who I thank God for during my sacred time of devotion as well as when we meet corporately, and I am asked to pray for our gathering. As we get together during the holidays or seasons of life, I remind God that these amazing people, called "our friends," are the truest riches and investments of time one could ever hope to be a part of or find.

I love my family; we are tight and always will be. But over the last five years, I've come to realize that both myself and many of my friends are losing some of our families' great patriarchs and matriarchs. We need the embrace and comfort of those who love us, and we, in turn, love them. I never had a biological brother, but I am so glad to know I am part of a group of friends who have loved, stuck closer to, and treated me kinder than any blood brothers I could have ever dreamed of or imagined having. That's why I love my hang-time friends!

I have lost some of my best lifetime heroes, mentors, and family friends within these four individuals: Paul Frazier, David Cavender, Landy Gardner, and Ernest Robertson. When I think of them, I'm reminded of the song "Friends" by Michael W. Smith.

Write out who your best friends are and what category you would place them as described below:

- Life-timers: Friends you have known for a lifetime
- Growth Friends: They love you enough to challenge you.
- Hang-Time Friends: People you do life with every day

Safety in Numbers

One of the best-kept secrets of our company is our board of directors, who serve as counsel to me both professionally and personally. I have been and am fortunate to have great men and women serve on the LifeCare board.

God was faithful to bring individuals with the expertise I did not possess to join in accomplishing His purposes for LifeCare. The diverse gifting and skills of those who serve have saved me from tumbling over a few dangerous cliffs due to lack of experience in many areas. Each one brings so much more to my life than just business savvy and experience. I view them a lot like the elders or deacons in a church. I'm reminded of Proverbs 11:14, "Where there is no counsel, the people fall; but in the multitude of counselors there is safety" (MEV).

These people were and are spiritual leaders, wise counsel, and accountability for the LifeCare family of companies, and in many cases, me personally.

Don Evans
Chairman of the Board
Life Coach and Mentor
LifeCare Foundations Board of Directors for Family Services
Visionary and Servant Leader

Don and his wife Barb have known me since I was ten years old when our families first met in Flint, Michigan. As a mentor and second father figure in my life over the last fifty years, he has been a gracious, unofficial life coach to me. Imprints of service, honesty, God, and family-first have been left on me simply by watching my friend live his life for Jesus.

One of his greatest attributes is having a servant's heart. Don would give you the shirt off his back if he thought you needed it. No act of service was too small, including quietly coming over and cleaning out our rain gutters and trimming hedges when I didn't have the time.

He's been known to take care of a task and never say a word about it later. Without a doubt, Don Evans continues to be one of the most giving men I have ever met and is a phenomenal chairman of the board.

Bill Campbell
Board Member, LifeCare Family Services
Business Life Coach and Entrepreneur
Mediator, Collaborator, and Man of High Integrity, Wisdom, and Foresight

I've known Bill and his wife Kathy for over twenty-five years. Bill joined the LifeCare Family board of directors in 2010, and he has served as our chairman since 2013. His focus on creating a financial environment built on strong positive cash flow has saved not only LifeCare but also many other companies who have found themselves in a distressed cash-flow situation.

His wisdom, troubleshooting, and mediation skills have been vital in finding amicable win-win solutions throughout the company, whether in a board meeting or dealing with contract issues. His most significant role in my life over the last eight years, however, has been in serving as my career and life coach. Raye and I count Bill and Kathy as a couple who has become a team of one of our most cherished friendships.

Dan Finley
Board of Directors, Secretary, LifeCare Foundations
Heart and Compassion

Dan's compassion for the disadvantaged fuels his advocacy for those with learning challenges, handicap challenges, and those suffering from mental illness. He's a man with a tremendous heart who serves from a place of love.

Dan does not hesitate to go the extra mile to accommodate someone in need. We have known each other for over twenty-eight years now since that first meeting at Trinity Elementary. If you'll remember, Dan was one of the confirmations God sent my way in those early Nashville days and remains one of my dearest friends.

Jeff Parrish
Board of Directors, New Project Management
LifeCare Foundations
Doer, Jack-of-All-Trades, Family Friend

Prior to joining our board of directors, Jeff was my neighbor. As I got to know him, I realized we needed his specific skill set in terms of buildouts and maintenance issues. Jeff knows how to fix just about anything. Not only that, he understands the world of renovation, construction, and building codes. When LifeCare needed a repair, Jeff was right there to offer a cost-effective solution. On top of that, he is also a confidant to me.

Jeff and his wife Darlene are treasured family friends. In fact, my parents and I have semi-adopted them into our family. Without question, Jeff is one of the hardest working men I've had the privilege of knowing.

Bruce Bode
Board Member, LifeCare Foundations
Kingdom Minded with a 40,000-Foot Perspective

Bruce has a passion for kingdom work. His "heart-and-head" approach to every decision involves both understanding God's purposes and thinking through every angle possible before moving forward. Many times, Bruce has asked the important questions no one else has considered, and it's prompted a shift or change in the direction we go. He doesn't merely work toward solutions. His goal is the absolute best answer, and he has an uncanny ability to see the bigger picture.

Bruce's understanding of government, housing regulations, and legal issues have been essential to the growth of LifeCare. His friendship is invaluable to both Raye Ann and me.

Eddy Richey
Former Chairman of the Board of Directors,
LifeCare Family Services
Wisdom, Discernment, and Business Sense

Although no longer an active board member, Eddy was a vital member during one of our most difficult seasons in the history of our company. His personal encouragement as well as his wisdom in charting a path through our most troubling circumstances helped our company remain intact.

His leadership and wisdom forged a plan that moved our company from being in jeopardy in 2009, to a safe harbor. I'm not sure where we would be today without Eddy's contributions to Lifecare during that time. So, if I've never said it before, I'll say it now—from the bottom of my heart, thank you, Eddy.

Rebecca Foster
LifeCare Advisor
Advocate for Senior Care Services
Character and Integrity

Rebecca is exceptionally knowledgeable in the area of aging and issues of elderly care. Over the last ten years, Rebecca has kept me apprised of assessments, transitions, and appropriate care issues for our seniors. She has tangible, firsthand experience in understanding and navigating these areas in the insurance and health care system, having been the primary caretaker for our Aunt Wanda and Aunt Marce. Even in the middle of difficult personal circumstances, my cousin has always been available with exceptional insight when I had a question regarding caring for the elderly.

Ernest Robertson
Treasurer, LifeCare and LifeCare Foundations
Encouragement and Dependability

I have been truly blessed by my in-laws Ernie and Anne. Ernie handled the buildout of our first office in Smyrna in 1997, with the help of my father Louie. Ernie also served on both our LifeCare Family and LifeCare Foundation's boards for over twenty-two years. In fact, he was the first official board member for our companies. In those twenty-two years of service, he missed only one meeting, and that was due to an email server going down, preventing him from receiving the email about a date and time change. On my birthday, June 4, 2018, Ernie passed away, and I miss him every day.

Navigating Your Story

I realize daily how blessed I am to live and walk through life with so many great people. Whether building a company or building your life, surrounding yourself with the right people is essential. Outside of family, these are the people you do life with, the people who know you, sometimes better than you know yourself, the people who aren't afraid to challenge you or present you with the opposing side or push back.

When I joined the Eagles, I didn't join a group of "yes-men" who all had the same opinions and beliefs. These men held varied views on government, business, religion, and the world. In sharing and expressing differences of opinion, an air of respect and a desire to understand was present in the room.

So how do you find your own crew? The saying, "Birds of a feather flock together" comes to mind. First, you need to be the kind of crew member you want to have.

Availability

Time. Such a valuable commodity these days. We are pulled in every direction by family, by work, by church, by the world. Many things that demand our time and beckon for our attention are good things, but are they all God things for us? That is the question.

To that end, I've learned that God is more interested in our availability than our abilities, accumulations, and accomplishments. While I've done my best to walk in wisdom, more importantly, I've simply tried to make my time and efforts available to keep myself focused and dedicated to the calling and purpose, to opportunities that furthered that purpose, to the people who help carry them out, and to those impacted by my purpose. I didn't know any better than to not give up. I just kept making myself available.

Are you available?

Passion and Purpose

What *are* the God things? Knowing the difference between a good thing and a God thing is so that you can save yourself from meaningless pursuits, wasted efforts, and lack of impact. It protects you from unnecessary overcommitment because purpose gives a lens that thoroughly evaluates every opportunity.

What energizes you? What stimulates your creativity? What excites you when you wake up in the morning? What do you find yourself wishing you were doing?

Conversely, what drains you? What sucks the life out of you? What makes you wish you were doing something else?

Knowing these things about yourself are crucial to keeping your decisions in line with your passion and purpose. I highly recommend you determine your mission statement so that you can define your passion and purpose further.

What are your passion and purpose?

Accountability

As the saying goes, so goes the truth. No man is an island. Men tend to be self-sufficient and self-contained. The power of wealth, lust, and love of money that men face are very real. It follows that it is of the utmost importance for you to have men who also face the same temptations as you yet overcame it. They are people who hold you accountable so you don't succumb.

For me, this was the Eagles, not yes-men. It's men who will check in with you, check under your hood, make sure you're running on all cylinders. I don't mean that as a sexist statement to the exclusion of women but one based on my own experience as a man.

Make no mistake, man or woman, the more you pursue your godly purpose and calling, the more the enemy pursues you. You need these people in your life.

Do you have accountability built into your life?

Faithfulness

Faithfulness is the cousin of availability. Faithfulness implies stability, dependability, and devotion to someone or something. Without faithfulness, being available can be a passing feeling, a whim, something that comes and goes. If your availability isn't secured faithfully to your passion and purpose, any task potentially becomes a burden. It gets less than your best.

When faithfulness is tied to your passion, to quote Winston Churchill, you will, "Never, never give up!"

Whether starting a business, developing a ministry, focusing on family, fatherhood, motherhood, or your marriage, faithfulness is the devotion and determination to walk with integrity and see it through to its full potential.

Are you faithful?

Charted Steps

1. First, think about the answers to the four questions above. Are you available? What are your passion and purpose? Do you have accountability in your life? Are you faithful to your passion and purpose? Write down your thoughts, pray over your answers, and ask the Lord for clarity.
2. Think about your crew or the people you invite to speak into your life. Write down the names of three to five individuals who support or would support you as well as share your vision and purpose. These are people with whom you do life and on whom you can depend. If you are already working toward a common goal, let them know how much you appreciate them and their contributions toward it. Share your dreams with them and let them pray for God's guidance as you move ahead.

3. Identify your Eagles. Name three to five people in your life who love you, who keep you accountable, provide guidance and support to you, and who you would give permission to speak into your life. If you aren't already in an accountability relationship with them, pray about approaching these people to put some structure and purpose around your relationships.

CHAPTER 10

The Admirals Club

"If I have seen further than others, it is by standing on the shoulders of giants."

— ISAAC NEWTON

"YA KNOW, KENNY, THIS DIDN'T JUST HAPPEN."

With a potted shrub in hand, my friend Don stood next to me on the sidewalk in front of my new home in a beautiful, wooded subdivision in Smyrna, Tennessee. He viewed the landscape, surveying the results of his green thumb in action while wiping the sweat off his forehead with his sleeve.

Shaking my head in agreement while handing him a drink of water, I agreed. "No, no it didn't, Don. Thanks so much. I'd be lost without your green thumb and help throughout the years."

"I don't mean the yard," he chuckled, nodding toward the beautiful home in front of us as he knelt down to pick up some bush trimming nearby where he had been working.

I contemplated his response while watching this wonderful mentor who has served others his entire life. Then my gaze turned to the house.

For decades, Don Evans has encouraged me to excel and challenged me to step outside my comfort zone. He and my dad taught me to play golf, but the lessons of hard work and service to others, these are the lessons I learned about life from them, lessons that were far greater than any games of golf we ever played.

When I considered following in his footsteps and getting my master's degree, he said, "You can do this." Don was instrumental in me landing my first teaching job. It was Don and his wife who helped Raye and me pack up when we moved from Flint to Nashville. Don eventually moved to Nashville and encouraged me when I had nothing but a dream and $750 to start LifeCare,

"You can do this," he would tell me.

After twenty-three years of working sometimes sixty-five hours a week, way too long, I realize there's an imprint since age ten standing right in from of me, my life mentor, one who's been an affirming influence, encouraging me, stretching me, and lending hands of support like this morning in my yard. I have watched him all my life doing what he does best, serving those he loves, and I smiled with a twinkle in my eye.

"No, this didn't just happen, did it, Don?"

Influencers

Influencers come into our lives and change our trajectory. They show us the possibilities, lead us to the edge of ourselves, and inspire us to become more.

Influencers challenge us so that we won't be content with the status quo. They motivate us to forge into new territory, to create a legacy like no other for those who come behind us just as they have done before us.

I've had many influencers in my life, a few of whom are listed in this chapter. Some, like Don, entered my life naturally through regular everyday circumstances. I was a student; he was a teacher. I intentionally sought out others for a specific purpose or advice, and in the end, gained a mentor and friend as I did with Dr. Tim Clinton.

Dr. Tim Clinton
American Association of Christian Counselors
President and Executive Director of the American Association of Christian Counselors (AACC)
CEO of Dr. James Dobson's Family Talk Radio and Institute

Making a difference in the lives of others was my primary goal as Director of Counseling at Christ Church in 1996. I set out on a quest to connect with as many like-minded ministries and people as I could. I wanted to learn everything possible from those who had already built counseling networks and were already making a difference in other cities, states, and even on the national level.

I scoured not only my home state of Tennessee, but also national databases for people and organizations that fit the bill. After compiling my list, I decided to start with a national organization in Virginia, to glean what I could from their incorporation of counseling and care into their national ministry. I went to The 700 Club to visit Pat Robertson, thinking maybe they had counselors there. Then I learned their focus was on prayer. I was a little disappointed until that next morning when I remembered someone I had heard speak at an AACC conference.

His name was Tim Clinton, and he was then the Vice President of the American Association of Christian Counselors (AACC). I thought, *It will only take another day to get from Virginia Beach, so what do I have to lose?*

I called and left a message for Dr. Clinton to please return my call. I shared I was now the Director of Counseling at a large mega church and felt I needed his guidance. After hanging up, I thought, *The worst thing that can happen is he won't return my call.*

To my amazement, not only did he return my call, he asked me to be sure and visit him in Forest, Virginia. So, I did. Tim showed me around the town of Lynchburg and Liberty University where he had completed his undergraduate work. He then gave me a tour of his own counseling practice in Forest and suggested we go to lunch after the tour. *That's when I learned Tim was a visionary.*

He talked about his role as a leader of the Liberty University Counseling Program and listened as I told him about my fledgling company and my dreams. More importantly, through the course of our conversation, Tim opened my eyes to the opportunities and the national potential for faith-based mental health professional services and organizations.

Turns out, Tim Clinton was the real reason I was supposed to go to Virginia. I learned something else that trip. Chutzpah. Sometimes, you just have to make the big ask... or the big call. If there is someone you know you can learn from, that you know will help you carry out your calling and God-given dream, in humility, get yourself in front of them. Learn from them.

What if I had chickened out and hadn't made that call, excused it away or even let my disappointment at my original reason for traveling to Virginia, shut me down? I would have missed out on not just a great learning opportunity, but an amazing mentorship and a lifelong friendship.

Tim is now President of the American Association of Christian Counselors. Under his visionary leadership, the AACC is now the largest and fastest growing international Christian counseling network and conference organization in the world. Over the last twenty-two years of our friendship, I've had the honor to take a front-row seat to the unfolding of his vision for his practice and the mental health care landscape in America and globally. Tim's an inspiration to watch, and his mentorship has been an indispensable asset as I have navigated the growth of my own large faith-based mental, physical, and health care company.

Tim and I have had similar experiences in our walk with God. Both of us realized the need to be ourselves and not attempt to follow after or emulate someone else's faith to encounter God personally.

Tim shared this special story about how his dad was his great influencer throughout his lifetime. He wrote:

> *My greatest influencer would have to be my father, Reverend James Clinton. My dad was a larger-than-life man and an integral part of my understanding faith and God. One of the greatest gifts Dad ever gave me was his emphasis on keeping God and family first in life. This is our Clinton family heritage.*
>
> *When Dad became seriously ill, I fell into a season of questioning. Why was God taking Dad now? How would I stand in my faith without him to hold me up? I shared my doubts and questions with my dad. I told him this was too hard, and I couldn't imagine my life without him in it. Dad encouraged me, telling me that my understanding would grow over time. Honestly, I wasn't exactly sure about that answer.*
>
> *After Dad's passing, I went away to a favorite retreat, an old family cabin in the Pennsylvania mountains. I needed time and space to process and come to grips with losing such an important part of my life. While there, I questioned God about a lot of things and actually left*

a little disappointed because I felt I hadn't heard back. But as I was coming down the mountain to head home, God spoke to my heart with this question: "Will I be the God of your father to you or be the God of you and your father?"

Breakthrough. In that moment, I released my heart fully and completely, a gift I'm sure Dad was smiling about from heaven.

Ken Abraham
Eighteen-Time *New York Times* Best-Selling Author
National Speaker

Ken was an Eagle and remains an "iron sharpens iron" friend. Through the years, we've encouraged each other as fathers, husbands, and Christian men walking out our faith in professions that constantly challenge our Christian worldview. I've watched Ken and his wife Lisa actively live their faith day in and day out for over twenty-three years and how they have poured into family, those they lead at church, and into their community.

Writing this book has stretched me every way possible, and my friend Ken's expertise and advice as a best-selling author have been extremely helpful on this journey. For a guy who is one of the most prolific writers, with publishers, well-known celebrities, and leaders clamoring for him to write their next book, Ken is one of the most unassuming, humble people I know.

A man of integrity, he carefully chooses his work, never compromising his beliefs just to take on a writing project or endorse a book when asked. You'll never hear Ken drop a name in a conversation. So, I'll do it for him. Ken's best-seller list includes: *Let's Roll!* with Lisa Beamer; *No Dream Is Too High* with Astronaut Buzz Aldrin; *Your Best Life Now* by Joel Olsteen; *Between Heaven and the Real World* with Steven Curtis Chapman; *Against All Odds* with Chuck Norris;

True Faith and Allegiance by Attorney General Roberto Gonzalez; and a wonderful book he personally wrote titled *When Your Parent Becomes Your Child* that chronicles with humor and care, Ken's own experiences and challenges in caring for his mother who suffered from Alzheimer's disease.

One of Ken's legacy influencers came from his college days, and he wrote the following about him:

> *Dr. Dennis Kinlaw, President of Asbury College, has been one of the most influential people in my life. Dr. Kinlaw's life itself was an example to me of what a Christian man should be. His ability to articulate his knowledge of God's Word encouraged me in my biblical studies at Asbury and encouraged me to be the best writer I could be.*

Don Marsh
University of South Florida, Assistant Track Coach

One of the most enthusiastic, encouraging men and influencers of my life is my former Kearsley High School Track Coach, Don Marsh. Coach Marsh personally invested himself in his athletes, coming out onto the track, arms pumped up in the air, whooping it up, and clapping as we arrived. He stretched out with us, jogged around the track with us (still clapping his hands enthusiastically), and gave us the proverbial slap on the back while exclaiming, "It's a great day, gentlemen!"

Coach Marsh ran right alongside us, striking up a conversation, asking how our day was, how we were doing, and spurring us onto a great practice. Coach was always prepared with a plan for each of us that was specific to our event. Even in a highly individualized sport, Coach Marsh always stressed the impact of our individual performance on the team as a whole.

Coach saw something in me even when I couldn't see it myself. I was a hard worker but didn't have a lot of confidence in myself as a runner. He pushed me beyond what I thought possible. It paid off.

Looking back, I can see how Coach wasn't just invested in me as an athlete; he poured himself into me as a young man off the track. He encouraged me to excel academically and found qualities in each and every one of his athletes outside of track to applaud. Coach attended my graduation party, came to my wedding, and bought gifts for both. I'm quite sure I'm not the only one.

His investment in me continued paying dividends in my life. When things got tough at Mott Community College, the University of Michigan, or while pursuing my master's degree, I could still hear Coach Marsh's words of encouragement reverberating in my mind: "Don't give up. Get back up and run like the wind. That hurdle was just another obstacle to fly over."

If I got discouraged by losing a race, I could always depend on Coach Marsh to remind me that there was another race coming soon, and that my team needed me to forget about the last running event and to get up and get prepared for the next one. This happened to me as a CEO as well, having to recover from a million-dollar loss incurred by our company. The qualities of perseverance and endurance my coach reinforced in me kicked in and carried me through. We eventually recouped most of our loss with commerce and insurance as our company weathered the worst financial time in its history. I had to shake it off and remember to "get up" and keep fighting. It was truly a "watermark" moment.

Don Marsh is in his twenty-first year as an assistant coach at the University of South Florida (USF), specializing in the pole vault and long jump. He has coached seven All-Americans, fourteen national qualifiers, sixteen conference qualifiers, sixteen conference champions, and four regional qualifiers. Before USF, Don coached three years at Saginaw Valley State University, where he had four All Americans in the high jump, pole vault, and 400 meters. Before Saginaw, Don coached at Flint's Kearsley High School for twenty-five years, building one of the premier track-and-field programs in the state of Michigan. He's Michigan's Track Coach of the Year for 1974, 1978, and 1992, in addition to the entire Midwest Track Coach of the Year in 1992. He was also a finalist National High School Track Coach of the Year in 1992, and was inducted into Michigan's Track Coaches Hall of Fame 1998, with multiple honors.

I asked Coach Marsh who he considered the top influencer in his life, and he wrote back with two:

> *Without a doubt, my dad is at the top of the list. A quiet, principled man, I learned self-discipline through his example. Dad attended all my high school and college meets when he could, always the encourager but never trying to motivate me by pushing too hard.*
>
> *My dad was one of the most intelligent men I knew and could do things I couldn't with a master's degree. The fact that Dad came from humble beginnings and only had an eighth-grade education only makes me love and respect him more for who he was and what he did for his family. I miss my Dad every day!*
>
> *Number two on my list is my own high school coach Mac Gobel, the legendary football and track coach from my high school in Charlotte, Michigan. When I went out for track in ninth grade, I was scared because of his reputation of being a tough disciplinarian. But we became close, and he helped me prepare to win the state championship in the quarter-mile and encouraged me to run at Michigan State University. He was also the one who suggested I teach and coach, which led me to fifty-eight years of coaching track. I still think of him and the life lessons he taught me to this day!*

Eric Strickland
Three-Legged Stool (3LS), President and CEO

In the fall of 2013, I began to think about the long-term interests of LifeCare Family Services employees and staff. Our company was doing great in terms of contracts and net revenue. However, I needed an exit strategy that provided an excellent retirement program for all our employees, not just the executives of the company who could afford an independent retirement plan.

An associate introduced me to Eric Strickland. He thought Eric's innovative strategies for retirement for his own company might be something that might work for LifeCare. On a beautiful fall day, I met with the young CEO and President of Omni Visions. I told Eric I was looking for a good retirement program for my employees and had been told he had some creative solutions.

Eric, in turn, explained that his company was an employee-owned company, offering each employee ownership in the form of stocks. Those who remained faithful for the long term would receive significant payouts at retirement. I spoke with some of the employees planning to retire who confirmed that the plan was indeed working well.

When I first contacted Eric, I didn't know that Omni was looking to partner with a company like ours. Turns out, our companies were a perfect fit. On October 1, 2014, Eric and I shook hands as LifeCare and Omni became one of the largest growing child and family programs in Tennessee, and the Southeast region. Currently, we are looking at working together to expand nationwide over the next decade.

I am ten years Eric's senior; nonetheless, he is one of the wisest men I know, not only in business but also as a leader. Eric knows how to empower those he leads. I am thankful God has chosen to bring us together as partners.

What began as seeking advice ended in finding not only precisely what I was looking for—a long-term solution for our employees—but also a long-term solution for the company, one that allows our legacy company to land safely under Eric's wise and visionary leadership. Eric will take our company to new heights in providing excellent care for millions of children and families.

When asked who the most influential person in his life has been, here's what Eric had to say:

> *The most impactful person in my life is my father Louis "Butch" Strickland, a humble migrant farm worker from Northwest Georgia, with a servant's heart. Butch wanted to study accounting but chose to work to take care of us, his family. His faithful commitment to family and his willingness to work long, hard hours characterize the great man my dad was.*
>
> *My father also coached me in baseball and basketball and served as a scoutmaster, guiding many young men to Eagle Scout honors. He earned the highest adult scouting honor as a "Silver Beaver," all while working more than full-time at a ten-to-twelve-dollar-an-hour job.*
>
> *I'll always remember my dad for his strong character. Every day of his life, he proved to me that no matter where you are by the world's standards, you can make a huge difference in the life of others!*

Mark White
Representative, Tennessee State House of Representatives

"May I call you Dad?" These five words written on a Post-It Note embody a lifetime of work for my friend Mark White.

I have known Mark White since he was elected to the Tennessee House of Representatives in 2010. As a representative for the Memphis area, Mark channels his passion for at-risk children into authored bills and amendments supporting our most vulnerable children in foster care, health care, and behavioral health care services. In an area that trends Democratic, a Republican and a man of godly character has earned the trust of his constituents and their vote by representing the district well. Mark is deeply respected on both sides of the aisle.

His passion for at-risk children took an unexpected turn on a mission trip with his church to Panama. Poverty created a cycle of teen pregnancy, children without father figures to look up to, and youth becoming enslaved in trafficking. Very few opportunities for education existed. Moved by the extended effects of poverty on Panamanian children and families, Mark immediately began laying the groundwork for a nonprofit to provide future educational opportunities with the goal of helping families break the cycle of poverty. Today, his nonprofit ensures children the opportunity for education at the elementary, middle, and high school levels, and even college.

Mark and his family have had the privilege of hosting children assisted by his nonprofit. One such child came to Tennessee, for a college visit with her mother and spent a few days with the White family. Shortly after her departure, Mark found an envelope addressed to him. Unfolding the letter inside, a bright-pink sticky note at the bottom caught his attention. It read, "May I call you Dad?" For hundreds of children in Panama, this is the real impact of Mark's work.

Mark's main influencer in his life was his dad. He wrote the following:

"While there are many people in each of our lives we could mention who influence us to be the kind of person we become, I will highlight my father Hoyt White as my main influencer. When I was five years old, my father moved our family from Union City, Tennessee, to Nashville to attend David Lipscomb College, and he never turned back from ministry or from his dedication to preaching the Gospel.

Growing up observing his faith, seeing it lived out as he led our family, taught me the importance of a strong Christ-centered father in the home. His example inspired my book May I Call You Dad: Why Fathers Are Needed in the Home. Having worked with children as a teacher, principal, and in mission work, I have learned that the absence of a father, especially a Christ-centered father, leaves a child lacking in their ability to meet the responsibilities and challenges of life. I learned from my father that we must be engaged in all areas: the home, the church, community, and politics. Most social ills that face our communities today could be addressed by a responsible, God-fearing father in the home."

One Thing in Common

Each of these people is an admiral in my book. From entry-level positions, each has worked their way up the ranks, plotted a course, built a powerful team, weathered the storms, and became successful in life. Each one of them has powerfully shaped my personal life and affected the course of LifeCare. Some I can say, "I knew them when..." Others were already at the top of their game when the Lord directed me to their door at just the right time, when I needed guidance and education on specific areas outside of my scope or training.

In each of these great individual leaders' stories, one thing stands out to me. One common thread the majority shared was that they all had an influential father figure. When asked about influencers in their own lives, the majority included their dad on the list. While having a strong parental figure is indeed not a prerequisite for success, it does emphasize the importance of the role many of us hold in our own children's lives while they are with us and then continue on once they embark on their own voyage.

My own list of top influencers would be incomplete without adding some of my individual family members, including my father and father-in-law. Not every man can count his father-in-law among the positive influencers in his life. I am fortunate to be one who can.

Ernest Robertson
My Father-in-Law
His Amazing Bronze Star Earned in Vietnam War, and We Never Knew It!

Action movies were a love of my father-in-law Ernie. That's why about a month or so before his passing, I had called him and suggested we spend the day together watching a few of his favorites at the movie theatre. During our lunch break, I decided to choose my words carefully and ask him about something he had never discussed. I said, "Ern, I know you might not want to talk about it, but I want to ask you about your time in the service and your tour in Vietnam. I don't want to push, but if you would, it would be an honor to hear your story."

Ernie stared off into the distance for a moment as if going back deep in time and then thoughtfully began. "Well, there was one time we were setting up for camp along a river, and we saw the Viet Cong on the other side setting up mortars and larger guns. We thought it might be a rough night because through our high-powered binoculars, it looked like the guns might be pointed at our position. We figured if we're watchin' them, they're watchin' us. So, we found a little bunker that was hidden behind some trees that we thought was out of the sight of any scouts. But only six men could fit comfortably in it and lie down if necessary, and yet there were fifteen of us that needed shelter. So, we told the men to go back and just act normal, like they were settling in for the night to sleep, but once night fell, to quickly and quietly fall back about a hundred yards to the bunker.

"Just as soon as night fell, sure enough, the shelling and rounds were coming in from everywhere on the area we had all originally selected to sleep. Machine gunfire was zipping, bombs exploding, grenade launchers launching, and all kinds of firepower came in all around us. We could hear it hitting our enclosed cement barrier outside. Yet all fifteen of us were safely crammed eye to eye in this bunker, not making a sound. The shooting finally stopped in the wee hours of the morning while it was still dark, and we snuck out of there as fast as we could, back to our larger unit."

Ernie sat there after talking, lost in his thoughts for a moment. Then I broke the silence and said, "Ern, you keep saying, 'we,' but I believe you were the only demolition expert in the platoon and the only one with binoculars that day who understood positions and traps from enemy artillery. It was you who saved those men that night."

He turned his head with an uncomfortable smile and watery eyes. That was my father-in-law's way, not wanting to take credit. Up until his death, I had thought Ernie had earned a medal of some kind, but he never talked about it with us. Not only did I find out he earned a bronze star, we now know he actually was awarded four bronze stars. I think I know how he earned them now—part of it had to do with what he did that night by saving all his fellow brothers in arms.

Ernie and my father were the ones who built out our garage as our first office in Smyrna, Tennessee, in 1997. That was just like him, using his skills as a carpenter to serve and love his family. Ernie also built a treehouse for the kids and a deck with a screened-in porch. When we opened up any of our new direct-care offices, he was there, building out rooms, putting together tables, computer desks, and filing cabinets.

Ernie loved spending time with his son Brent, fishing and hunting. He hid little miniature cars in his pockets for his great-grandchildren to find and loved to beat all of us in the card game Euchre. His wife of forty-two years, Ann, his daughter Raye, and his son Brent and their families were his life.

My father-in-law Ernie Robertson died on June 4, 2018, while I was in the middle of writing this book. Ernie served on both boards (LifeCare Foundations and LifeCare Family Services) for over twenty-two years.

Brad and Candy Rainwater
My Sister and Brother-in-Law

Brad and Candy have huge hearts and an exceptional ability and capacity to love unconditionally. For years, they have done just that. Brad's varied coaching positions in both track and football and his enjoyment in taking advantage of the opportunities to show his unconditional love on student athletes were important to him. Some of these athletes had been given a clinical label of a learning or social disability, yet they have managed to overcome the stigma due to both my sister Candy and Brad's affirming ways. Many times, they have been more of an adopted mom and dad or aunt and uncle image to kids who come from broken homes or who might need to build more confidence in their lives.

An Exceptional Grandson and Grandchildren

Brad and Candy's love is not just centered on helping other children. It starts in their own home. They love all the grandchildren with the love of not just grandparents, but true roles models as evidenced by Candy picking all seven of them up every Wednesday night for church or for the musicals she conducted and wanted them all to participate in. As a result, they recently went to a national drummers talent contest in Florida. Their grandson Bradley has been diagnosed as legally blind since birth. Yet with Brad and Candy cheering him on and being present with hands-on assistance, Bradley has learned to ride a bike, become an excellent student, wrestled, played piano, and recently was granted only one of four Michigan gold-star medal as an exceptional athlete recognized as to his abilities in the pole vault. Bradley has no fear in pole vaulting, thanks to the love that Brad and Candy have modeled before him.

Finally, Brad and Candy took me in as a young University of Michigan student finishing my bachelor's degree with no other place to live. It's a way of life for them—providing a safe place, meals, and a bed, and for listening to and actually helping someone in need. I have watched as my sister and her husband put love into action by doing and being there for so many like myself. Their imprints of love are known throughout their entire community.

Brad and Candy have not only provided a safe harbor, but a lighthouse and beacon of hope to so many.

"Big Lou" and Melonee Mauck
My Parents

Without question, my parents have been the most influential of anyone in my life. Every day, I carry with me the love, support, commitment, and encouragement I experienced as a child.

My mom has been a living example of true "unconditional love." She has prayed with and for me since I was a child at bedtime and while I slept. She fixed my favorite foods, pretended to feed my imaginary friend, and made sure I always had clean clothes for school and church and a clean uniform for all my sports practices and games.

When I was sick, Mom fixed me her famous potato soup, her favorite healing recipe. I aced writing papers all throughout school, mainly because Mom applied her editing skills and attention to detail before I turned anything in, helping me correct what I had missed.

More importantly, it was watching the way Mom lived her life and sowed into others that influenced me most. I heard my mom spend untold hours on phone calls while I played on the kitchen floor. She wasn't talking as much as she was listening to friends and family pour out troubles and hurts. Mom gave her friends encouraging words of comfort, affirmation, and prayers. She was there for them. All those caught listening skills built by watching my mom just be who she was growing up are now a part of my DNA.

I don't believe I would have been a therapist, writer, or a speaker if not for the influence of my mother's example. Although a sermon from my pastor and a promise to an inner-city child pushed me to start a faith-based agency, it was actually my mom's continual encouragement that prompted me to actually walk out the door and start the process of beginning our company at LifeCare.

My father was a wonderful influence on my life as well. We always enjoyed tossing the football or him showing myself or my sisters how to ride a bike.

The pain of his own story gave him perspective and purpose in his own life and only strengthened his commitment to our own family. Growing up without his own father and lacking the paternal affirmations we are wired to receive fueled my father's determination not to repeat the same pattern. Unlike his father before him, he has kept that promise for over sixty-three years. That kind of commitment left an indelible mark on our family.

When Dad moved to Nashville from Michigan, after retiring, I approached him with the idea of assisting with the building and grounds needs of LifeCare. The company had started purchasing buildings instead of leasing space, and the demand for someone to oversee the facilities was growing. The ex-CEO in Dad rose to the occasion, accepting and accomplishing every task asked of him, and he has continued to do so for over eighteen years.

Dad has made his mark on not only the company but also the people of LifeCare during those years. His commitment, encouragement, and sense of humor have earned him the nickname "Big Lou."

I love both my parents and would never be the man I am today had my father and mother not influenced my life in so many great ways.

Navigating Your Story

Each influencer listed has spoken into my life at a critical juncture, at a time when I needed to know more, do more, be more than I was in that moment. I wish I could say that every time I found myself in that place, I was prepared to hear what I needed to hear and see what I needed to see.

Three words come to mind when I think about those times. I've had to be completely open when I've heard and seen beyond myself and moved forward in significant ways.

Motivation

Both external and internal forces motivate us to pursue knowledge and change. For me, they were do or die, sink or swim, stay where I was and be safe, or step out in faith and take the risk to go to the next level. These were times when I found myself highly motivated, and the Lord brought just the right person into my life, the person with the skills and knowledge I needed to learn to take the work He had given me further than I ever could have on my own.

When we lost our largest client and were sitting on seven digits of accounts receivables owed?

I was literally faced with layoffs, major cutbacks, and potentially closing the doors. This was the season I gave the used children's book to Dave Ramsey. My motivation to survive was extremely high. That's when Mark White came into my life, helping us navigate the legal system... and I learned.

When I realized the vision the Lord had for Lifecare far surpassed my own?

I had a choice to settle for where we were or pay attention and be obedient to the calling on my life. The promise I made to Carlos continued to be my motivation to move forward instead of settling. It drove me to learn everything I could about the national platform for mental health care and guided me to Virginia. It was the Lord who led me to Tim Clinton while there... and I learned.

What is your current motivation?

Teachability

All the right information can be swirling around you; all the right people can be in proximity; everything you need to succeed at whatever it is God has called you to do might be right there at your fingertips. But it's worthless if you don't have a teachable heart.

Being teachable is a foundational part of growth—in character development, personally and in business. Without the quality and heart position of being teachable, it doesn't matter who comes across your path; you won't hear or accept what they have to offer.

Listening is a skill so lacking in today's culture, but it is an essential quality in a teachable person. A good listener *is not distracted and is present in the moment.* Are you focused on what the other person is saying or on what you are having for lunch, what you are going to say next, or your to-do list for the rest of the day? Are you constantly checking your phone, or do you put your phone on *Do Not Disturb* during meetings and conversations with others? Better yet, do you leave it out of sight all together? Are you continually paying more attention to what's going on around you and who is walking by than the person in front of you?

A good listener does not interrupt, finish others' sentences, or derail the conversation. It follows that if you're actively listening, you'll have questions. You'll respond to what's being said authentically, both verbally and through body language but not at the expense of finishing the other party's sentences.

Are you teachable?

Humility

Above all else, humility. Humility goes hand in hand with being teachable and a good listener. It's a biblical mandate for the believer. "... Clothe yourselves, all of you, with humility toward one another, ..." (1 Peter 5:5b ESV).

Humility knows, well, that it does not know it all. You can't think you know it all and be teachable. Humility considers the needs of others. One can't always be thinking of themselves in a conversation and truly be listening. Exercising humility implies action. It implies self-restraint. It implies intention.

Humility also recognizes the grace, the gifts, the forgiveness, and the favor that has been bestowed along the way. It considers itself not more worthy than the next person to receive any of it. Now that I own my own business, I find people come to me from time to time as I have gone to my influencers. More than ever, the above principles still apply.

Do you exercise humility?

Charted Steps

IMPRINT: Influencers and Mentors

This chapter and the previous have similarities. Both are about finding *your* people as you carry out your life purpose and mission. Remember these?

Rule number one: Don't just find people. Find your people.

Rule number two: Find your Eagles, people who encourage and inspire you to higher heights and greater depths.

Now add:

Rule number three: Find your influencers, people who mentor you by both the actions and deeds in life.

Let's explore who the influencers are in your own life. First, think about the answers to these questions:

1. Are you motivated to learn?
2. Are you teachable? Why or why not?
3. Do you exercise humility?
4. Write your thoughts down, pray over your answers, and ask the Lord for help. Be completely honest about where you are in this.

5. List five people who come to mind who have been a major influence in your life.
6. Write a paragraph or two under each name, briefly telling each story.
7. Be intentional. Make a plan to reach out to each person on your list, and thank them for what they have meant to you. Ask if they would be willing to share about the person who has had the greatest impact on their own life.

CHAPTER 11

Captain's Log

"Letters are among the most significant memorials a person can leave behind them."

— JOHANN WOLFGANG VON GOETHE

"DADDY, YOU WANT TO HEAR my Scripture verse I learned today? It's not too hard." My "Kelsey Girl," the nickname of my youngest, in all her beautiful curls, smile, and bubbly personality, sat in the back seat looking at me in the rearview mirror.

"Well, sure, honey. What is it?" I waited in anticipation of some cute misquoted paraphrase.

"Psalms 139:14. *We are awesome and wonderfully made,*" she stated clearly and concisely with the cutest childlike confidence.

I remember that car ride as I walk the wooded paths behind our home on this gorgeous fall afternoon with tree leaves of all colors. I had picked up Kelsey from church after Vacation Bible School one afternoon. I remember buckling her in as she sat there examining her hands. We then talked about the uniqueness of each person God created, the fact that *no two fingerprints are alike in the entire world.*

I sat down on a nearby log, feeling the breeze pass, and breathing in the clean air. I am reminded just how fast my life and that of my family is passing by right in front of me. My oldest daughter Megan, a teacher of ten years, now has three children of her own. My son Landon, an executive with a nursing home facility, constantly travels, following the demands of his job and is soon to be married. My youngest daughter Kelsey is finding her place in this world as an adult and will soon be working as a speech pathologist. *Wow!* Where has the time so quickly gone?

All these thoughts swirl around my head as I look down at my own hands and my fingers. Then it hits me—DNA. God makes each of us with unique DNA, just as our stories carry unique DNA. They carry both a strand from our past and a strand from our present. We not only carry a unique physical DNA, we carry a unique story DNA that in God's hands is being shaped into something miraculous and beautiful, even if we can't see it yet. One person's story DNA is a distinct imprint like no one else.

So, yes, my sweet Kelsey girl, we truly are all awesome and wonderfully made!

A New Tradition

A few years ago at Christmas, I unknowingly initiated a new tradition in my family. I had been searching for a way to make sure my children knew exactly what they meant to Raye and myself. As much as I was capable, I wanted to let them know their God-given uniqueness, their awesome-and-wonderfully-made-ness, exactly what we saw in each of them that made them special in the world and significant in our eyes, to have something they could turn to, hold in their hands, and reflect on when life told them otherwise, a tangible encouragement that would last beyond our lifetime as parents. So, I decided to write them each a letter.

Christmas Eve, I gathered the family around and had each one open their letter, and we read them as a family. Imagine one of those warm Christmas movie moments, family gathered by a cozy fire, grandchildren scattered at the feet of the patriarch of the family. Everyone smiling with misty eyes as each letter is read by Pop! (Their nickname for me.)

Unfortunately, the first time didn't turn out exactly that way. It wasn't a flop, but no home runs either. I had never done it before.

Each one listened, and the letters were tenderhearted with everybody getting a little more emotional at the touching parts. The first letters were a little harder to write and probably a little too long. So I stepped it back and instead of having them read it, I read it out loud. I lightened up by sharing humorous Christmases or memories from when they were young. Then my letter stressed my hopes and prayers for them in the future. As each year progressed, they not only began to enjoy the letters, but now they look forward to them. I quit trying to find the right words and instead just dug deep down into the memories we've made and reshared in these great family keepsake stories.

I believe this gift letter at Christmas from me to them has now become a great family tradition and imprint. I hope someday our adult children might want to emulate it with their own kids someday.

Raye Ann Mauck

My wife Raye Ann is one of the most giving, caring, and loving individuals one could ever meet. Her wonderful attributes had made her the best wife I could have ever dreamed of, a great mother to our children, and the best grandparent a kid could ever want. Our grandchildren love to respectfully and joyfully call her "Nan."

For me personally, Raye Ann's help to start LifeCare was essential to me due to her great attention to detail and ability to prioritize what things needed to be accomplished. In addition, her great experience as an executive assistant in personnel at General Motors helped us considerably as she became our primary human resources coordinator during those formative years of our company.

Raye has a big heart, so much so, she readily admits that if it was up to her, we would have had to close our doors. She would have given everything away due to her love for hurting children and families. Her classic favorite song, sung by the late Louis Armstrong, is "It's a Wonderful World"; that's how she views the world.

Being a mom and working full-time was a difficult juggling act, but she somehow pulled it off. Our kids and I have great respect for her commitment to excellence and knowing exactly the right gift to get all of us each year for our birthday or Christmas. Raye doesn't forget anyone's birthday in our family, is always thoughtful, and makes sure each seasonal occasion is special by the evidence of wreaths, garlands, and decorative lights. In short, she makes things special around our home!

As for the grandkids, there's hardly a need that she hasn't somehow fulfilled and bought for them. I have never seen such a thoughtful and caring grandmother as Raye Ann.

Years after she left our company in 2008, to help watch our twin grandsons Easton and Cooper, I was sitting in the car with them when Cooper looked over at me and asked, "Pop, how can Nan be so rich? She buys us everything we want or need."

I laughed. "Well, I'm not for sure. Maybe you can ask her that yourself someday."

Raye Ann, I hope the following letter lets you know how deeply I appreciate you as your husband and that it adequately conveys what you mean to each individual in our family. We do indeed note all the special caring ways whereby you remember each one of us. Your imprints in our lives will never be forgotten....

Letter to Raye Ann—inspired while walking in Rome, Italy, a celebration trip due to our thirty-five-year anniversary trip in September 2018.

Raye,

I don't know why you married me? It was 1982, and I was in my last semester of college with a degree in teaching and working as a substitute teacher making forty dollars a day, which was much less than you earned with General Motors. I wasn't making enough to support myself, much less you.

As you remember, I even tried to break up with you when we first started dating, stating you had a better job and thinking you would need someone else who could take care of you financially. I thought it best that we end our short time together amiably. But when my breaking-up offer was not accepted, I made a crazy promise to you: If you remained with me, the time would come when I would become your sole provider if you chose not to work again. Although it took me a few years longer than anticipated, I kept my commitment over ten years ago in 2008. Thanks for staying and making LifeCare extra special and working all those years to help our family.

When we took our eighteen-day trip to Germany and Italy in September 2018, to celebrate our thirty-five years of marriage, I had an epiphany moment of our life together while walking with you in Rome and watching all the trees and colors that represented this fall day. It reminded me of all the various seasons of our life that we have lived together. Watching families riding bikes and walking together reminded me of why I appreciate you so much. I shared with you the great attributes I loved about you, like hanging with me all these years through each of our ups and downs of marriage, having children, moving, and all the other issues that life can throw at a couple. I had no idea how great a mom you would become to our children and Nan to our grandchildren. I realized how challenging it was for both of us, yet I realized that the things I didn't like were because we were so different from each other. Over the years, I have begun to appreciate those differences and how you complement so many of the things I can't do. Your faithfulness despite all my shortcomings, forgetfulness, and busyness speaks a lot about the person you are.

God truly looked beyond all my faults and missteps and has blessed me by having you in my life. We started with humble beginnings within a small 1,000-square-foot home. At the time, we thought that monthly mortgage payment of $350 a month might be over our budget. Now we're living in our dream home, more blessed than I could have ever imagined we could afford. It's all part of our humbling story now!

Thanks for being all the great things I couldn't be at LifeCare, for taking care of all those details and areas of our family, our home, and me. We all needed your special touch, and you freely gave it.

I love and appreciate you, Raye. You could have married someone more intelligent, a better fixer upper around the house, someone better organized or super wealthy. But thanks for the richness of our years together and making our story special. When I look at our three grown and healthy children and wonderful grandchildren, I realize how so very truly blessed we are as a family!

I love you!
Kenny

Landon Kent Mauck
April 17, 1985–Present

Landon is my firstborn and my one and only son. When he came into this world, I'm pretty sure Hans and the rest of my great-grandfathers were high fiving and throwing a party up in heaven—the Mauck name would live on. Well, I imagine they would have, but in all seriousness, carrying on the family name was extremely important to me, and Landon was a fulfillment of that desire.

Landon's birth was not an easy one. Weighing in at nine pounds, eleven ounces, he was a big baby, and Raye Ann is a little woman. After hours of labor with little progress, the doctors determined she would need a cesarean delivery and fast.

Honestly, I was not prepared for what happened next. I remember standing by her side, holding her hand, watching the doctors begin the operation. As the doctor wielded the knife and begin making the incision, I began feeling a little dizzy. I must have turned white as a sheet because the nurse took one look at me and said, "Honey, you might want to sit down."

Working quickly, the doctor soon reached inside Raye Ann and exclaimed, "Wow! I think this kid has a helmet on!" Pulling and pushing in a manner that did not seem natural (or physically possible), the doctor attempted to get Landon turned around and out of Raye Ann.

Our usually jovial doctor was now no longer smiling. The atmosphere intensified as he asked for the forceps and continued pulling, pushing, and maneuvering what seemed like the entirety of both his arms inside my wife's abdomen. Finally, after a few very intense and scary minutes, the doctor, sweating now from the workout, let out a huge sigh of relief and said, "I think he's finally turned upright."

Seconds later, the doctor pulled out our beautiful, wonderfully handsome baby boy. (No biased parent here.) Immediately, Landon let the whole world know he was not happy to be removed from such a dark, warm, and secure place, plopped into this cold, bright place, and then poked, prodded, measured, and wiped down.

When the nurse asked if I wanted to hold my son, I chuckled to myself. I don't know why they ask a father, who's been waiting hundreds of days and spending considerable time and money buying the baby bed, baby rocker, stroller, diapers, and every other little thing needed, if he wants to hold his baby. Seems like a no-brainer until I realized she may have been inquiring because I was speechless and apprehensively holding out my hands in a nonverbal cue. Landon didn't seem all too happy to see me as I embraced him, laughing and crying.

I was able to hold Landon only briefly before the nurses whisked him away to check his bilirubin count and run through another gamut of newborn tests and checks. I was so excited I couldn't wait to tell everyone. Instinctively falling back on my track days, I burst through the swinging double doors and down the hall at a full sprint. I didn't even stop to take off my scrubs.

I raced to the waiting room, excitedly announcing to friends, family, and anyone else in my path, *"We have a baby boy!"*

As everyone hugged and celebrated, it really began to sink in. I was a dad for the first time, and it was a boy. Raye Ann and I had made a deal. She named the girls, so I had the honor of naming our son. The name had been picked out months ago. Our favorite show at the time was *Little House on the Prairie*, and Landon would be named after the actor who portrayed one of our favorite roles, Michael Landon.

Living life with Landon has been a joy. To my great delight, we share a love of sports, which has been the catalyst for many great memories. At first, he loved two things, his pacifier and playing with a ball. We started with a soft cushy baseball and bat, which he mostly chewed while teething.

In the toddler years, we moved on to a preschool-sized slam-dunk basketball hoop and wrestled once I got home from work each night. When Landon turned five, the fun really began. I would take him to the elementary school across the street from our house, and we'd play for hours on the playground.

In his teen years, Landon developed a love for basketball. We played often from daylight to dusk. He had a great shot, scoring often from outside and near the basket and was one of the most unselfish players on his team, always looking for the open man.

Over the years, Landon has learned to be a true team player in life, and to this day, his competitive and kind spirit have served him well. He has expertly transferred those life skills learned from competitive team sports to the corporate world, improving the quality of the work environment.

As a human resources administrator, and more recently as management at a senior-care facility, he searches for creative ways to include the entire team's ideas and input whenever possible. Landon has so much to offer, and one of the greatest values he has spoken into my life is his extreme faithfulness to family and friends.

> *Dear Landon,*
>
> *One of the greatest joys in my life is being your father. I have so many great and wonderful memories made while spending time with you. Holding you in my arms that first time, I never realized how fast my life and yours would fly by. It's hard to believe it's been over thirty-plus years. From hearing your belly-laughing giggle while your sister unsuccessfully tried to tumble or roll over, to countless high fives and games of H-O-R-S-E, to admiring your great shooting ability as we played Around the World, I've treasured it all. Every moment you*

chose to hang with Dad as a little boy is a cherished memory, such as following me around every time I cut the grass, pretending to do the same with your toy mower. You were only four years old.

When winter brought piles and piles of Michigan, snow, you were right there with me with your little shovel, working up a sweat trying to keep up with me. Watching the video of you riding your bike without the training wheels for the first time, me running beside you until you trusted me to let go, brings me great joy. Even when you fell, you got right back up. You never give up, a trait I know you will pass on to your own children.

The times you and I went swimming, played one-on-one basketball games until it was dark and your mom called us in for dinner, all are priceless imprinted memories. Now we enjoy golfing and watching a great college football game together. The best part is not the game but simply throwing the football at halftime to each other.

I never thought about getting older until I put on my good running shoes and caught some of those passes from you. I was sore the next day, but I didn't want you to know it; I just so loved being with you as your dad and enjoying our times together. Remember a few years ago while watching the bowl games? You said, "Dad, something I've always wanted to do is go to the Rose Bowl. Can we go?"

Your spontaneous request caught me by surprise, but somehow, we were able to convince your mother this wasn't a crazy idea and even to go with us. Just like that, we were on our way New Year's Eve day to see Michigan play USC at the Los Angeles Memorial Coliseum. I didn't even care that Michigan lost. I'll never forget our momentous trip.

When your mom and I watched you in the ceremony after earning you MBA from Indiana Wesleyan, I was so proud. I am amazed at what you have accomplished so early in your life. Landon, don't ever compare or let others compare you to me or anyone for that matter. God has a special calling specifically for your life, a wonderful journey meant just for you and your family.

I hope you have great memories of you and I working together at LifeCare and your great work as our human resources director. Son, I gave you the most simplistic and menial entry-level job to start, and you soared with it. I watched how you initially passed on better paying offers out of allegiance to myself and LifeCare. Then finally, you moved onto your current administrative position with another company. Although LifeCare wasn't able to compete with those salaries, I will never forget your faithfulness to our legacy company for fourteen years, helping build up and hiring our company's diverse and excellent staff.

But what makes you stand out, other than your six-foot-four-inch height and great looks, obviously from your mom's side of the family, is your heart. You generously and quietly give to others financially or otherwise, never seeking public acknowledgement. I know you do these things as unto God, not anyone else. But I do see it, and I know more importantly, God sees your heart, and that's what makes you so special to us as your family.

By the way, I am so thankful that you have finally met the love of your life in Brittany. Your mom and I don't want to put any pressure on either of you, but to keep the Mauck legacy going, we are hoping for at least five grandchildren over the next five years. LOL

Landon, you're the best son a dad could hope for. I'm blessed and honored to be a father to a son who has exceeded way beyond all my expectations—thank you! I love you, Landon. Dream deep. Enjoy each moment of the sunrise, every soft breeze in the afternoon, and sunsets with a family as great as you three have been to your mother and me.

Thanks for being such a great part of our legacy story, Son!

Love, Dad

Megan De Ann Mauck-Hinson
July 7, 1987–Present

I nicknamed our first daughter Megan our "Sunshine" because that's exactly what she brought to us as a family, a "bright warming light" of joy into our lives. Megan was always full of surprises. Her middle name is a combination of my mother's middle name Delois and Raye Ann's mom's name Ann. As a baby, Megan was always ahead of the curve academically. Whether talking, walking, or reading, Megan did it sooner than the rest of our children.

Megs, a name we sometimes called her, was an active child, always on the go, the one who got into every single unlocked closet, opened (and emptied) every drawer she could reach, and tried to climb out every window. At the age of two, it was not uncommon for our little busybody to make it all the way to the neighbor's house and knock on the door before we even realized she was gone. That's the way she rolled. We were that family that had to install all the extra special safety latches on our cabinets and baby gates on our steps.

Hand in hand with that activity was a stubborn streak. I'll never forget the day I realized we were in it for the long haul on that front. Megan, who was two at the time, kept pulling her four-year-old brother's hair while he slept. I had already asked her twice to stop pulling his hair. She didn't.

I looked her square in the eye and shook my finger as I said, "If you don't stop, I'm going to spank you," to which she turned her backside to me and bent over. I swatted her once on her pampered bottom.

Megan straightened up, looked at me, and proceeded to turn her back on me again. She bent over again as if to say, "Is that all you got?"

I was completely taken aback, and I tried so hard to keep a straight face and follow through. But I burst out laughing instead.

Right then, I knew she was going to be my challenging one. On a side note, somehow, we got all of that on video, and yes, eventually, I followed up with a more serious consequence when it came to correcting her.

Because of her bouncy curls, Megan had always reminded me of Shirley Temple. She really loved to sing. We bought her a little karaoke machine, and she and her sister presented many a performance to the family. She also loved dancing. Raye Ann would help with her dance routines, and she won first place several times at her school talent shows. Her love of performance stayed with her throughout her childhood and into high school. More times than I can count, I would watch her sing and dance her way through the house, and she would ask me to video her, to dance with her, and to sing with her. She was an actress, a dancer, a singer, a reporter, a teacher. Whatever it was, she was in charge.

In high school, Megan was the flier for her cheer squad. Don't ever let anyone tell you cheer isn't a sport. Wait until your daughter is tossed twenty feet in the air, plummeting back down with only the arms of a few high schoolers to break her fall. I think Raye Ann and I aged ten years in those four years, but she wouldn't have wanted any other position.

In addition to being the most active of our three children, Megan is without a doubt the most driven. All of that determination, tenacity, and spark have served her well in whatever she has chosen to pursue. For ten years, she has somehow juggled being a teacher with a side home business. Her teaching, coupled with her natural performing abilities, have opened the doors for many opportunities, including a national commercial titled "ABCMouse.com".

On top of her multifaceted careers, Megan is a wonderful mother of three—our wonderful twin grandsons Easton and Cooper and our two-year old baby granddaughter Gracelyn Hope. When I think of Gracelyn, I just have to smile. God has such a great sense of humor. Gracelyn is giving back to Megan the energy level she had when she was Gracelyn's age in heaping spoonfuls.

> Megan,
>
> I love you dearly. Your joyful energy from the time you were little has been such a delight to experience. The great delight you bring to our family is special to all of us. You will forever be "my sunshine." Always the one to get up early and kick the covers back, you greeted each day as if to say, "Watch out world, here I come!" I loved that then and now, I love that you, like me, are a dreamer, visionary, and creator, and that unlike me, you can fly by the seat of your pants with the ease and confidence required of a mom with twin boys and a little busy bee like Gracelyn. Those precious grandchildren you have given us are an absolute joy in your mother and my lives.
>
> I will always love your special laugh, wit, and beautiful smile you share with family and friends. In each picture album I leaf through of your growing-up years, your beautiful, bouncy goldilocks curls, embody memories that I will always cherish. Your love for God, your friends and family mean everything to us.
>
> I cherish all the great family trips we have taken to Florida with you. We used every kind of camera to capture everything about you, including the handprints we made at the beach with you, Landon, and Kelsey as children and now with our grandchildren. My best remembrances prove that father time needs to be seized in the here and now, not when I can find the time.
>
> We don't often have enough time now due to your life as mom and wife. So, I was so happy we intentionally set aside a day together, doing what you wanted, no kids or other family members, just a dad-and-daughter lunch date at your favorite restaurant. Without phone distractions or concerns about social media, we were able to relax and

talk about your life goals, ambitions, and your new home. We discovered that two very intensely purpose-driven people can take advantage of a moment to be together as father and daughter with no agenda. And I want us to maintain these times as well in the here and now of life!

Megs, I really couldn't be prouder of you. When you finished your student teaching at Middle Tennessee State University, I beamed. The fact you have been such an esteemed teacher all these years at Brown's Chapel makes me so proud to be your father. I enjoyed so much coming and watching you teach and reading to your class last year. Your students loved you, and I knew you loved them dearly as well.

What a great part of our family story you are to all of us, and you will always remain special within my and our family's hearts. Now and forever, there will never be another sunshine in my life—that's only you, Megs!

I pray God shines His love on you and your family, and may His glorious face brighten and awaken you each morning. May His beam of light guide you through every challenging situation and His bright countenance point you toward a lasting future.

Love you always and forever, darling!

Dad

Kelsey Rae Mauck
August 28, 1991–Present

I cannot imagine life without my youngest daughter Kelsey. Early on, I affectionately dubbed her as my "Peanut."

Kelsey was an unexpected gift to us all from heaven. The four of us—Landon, Megan, Raye, and myself—welcomed her home and into the family with open arms. Many times, we would all stand over her bassinet, watching her sleep. I think Landon and Megan felt more like another set of parents at times. They were so cute, making faces in an effort to get Kelsey to smile and laugh, and wanting to help with everything. Kelsey was their baby as much as she was ours.

As Kelsey grew, she captured our hearts as she tried desperately to outdo her sister in dancing, singing, and special drama presentations they both created for the family.

I remember how close I felt to losing her when she was born. An experience like that can make any man an overprotective father, and I've probably leaned that way more often than not when it comes to my Peanut.

Those first twenty-four hours were some of the roughest hours of my life. Due to a low bilirubin count, Kelsey spent her first few hours in the NICU in an incubation unit. It wasn't long before the doctor decided she could be in the main room with the other babies.

On my way out to run a few errands and run by home to pick up a few things Raye needed, I went to admire my baby girl. I immediately noticed Kelsey's breathing seemed slightly labored. I banged on the window until the attendant responded, motioning toward Kelsey and mouthing, "Are you sure she's okay?"

The nurse nodded yes. I lingered a few moments more while she attended to Kelsey until I was satisfied that everything was indeed okay.

As I walked in the door to our apartment with the list Raye Ann had given me, the phone rang. It was Raye, and she was crying. All I could make out was something was wrong with the baby and the phrase "turned blue." The rest was a blur.

I remember driving fast, running, pacing, and crying out to God to save my baby girl. What seemed like hours in the hospital waiting room turned out to be only about fifteen minutes. When the doctor finally came out and gently put his hand on my shoulder to reassure me, I collapsed in a nearby chair. "Mr. Mauck," he said, "take a deep breath. It's going to be all right. Kelsey is going to be just fine."

I stood keeping watch over her incubator for the longest time. I don't remember how long; I just remember I did not want to leave my baby girl!

Kelsey's nickname shifted from Peanut to my "Kelsey Girl" somewhere around the age of five. It's a name I call her even now at twenty-seven years old. Growing up, she was both tomboy and cheerleader, sugar and spice. She loved to play basketball, and I was fortunate to be her coach. Many underestimated her because of her height (or lack thereof), thinking her too small to even play guard. Her deadly outside shot quickly won them over. Those three pointers helped us win more than a few games. I can assure you, no one overlooks Kelsey now.

She has an uncanny ability to make people smile, even people she has just met. Her laugh and carefree spirit invite everyone to enjoy the fun. I believe this light heartedness and ability to put people at ease have added to her being one of the premiere nannies in Nashville for several years.

Kelsey's knack for getting herself into hilarious situations have left her with many funny stories to share. I'm sure as she enters the University of Tennessee to study speech pathology, she will add many more humorous chapters to her story.

> Kelsey,
>
> Since your first breath, I knew that you would become something very special to us. Without a doubt, your birth was not just a physical one but a love birthed in our hearts. As your father, I realized you were meant to complete us as a family.
>
> Some of the richest memories of my life are the times in the evenings when your mom would be working her Mary Kay business, and you and I would spend time together. We would do flips with Megan and Landon on the trampoline or ride bikes. You and I would get on the

fastest rides at Kentucky Kingdom, Disney World, and any other theme parks where the family vacationed. We were the crazy ones of the group. As you grew, you knew how to bait me into doing things none of us should have attempted, like the bungee cord virtual ride that threw us hundreds of feet high in the air and had me screaming at the top of my lungs. I enjoyed every minute of it with you.

Kelsey, there is a serious side to you as well. When you completed your bachelor's degree in elementary education, you were voted by your peers in your entire senior class at Lipscomb University as the teacher most likely to succeed. You followed your heart, though, another trait I admire as you seek to become a speech therapist. I'm overwhelmed at your love and care for children with exceptional needs and those experiencing physical and emotional issues, such as autism, speech, and hearing.

I also remember very clearly when one day you thought you had disappointed me and came running down the driveway into my arms, evidence of your tender side. I hope you will always remember my response, "There's nothing in this life you could ever do that would stop me from loving you!"

When you suggested I pick an adventurous place for our dad-and-daughter time this year, I had to one-up you and take you to one of the highest and fastest zip lines in Tennessee. On our way, we sang, we laughed, we shared funny faces and ended up staying at a bed and breakfast where both of us had beautiful rooms and views from our windows. The food, the ambience, and the mountain atmosphere were so very special and beautiful, weren't they? The zip line's seven stations and lines became increasingly more challenging, the fastest one running sixty-five miles per hour over half a mile. I think that was one of my favorite ones. But each one had its own challenges and brand of fun. Watching you doing flips while taking off down the zip line was a highlight for sure.

The Dollywood Splash Country water park was amazing as well. I've never ridden a semi-water roller coaster before that day. Above all these things were the dad-daughter pictures we took that looked out over the mountains where we had dinner that night. They weren't just pictures, but the imprints planted on my soul. Your see, I know your days hanging like this with me are numbered now. I wasn't just looking at memories captured, but I was seeing my little girl, now a young lady, so beautiful, and hearing you admit you wanted to have a family like ours.

I shared with you my thoughts on how precious life is and that each day needs to count. I tried to keep it light, but you know me, I'm a sentimental man. I remember you jokingly mentioning that I'm there for my parents in their eighties, and someday that might be you and me.

We laughed together until you brought it all home in a more serious tone, saying, "Dad, I will always be there for you just like you have been there for me."

Kelsey, you have made your mom and me so proud. I know soon you will be married, and we couldn't be happier for you. I will tell you the same thing I told your brother, but I will lower the expectations somewhat. We would like, at minimum, a three-seated bobsled with grandkids in it. Just teasing! But you do know twins do run in our generational family!

Love you!
Dad

Leaving My Forever Sea Bottle Letter Capsule

I want my children to read the following imprinted letters to their children and for their children in turn to read it to their children, my great-children, yet to be born.

In 2019, I wrote this futuristically driven letter to you as your grandfather for you to become the keepers of the story. Maybe you will someday benefit from your Nan and Pop, or from your parents from the material things we left, like land, investments, and property. However, I want you to know we are leaving all of you something way more important than any of those material possessions. I will instead be leaving you a treasure chest of letters and a hidden trove of stories that I pray will last not only beyond my lifetime, but yours as well. You see, no money or monetary inheritance could ever fulfill the endearing and invaluable everlasting joy of sitting in a quiet place and embracing your, my, and our endearing family story.

So, Megan and Michael, Landon and Brittany, and Kelsey and Jon, please read it to your children and teach them to cherish their heritage. Encourage them and your grandchildren to read it to their children as it's part of their and our family legacy. I hope it becomes like a treasured "sea bottle" letter that keeps it fun for them, like discovering a precious jewel washed ashore in a marked barrel that reads, "My Family's Life Imprints. Within this bottle, I pray they will not just read this book but will find pictures, letters, and stories as something they can keep for a lifetime."

My Letter To My Grandchildren

To Easton, Cooper, Gracelyn and my soon-to-be grandchildren, great-grandchildren, and children yet to be born who I hope will one day read this: I am writing this forward-thinking letter purposely so that one day you will realize how far and wide my love is to you as your Pop!

Easton, you're the oldest of your twin brother by a few minutes. I hope you will encourage him, your sister, and all your Mauck and Nance cousins yet to be born to not only read this book, but someday answer the questions so that you can eventually add your own paragraphs, chapters, and stories. I hope you will find memories within the paragraphs and pictures and that they somehow will inspire you to write, speak, draw, and dream so that your own story continues for generations to come!

As you and your parents commit to become the "keepers of this story," regardless if you're a Mauck, Nance, or Hinson, I hope as you include pictures of us together, you will sense a part of myself, and our most cherished memoires will live with you beyond my own lifetime. I hope these reflected pages become part of your own imprinted legacy story one day, one whereby your most cherished memories, prayers, and precious loving thoughts are captured.

After several years of researching the lives of your ancestors, one of my greatest joys and hopes is to be granted a view from heaven. I want to watch your brother, your sister, and cousins listen as I share all about our Mauck and Nichol families' heritages. I couldn't help but smile widely and joyfully as when I read to you from my reclining chair at Christmas, and you and your twin brother kept scooting closer and closer until you were right at my feet. You listened intently to each word. Then as I began asking questions, you were right there with the answers. I pray this tradition will continue way beyond your and my lifetimes. Sharing our heritage story is a wonderful pastime.

Please know, my greatest wealth and treasures will be the remembrance of our walks, the treasure hunts in the woods, playing hide-and-go-seek, throwing the football, playing basketball, golf, soccer, and wrestling with you. It will be the memories of hugs and kisses, the tickle bugs, laughs, and the pleasure of being present as you talk about your day, reading a devotion or wonderful story with you at night, saying prayers over you, or holding you on my lap. I hope the songs and music we have shared as your Nan and Pop will someday be shared with your own children.

In closing, a story like ours must include our everlasting Heavenly Father and Creator if it's to live throughout and beyond your and my lifetimes. So, I leave you my greatest imprinted secret of all, and I pray you will hold it deeper than any other story. I pray you will give your heart completely to our most loving, redemptive Author and Finisher of our family story. He is Jesus Christ, and He will forever be your and my true joy and peace, one that has conquered death and the grave. He is the one who planned to prosper us, to give us hope and joy in our life.

> There will never be a greater imprinted redemptive storyline that will keep our story alive forevermore than that of Jesus Christ. Remember a life without God is one filled with disjointed pieces that will never become whole, but with Jesus Christ, you have everything you need. He's preparing a beautiful place for each of us, an eternal home with great and loving stories that will never end!
>
> Love you to moon, stars, heaven, and back!
>
> Love, Pop

The Lost Art of Letters

Back in the old days when families gathered at the end of the day, instead of movie night or reading a bedtime story, fathers, mothers, or grandparents—the keepers of the story—talked about their younger days. They reminisced about distant relatives, travels, sorrows, and joys passed down from generation to generation. Legacy and heritage came to life through animated storytelling, a once time-honored tradition filled with personal contact and sacred family moments. It's a lost art I pray will regain prominence in a world where social media has taken over as the cold, impersonal story keeper.

With the fast-paced, technology-infused society we live in, letter writing is also becoming a lost art. Texts, emails, tweets, and Facebook posts all happen in an instant and are as quickly forgotten as soon as the next one comes along. But a letter, intentionally written and delivered, says something to the recipient. It says, "I value you. Giving time to you matters. You matter, and I want you to remember that you do."

When the kids were little, we notched and dated their growth on a doorframe somewhere in the house. We logged all the firsts, hung the baby pictures and school pictures, and made sure family vacations had a photo album. It was easy to find the good, the things to love in the early years.

But when was the last time you put in writing how much you appreciate your aging parent or children? Write out what you love about them and share those things with them? Have you put your deepest feelings about your children in writing?

For me, letters are the Captain's Log I'm leaving behind, the printed manual of who the people I love are. How much they are loved will guide them through hard times and be a map for doing the same for their loved ones. Tangible vulnerability.

I hope my children and grandchildren will hold onto these tangible pieces of encouragement and turn to them often, knowing these are the kinds of brandings upon and in one's life that really matter!

Charted Steps

Viewing on paper everything a person means to you is sobering and humbling, even therapeutic in a good way. No matter who your family is—a wife and children, extended family, or friends—putting your love for them in writing is a gift not only for them but also for you. You're adding to your family story and the importance of being a keeper of the story.

1. List the people you consider your immediate family and what it is that makes each person unique in the world and special to you. Think back to your first encounter with them. Jot down the highlights in the relationship and try to articulate why those stand out.
2. Take your notes and put them in letter form. This process is not easy or quick. Don't rush through it. Revisit it regularly over a period of weeks. Allow yourself complete freedom to show vulnerability.

3. Pray over each letter as you write it, asking the Lord to give you the words and bring to mind the things He knows each one may need to hear.
4. The big one... once your letters are written, find a time to honor your family and share the letter(s) with them. Don't be disappointed if you have a less-than-postcard moment your first time. It's the long-term and unspoken impact that's important, the fact that you have left affirming value in this person's life and what they mean to you.

CHAPTER 12

The Wind in Your Sails

"I find the great thing in this world is not so much where we stand, as in what direction we are moving: To reach the port of heaven, we must sail sometimes with the wind and sometimes against it—but we must sail, and not drift, nor lie at anchor."

— OLIVER WENDELL HOLMES, SR.

THE SUN SETS BEAUTIFULLY as I reflect on all I have discovered about my ancestors. I have embraced and learned from my own immediate and extended family as well as my entire life journey, calling, and vocational ministry. I see more and more how God has connected and interwoven these three areas into one that completes my imprinted story.

While Hans' life imprint may have passed over a few generations, it certainly did not escape me or my life upon unearthing it.

God used Hans' story to reach my heart by helping me realize His kingdom purposes are the most powerful and important calling in our life. Above all else, I conclude that God and His purpose for our lives are what's most important in that they provide everlasting value to us. How powerful is the God I serve who reaches down through generations to touch the heart of one person by breathing new verses, paragraphs, and chapters into their redemptive story. How much more powerful and productive will our lives be if we stay focused on His eternal purposes? We are investing time in what will live beyond us.

Let's look at what God says about the importance of imprinted seasons and time clock events of our lives.

Answering the Call

One of my favorite Scripture passages is Ecclesiastes 3:1-8 (KJV):
1 To everything there is a season, and a time to every purpose under the heaven:
2 A time to be born, and a time to die; a time to plant, and a time to pluck up that which is planted;
3 A time to kill, and a time to heal; a time to break down, and a time to build up;
4 A time to weep, and a time to laugh; a time to mourn, and a time to dance;
5 A time to cast away stones, and a time to gather stones together; a time to embrace, and a time to refrain from embracing;
6 A time to get, and a time to lose; a time to keep, and a time to cast away;
7 A time to rend, and a time to sew; a time to keep silence, and a time to speak;
8 A time to love, and a time to hate; a time of war, and a time of peace.

I love how these passages were inked during Solomon's reign and the BC period. He talks about the seasons of our life. "To everything, there is a season and a time to every purpose under heaven." I hear this as a call from our Heavenly Father reminding us that each season of life is significant enough to be recorded and passed down to our children. It's not just remembering dates, births, deaths, records of marriages, or historical events, but the life that happened around these events, the difficult decisions made, the live-or-die moments, and the struggles. We need to share with our children and grandchildren the humor, the laughter, the tears, the mending of broken relationships found along the way. For me, it's a call to be the keeper of the story.

Friends, there is no better time than now to accept this call and responsibility to be the keeper of the story for your own family. My prayer for you has been one of transformation as you've worked through and journaled the steps to find your own story.

This is not a call to merely take more family pictures for the sake of having a record, to gather family recipes from moms, aunts, and dads, or gather statistics. This is a call for context, for memories, for the backstory behind all of these things. It's a call to have conversations, ask questions, record and journal the thoughts and feelings, the sadness and the humor, to capture life in a lasting way, and to make and take the time to share it with friends and family. It's a call to be intentional in creating the life imprint you will leave behind.

Mr. Winchell's Pictures and Their Context to Our Seasons in Life

My first real experience with context surrounding pictures came as a ten-year-old boy. Our neighbor Mr. Winchell invited our family over for dinner one night. Afterward, he brought us into the living room where a projector and screen were waiting. He asked if his family could share with us an amazing trip to China that they had taken.

At first, I thought, "Oh, yay. A slideshow of the family vacation. This is going to be so boring," and settled into a comfortable spot ready to daydream about anything else but what was in front of me on the screen.

As the images passed one after the other, Mr. Winchell shared stories. Adventures unfolded. Pictures came to life. The whole Winchell family chimed in, and it made me want to learn more about the Chinese people, culture, and places.

It wasn't the pictures that drew me in and kept my attention; it was the storied context that captured me. I began to feel like I was a part of their party as Dad, Mom, and kids excitedly reminisced about the Great Wall, jumping into paddle boats and almost tipping over, gliding down the river. They described the beautiful scenery and gave the lowdown on the different kinds of interesting and strange food they ate. Mr. Winchell's presentation made a lasting impression on me, not because of any particular picture, but because of the life in the stories behind each one.

This is the goal of the keeper of the story.

The Least of These!

After almost two decades of growing LifeCare, I experienced a short period of time where I felt very disconnected from LifeCare's initial mission promise. I began to wonder if we were still making those positive impacts on the lives we were serving. I was no longer a counselor, case manager, or treating people. I was now strictly in an administrative role as president and founder of the company. We had helped thousands and thousands of people, but I couldn't see how we were actually making a difference. I started beating myself up, wondering how I could have done things differently, how I could do things differently moving forward. I just wasn't seeing the results.

About four years ago, I was working in my office upstairs when I got a call from our adult daycare staff asking if I would come down to observe something very special during my lunch hour. Our Life-Care Foundations adult daycare center specializes in rehabilitative services that assist acute handicap or brain-injured individuals with their socialization and daily care needs.

One of our support staff introduced me to an exceptional young man, nineteen-year-old Willie. I have to admit, despite my twenty-two years of training and working with special-needs youth and adult, I have never witnessed the challenges that Willie faced each day. His physical condition was overwhelming, hopeless at first glance. Willie had no legs; both his arms were deformed, and he couldn't talk. His assistant was in the middle of feeding him when I arrived. I asked if it would be better if I came back after he had finished, but both staff members encouraged me to have a seat and assist them during his lunch.

I sat next to Willie trying not to show on my face my feelings of total sadness over his conditions. Willie was totally dependent on our staff for all his needs—restroom use, eating, and movement about the facility. He couldn't even wipe his mouth or ever wash his hands without assistance. Without any legs to support his body and hold him up, he had to be belted to his wheelchair in several places; otherwise, his body would slump over due to the weight from his upper torso.

I held Willie's cup for him as he drank. When he finished eating, I stood and stacked his dishes on a tray and turned to set them on another table. My back was to Willie while I spoke with a staff member.

All of a sudden, several staff came over to me smiling and pointing behind me at Willie. They excitedly exclaimed, "Look, Mr. Mauck, this is what we wanted you to see!"

As I turned around, I saw Willie with the most enormous smile I had ever seen in my life. It filled the entire room.

I learned that Willie had no family who were blood-related, no one who came to visit and show love and concern. When the staff asked him about his family, he communicated to us in the only way he could—with a guttural sound and nod, conveying that we were his family.

I was again caught off guard by the sincerity and genuineness I saw in his eyes and in his smile. It was so big and contagious that none of us could help but smile right back at him. His face brightened up the entire room for anyone who looked his way.

After a few minutes, I had to leave the room and go out into the hallway in an attempt to hide the tears that began filling my eyes. As I walked, God began whispering this Scripture and branding it into my heart and mind, "... Inasmuch as you have done it unto one of the least of these my brethren, ye have done it unto me" (Matthew 25:40).

At that moment, the last two decades flashed through my mind all the way back to Carlos and me standing on that playground. More than twenty-one years later, it was as if God was smiling back at me, speaking straight to my heart through Willie, peeling back another layer of understanding. My calling wasn't about the millions of dollars raised to serve thousands of people each year. No, it was all about moments like this where God desired to speak to me and me simply being available to see that it was always about serving one exceptional person at a time, each child, adult, and maybe an exceptional angel-like figure that resembled someone like Willie. I realized it was all about honoring and hearing God smile and affirm our work by using "the least of these." He values His love and mercy more than anything else.

It's not about us attempting to be more perfect. God teaches and speaks to us within our imperfections. He chooses to show up in the most unlikely and special ways to embrace us within His amazing grace. Then He SMILES upon us!

Finding My Own Compass

Fully realizing the depth of God's love continues to be a lifelong pursuit of mine. Defining moments stand out, such as the time at the daycare center with Willie and the night I fully committed my life to Jesus Christ.

After finding freedom from religion and indoctrination during that questioning season, I could then focus on my giftings—music and writing songs—and spend quality time on prayer walks around the grounds.

I knew I had found a more mature walk with Christ, one of clarity, peace, and purpose. It caused me to enjoy and reflect on times to love, to embrace, to laugh, to meditate on God's Word and time to enjoy silence without rushing the moments of life.

This journey led me to a welcoming place where I could undeniably feel His presence, to know Him for myself, and hear that reassuring voice that said, "Be still, and know that I am God."

When I awoke that next morning at Jackson College of Ministries, my confidence in my own faith was absolute. My faith was my own. The clarity of the work Christ did for me on the cross was crystal clear. Nothing I or anyone else could do would ever be good enough to earn a place in heaven. Only by the amazing, selfless sacrifice Jesus made on the cross would I enter into eternity with Him. I knew without a doubt that I was saved by grace through faith.

From that day on, I also knew I would be expected to carry that message to others, not only that He died, but also and even more importantly, that Jesus rose to conquer death and hell and the grave, that the only way to spend an eternity in heaven is not through our own good works or power, but by the power of the blood of Jesus shed on the cross for us all. There never has been nor will there ever be a greater imprint on my life than that of accepting Jesus as both Savior and Lord of my life.

Coming Full Circle: Route 171

The afternoon of Christmas Day 2018, I got an unexpected call. My last living aunt, my mother's oldest sister Marcell, or "Aunt Marce" as we called her, passed away. After helping Raye Ann clean up the post-Christmas morning chaos, I quickly packed and began the trip south to DeRidder, Louisiana, where my aunt had lived her entire life, some eighty-eight years. My plan was to drive all night straight through to DeRidder, but after eight hours of non-stop pouring rain and lightning, I decided to stop over in Natchez, Mississippi. The storm continued all night.

The next morning, the sun was trying to break through the clouds, and the day seemed brighter. I grabbed a quick breakfast and hit the road. The streets were still wet, and in some places, covered by runoff from the night's relentless rain.

I didn't usually use my GPS on the main roads, but since spending the night in an unfamiliar city, I went ahead and entered DeRidder into it anyway. Expecting my old familiar route to pop up, I was surprised when a much longer, unfamiliar one appeared. I tried again. Still not my usual route. A third attempt brought the same result. That was when I realized the flash flooding in the area must be worse than I thought.

So, I took the *less-traveled road*, heading southwest about forty-five miles out of my way. I listened to all the great old-road trip-worthy pop songs and Christian radio on Sirius XM. I thought about my Aunt Marce's life, trying to figure out exactly what I was going to say at the service. What should I talk about? What stories should I tell? Aunt Marce had been such a great family-member influence on my life.

Narrowing down the list of options seemed daunting. Should I talk about how I admired the way she navigated being single, or when she was about the age of twenty, she married a man who unfortunately was not only an alcoholic but also unfaithful? After that relationship ended, she remained single almost thirty years before meeting and marrying a widower named Eddie Lee Hinson. They celebrated twenty-five years together before Eddie passed away.

In counseling others going through loss, transition, and change, I would often refer to Aunt Marce as someone who believed that finding true love should never be determined by a time line. It was worth the effort to find the right person, no matter how long the wait. Or I could share about her example of what being a good sibling really meant? Maybe I should talk about how she lived with a kingdom mindset, or maybe the intentionality of her life, always finding ways to serve or be of help to others.

My GPS rerouting again snapped me out of my thoughts, and I started to be concerned about just how far out of the way it was taking me. So, I called my mom and dad and asked what the best route would be to get to DeRidder from where I was. Immediately, both my parents said it was a straight shot due north. I should look for State Route 171 and take it to DeRidder. For some reason, I felt like I had previously heard of that road. So, I asked my parents if there was any significance to it.

Laughing, my dad said, "More than any other road you will travel, Kenny." Well, that intrigued me.

Then I started putting the pieces together with the help of my parents. "Is this the same road that leads to Lake Charles where I was born?" I asked.

In unison, my parents answered, "Yes, the same one."

Dad continued, "Your mom and I drove down 171 when we eloped, and Lake Charles is where your mom and I lived our first year of marriage. Your Pa Paw, Ma Maw, and Aunt Marce came down 171 to see your sister Candy when she was born in 1956. That's when we reconciled with them after leaving DeRidder."

Mom added, "It wasn't until that trip that Ma Maw and Pa Paw finally understood that your dad's first wife was unfaithful and left him for another man. Divorce was not something he wanted. He just wanted to start over."

Slowly, these pieces of family history swirled around me. DeRidder... Route 171.... That afternoon along 171, I had driven right by the place of the camp meetings where all of my aunts had accepted Christ. I made a brief stop at the very cemetery in which my Pa Paw and Ma Maw were buried. Next to their graves was the place my Aunt Marce would be laid to rest tomorrow. So much of our family story, spiritual roots, and heritage resided in this place. I went to bed feeling a stirring in my soul, a fresh wind bringing a fresh perspective on my family.

I eventually made it to DeRidder. As I settled into my hotel room that night, I was still trying to piece together my part of the eulogy for Aunt Marce, but my phone call with Mom and Dad kept interrupting my thoughts. I had grown up with the stories of the singing days of Mom and her three sisters—Aunt Marce, Wanda, and Casille. I chuckled as I remembered Mom's childhood nickname; her sisters called her "Pouchie" instead of Melonee because she was so small. Mom and Dad's elopement and the events surrounding it were family folklore.

The day of the funeral, I decided to catch one last glimpse of Ma Maw and Pa Paw's house before the service. My heart skipped a beat remembering all the games of tag I had played as a boy in the yard. I closed my eyes and smelled those delicious meals Ma Maw cooked. I saw the big garden out back that Pa Paw had planted to care for his wife Mertie Mae and their four girls.

Standing in front of the house taking pictures, the whole story flashed before me, not as individual pieces but like a movie reel: my mom and dad meeting at the First Pentecostal Church off 171, seeing each other at church, struggling to be together, then trying not to be together, beginning their marriage by running away off Route 171; Ma Maw and Pa Paw coming down this road to visit when my older sister was born, opening the door for reconciliation. What my parents thought was all lost, by grace was found a year later along that same road, Route 171.

The time pulled me back to reality. I wanted to linger in these memories. I felt God's presence, that He was trying to show me something, but it was as if a veil had not been lifted yet.

However, I didn't want to be late for the service. I was emotionally exhausted from these trips down memory lane, from trying to put my finger on exactly what it was that I was feeling. I was going to need everything I had left just to hold it together and try and give my aunt my best at the service.

What Really Matters

On the way to the church, I thought about my last visit with Aunt Marce. I had walked into the nursing home to see her. She was dressed up, playing the piano and singing an old-time favorite "I'll Fly Away."

I found an inconspicuous spot behind a pillar, pulled out my phone, and started videoing her performance. Her dementia was acute, and I didn't want to disturb this moment or upset her. After a bit, I put my phone down and walked over to the piano, singing harmony. She finished the song and looked up at me with her smiling, dark-brown eyes and said, "You can sing good harmony."

I was a little disappointed. This was one of those times she didn't recognize me. I smiled back and said, "Thank you. My Aunt Marce and my family taught me how to sing."

Aunt Marce turned fully toward me. "Kenny, is that you?" she asked, laughing and crying at the same time.

"It sure is, Aunt Marce," I replied with a big smile, grateful that she recognized me.

It was an amazing afternoon. We ate lunch together, we laughed, we cried, we reminisced about old times. Before I left, I asked if she would speak with her younger sister Pouchie. I watched as Mom and her older sister talked on the phone for a few minutes. Then Aunt Marce said, "Melonee, I just want to go home."

Pretty much every day since entering the nursing home in Texas, years ago, Aunt Marce wanted to go back to her home on Devilla Street in DeRidder. This time, however, she was not referring to that home. She longed for the home she had prayed and sung about her entire life—heaven. She just wanted to be with Jesus.

I looked out at all of the friends and relatives who had gathered to honor my aunt, searching for my next words. The veil was lifting. I saw Hans on the *Samuel*, Frederick on the trail to Ohio, and Samuel on his deathbed. I felt the pain as Joseph watched his Uncle John walk away for the last time and Wild Bill ignoring the needs of his family. I saw Great-Grandpa Tom's farm and Grandpa Lewis' lifelong search for significance. I saw Route 171 that connected us all and the story of my parents held together by that same route. I saw God's hand of providence through the generations.

I understood what it was He was trying to show me, what it all meant. I did my best to control my emotions, but my voice broke with a smile as I concluded, "My Aunt Marce used to take me to the cemetery, to the graves of our relatives, to honor the faithful saints of God and our family. I often wondered why, but today, here in DeRidder, standing up here, I finally get it.

"I stood by a freshly dug grave yesterday, knowing today I would share in honoring her memory but not sure how I would do that. Today, I realize that my GPS taking me way out of my way to get here and coming in via State Route 171 was no mistake. God had it all planned out a long time ago. In fact, He has a time and place for each of us.

"I took the less-traveled road to get to DeRidder, Louisiana, but I see now it's made all the difference in my life. Right here in this little town along Route 171, seeing the church where she was raised, the graveyard where we will soon honor her one last time, it's here I'm reminded of the things in life that really matter."

As I headed home toward Nashville, Tennessee, going north on the route my Pa Paw traveled as a truck driver, I sang some of the great hymns of old, the favorites of the Nichols family. I smiled as memories paraded by of Ma Maw and Pa Paw asking us to kneel together for family prayer, thanking the Lord for watching over us another day, and being living examples of the Christian life. The impression of my childhood was not one of the Mauck family in isolation or separation, not one of anger or unforgiveness; the greatest decision my father ever made was marrying one of the Nichols girls.

The faith of my Ma Maw, Pa Paw, Aunt Marce, and the entire Nichols family shaped my father, my family, and me. The imprint of faith on my heart and soul passed down to my own children is God's redemption of what could have been a completely different story.

Imprints of Prayer
My Meeting with Dr. James Dobson

Recently, I got to complete one of my bucket-list items by obtaining a providential meeting with Dr. James Dobson, famous author and founder of *Focus on the Family*. Thanks to several people who worked with him, I was able to sit down and visit with Dr. Dobson in his office after one of his *Family Talk* tapings. I got the honor of him personally showing me his famous first book *Dare to Discipline* displayed right outside his office within a glass case, denoting his original manuscript written within his own handwriting.

He asked about my book *Leaving Your Life Imprint*, and we began to discuss his new book *Your Legacy*. I shared how proud he must have been to have such a wonderful grandfather who prayed over the life of his father, his brothers, sons, and grandchildren. He replied, "Yes, most all the males in our family became pastors except for me.

"I look back now and realize the great significance and difference my grandfather made in all of our lives through his consistent daily prayers during his lunch hour. I obviously wasn't meant to be a pastor. In hindsight, we have far exceeded what most pastors could have accomplished. I credit God and those early prayers of my grandfather for making me who I am today."

Dr. Dobson asked about me and my story as well, so I shared with him how prayers had also covered my life. Thanks to my grandparents' and mother's prayers, I was able to found two nonprofit legacy companies. I told him how they prayed every day for each of their children and grandchildren. These were not sixty-second prayers either. Instead, they were heavy, deep passionate calls to God with hearts and heads looking above, praising and thanking God for His blessing, affirmation, and touch. They cried out to

God to oversee and protect each of my aunts, uncles, and cousins with His grace and everlasting arms.

We both smiled and shook our heads acknowledging our ancestors. Prayers had continued to have a residual impact. They represent the valuable imprints to affirm a world desperately in need of God's grace and love. This can only happen by reaching up and praying to the true God who can do above and beyond all we can think or ask!

This meeting was a reminder to me that we all have a story. Each one is special, unique, and different. None should be minimized or dubbed as insignificant, and prayers can be a central part of finding its correct time and place to be shared!

The Greatest Story of All—Christ, His Imprints on the Cross, and His Eternal Home

Of all the great imprinted stories, nothing can compare to the greatest one ever told about Christ, the cross, and His greatest imprint of all time. It can be found and described in John 1:1-14, "In the beginning was the Word, and the Word was with God, and the Word was God.... The Word became flesh and made his dwelling among us ...." (NIV).

His name is Jesus Christ, the perfect Lamb, the Son of God, who came down from His glorious home, lived and walked on this earth, gave His life, and paid once and for all the debt owed for sin. His hands and feet were nailed to a cross for our sins. His resurrected spiritual body still carries the imprint of His suffering, His nail-scarred hands the evidence of His love for us. Upon seeing and touching Jesus' hands, even Thomas the disciple who doubted, proclaimed, "My Lord and my God!"

Friend, this love, this gift is available to all, but it will never be forced upon anyone. You have an invitation to be a part of the greatest redemptive story, to have your own story carry the imprint of redemption through the eternal Keeper of the Story, the King of Kings, Lord of Lords, Jesus Christ. He even charged others with the responsibility of becoming the keeper of the story, of chronicling His life-imprinted story for you from four different perspectives in the gospels of Matthew, Mark, Luke, and John. In fact, the entire Bible is the story of Jesus Christ, His life imprint left for all so that all have the opportunity to hear.

If today you are unsure about where you will spend eternity, I invite you to consider Jesus Christ. There is a hymn often sang by Mahalia Jackson and George Beverly Shea during Billy Graham Crusades: "Just As I Am." It has become a favorite of mine. I pray these words will bring life to you as they have for me and countless others.

"Just as I am, without one plea, but that thy blood was shed for me, and that thou bid'st me come to Thee, Oh Lamb of God, I come, I come."

The tug you may feel on your heart is not from me. God is calling you to a place of true repentance and freedom. The answer of submission, repentance from sin, and acceptance of the greatest gift ever known can be found in this simple prayer:

> God,
>
> I know I have sinned and that my sin separates me from You. I believe Jesus came to this earth, lived, died on the cross, and rose from the grave so that I could be forgiven and live a redeemed story.
>
> Please forgive me. I confess my sins before You knowing the blood of Jesus is washing them away. I know You live today and are calling me now to live for You. I ask You to come into my life and be my Lord and Savior. Amen.

If you have prayed this prayer and wholeheartedly accepted Jesus Christ as Savior and Lord of your life, you have accepted the greatest imprint ever within your life. God wants you to know that you are fully forgiven and that He looks forward to you spending eternity with Him. I encourage you to find a good Bible-believing church now that you have made your commitment to Christ.

My dear friend, we've come to the end of our journey together. I've done my best to give you everything you need to start recording, writing, and sharing your own voyage of family, self, and faith discovery.

Leaving your life imprint requires intentionality and purpose. Living purposefully means being present in the moment, catching glimpses of heaven in our everyday life by looking at opportunities to love and care for others as God has loved us. It's now up to you to catch the wind in your sails and head for destinations known and unknown, to uncover the themes of love, heartache, and joy, to search for significance and redemption that make a story compelling.

Chapter after chapter is just waiting for you to pick up your pen, and with the help of the guided questions, lead you to finding and embracing your own personal story. This priceless treasure, this story of yours and your ancestors', this journey of faith and family once written will live beyond your lifetime and help generations to come live with purpose.

I leave you with one final inspirational question: Will you join with me and become the keeper of your imprinted story?

Imprints—The Marking of True Inheritance

"The greatest travesty in life is not to have feared death throughout one's life, but rather to have come to the end of life and realized you never truly risked living!" –Kenny Mauck

The Tale of the Two Brothers' Tombstones

The graves of two brothers were but four feet apart from each other. One brother was very rich in terms of money, possessions, and land as evidenced by the gold-plated marble stone that arrayed his larger-than-life tombstone. On display were all the accolades and accomplishments, the corporations founded, charities and foundations to which he had given toward. A footnote by his attorney stated he left a hefty portfolio of money in his Last Will and Testament to his children and grandchildren. This grave was a magnificent monument signified by a beautiful large brass gate whereby no one could get close enough to touch.

His brother buried next to him couldn't have been more different. Though laid to rest within the same well-kept cemetery, his tombstone was overwhelmingly ordinary in comparison. The area surrounding his grave was open wide for all to walk around with a small bench facing toward his grave. The grass had withered due to the footsteps from a multitude of visitors who ended up taking some time to read and stay. Fresh flowers and cards were often left underneath the engraved message he had left to his friends and family on his tombstone. Also carved in at his request were the imprint of little feet and hands and an open letter with these words for all to see:

To all my beloved children, family, and friends, may these imprints recall all our fun in the fall, playing hide-and-go-seek, or riding our bikes in the street. Always laughing, we had such a ball! I dreamed of you grow-

ing tall as the trees, whether fishing with you on the lake, or holding you up high on my knees. There's no better feeling than moments like these.

During these gifts of time, I taught you what it takes to live, but I hope above all else, I taught you how to give. May this seat facing my tombstone remind you to take a rest and think on the things we have done, like the books we have read, things we have shared. Yet as the night calls us to bed, we ensured nothing else was ever left unsaid. Remember the years of laughter and tears, our special letters, both happy and sad, but mostly reflecting all the fun we've had! Best of all, we captured great pictures of all the memorable things we saw. Oh, the joy of watching you take risks both large and small, watching love conquer all your fears. You, just like me, will one day dry all your children's and grandchildren's tears.

Even though we worked tattered till day's end, watching you help in the garden was all that really mattered. Yes, I will leave you all my goods and possessions here, but unfortunately, like sand, the wind will take them away, whereby they will soon quickly disappear. So you see, there are no greater riches in life we can share than showing each other how much we care, like singing to each other or kneeling during our evening or bedtime prayer. These are the imprints neither gold nor sliver can ever buy. Like our Savior's story, no tombstone can hold down a life that was destined to forever live and rise.

So take comfort in knowing, my head now rests within Christ's everlasting arms. There is no more reason to worry or fear, for heaven awaits beaming with joy. There's no more weeping or wailing alas! So keep passing on our redemptive story with gleam for all our dear loved ones to see that living with Jesus is the greatest eternal gift for you and for me.

Feel free to keep leaving your notes and letters here on the ground because one day we'll read them together once you become glory-bound. I leave you with this last thought in mind: We will live, laugh, and love forever beyond time. For this my dear beloved precious family and friends is a life-imprinted story that will never, ever end!

—KENNY MAUCK

ABOUT THE AUTHOR

Kenny Mauck is an author, speaker, singer, songwriter, ordained minister, and counselor. He's also the owner of a commercial real estate management company and the founder of Lifestone Springs Community Missions Church and two faith-based nonprofit organizations, LifeCare Foundations and LifeCare Family Services.

Kenny received his master's degree in counseling in 1990, from Eastern Michigan University and took doctoral classes at Trevecca University in both counseling and leadership development. Understanding the needs of nonprofits, he takes his decades of experience to raise funds for those in need and helping other nonprofits through his new missional organization LifeStone Springs. This organization provides homes to seniors, support to veterans needing adult day services, and helps raise money for handicapped children living in the Dominican Republic.

Kenny has been married to his wife Raye Ann now for thirty-five years. He is also the proud father of his three endearing adult children, Landon, Megan, and Kelsey. Landon and his wife Brittany will be newly married September 1, 2019, and Kelsey will be marrying her fiancé Jon the following September in a destination wedding. Kenny dearly loves his three grandchildren, twins Easton and Cooper, age eight, and Gracelyn, two years old. He creates and plays treasure hunts with his grandsons in the woods, takes them horseback riding, and plays sports with them. He also enjoys playing hide-and-go-seek with his little Gracelyn and the twins as well. All his grandchildren honorably call him "Pop."

His love and passion about living out one's story with purpose is evidenced by him residing thirty-five miles south of Nashville out in the country. His home is near a beautiful pastoral setting surrounded by horse farms, a pond, and every outdoor animal imaginable, such as deer, turkeys, ducks, cranes, and geese. He says they give him his early morning wakeup call due to their incessant honking noises.

Kenny has recently resigned after twenty-three years of running his largest nonprofit. He will now have the opportunity to travel, speak, and share his passion about leaving one's imprinted story as a legacy with those we love, work with, and with whom we have long-lasting friendships.

His love for the outdoors, sports, and music has continued. He still enjoys running, playing golf, touch football, and basketball, riding bikes, rock repelling, hiking, and recently, flying on a sixty-five-mile-per-hour zip line! His love for contemporary jazz and gospel music, as well as attending the orchestra in Nashville, exemplifies his love and zest for life.

Kenny's priorities are simplistic: his love for God, family, and friends comes first. Secondly, He enjoys meeting a wide and diverse set of people. You can also meet them on his podcasts that are available on YouTube and Facebook. It's one of the ways he expresses his love for Christ and His amazing grace on his life as demonstrated in the final chapter of *Leaving Your Life Imprint*. Here, he summarizes that we all are in need of a redemptive story, and Jesus is the only one who can provide that.

CONTACT INFORMATION & WAYS TO GIVE

Please contact Kenny Mauck at kenny.mauck@lifecarefoundations.org should you desire to invite him to speak at your next event.

As an entrepreneur and CEO of both commercial and nonprofit ventures, Kenny can speak about the tenants of what makes up a legacy company through its own imprinted story tailored to your company, school, church, governmental entity, or other community nonprofit organization. Through consulting, he can also help develop and share the principals on how to grow a corporate- or mission-oriented imprinted story that's waiting to be inspirationally shared or recorded as well.

Be sure to download or visit Kenny's website to view him speaking at churches, businesses, or national conferences, as well as conducting interviews on national radio broadcasts like *Family Talk* and Bott Radio Network. Kenny also has conducted podcasts with *New York Times* bestselling authors, such as Ken Abraham, national political leaders, like former Attorney General Roberto Gonzalez, various artists, and he has been endorsed by nationally syndicated and radio talk show host Dave Ramsey.

Kenny was honored to speak at the annual New York City Book Expo event for writers and publishers in 2018, and then in 2019, he began interviewing various legacies. In addition, Kenny is available on other social media that includes Facebook, Twitter, Instagram, and LinkedIn.

You can order your copy/copies of his book *Leaving Your Life Imprint* through an online retailer, or visit Kenny's website at **kennymauck.com** (Visa and major credit cards are accepted), or call 615-836-8301 or 615-781-0555, whereby a LifeStone Springs representative will help you. A suggested minimum donation of $25.00 per copy is requested. (Postage and handling fees are included.) Finally, should you request a tax-exempt receipt from LifeStone Springs, it can be e-mailed to you directly. If paying by check, simply write in the memo that your donation is for LifeStone Springs.